THE INVINCIBLE ED

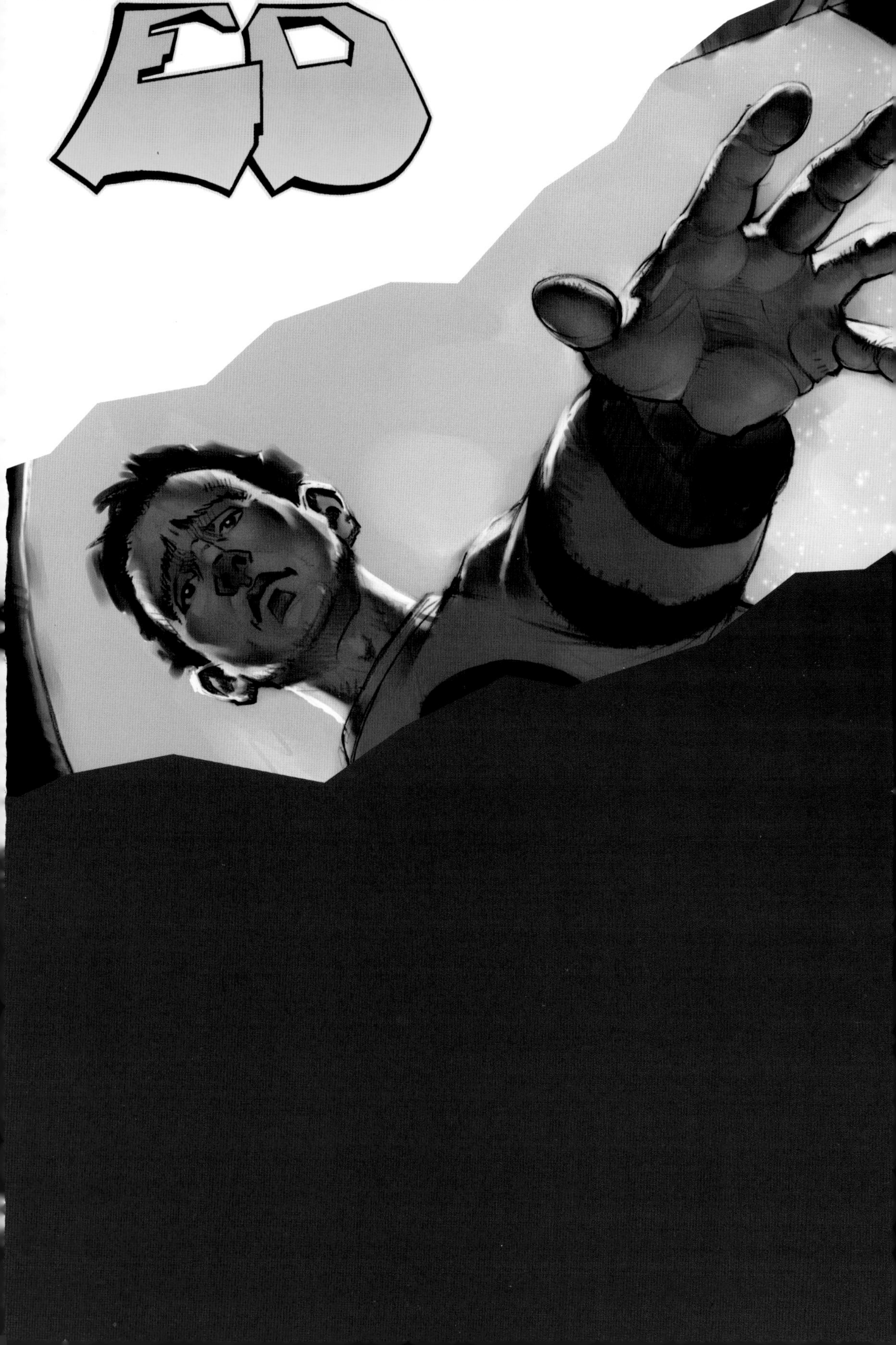

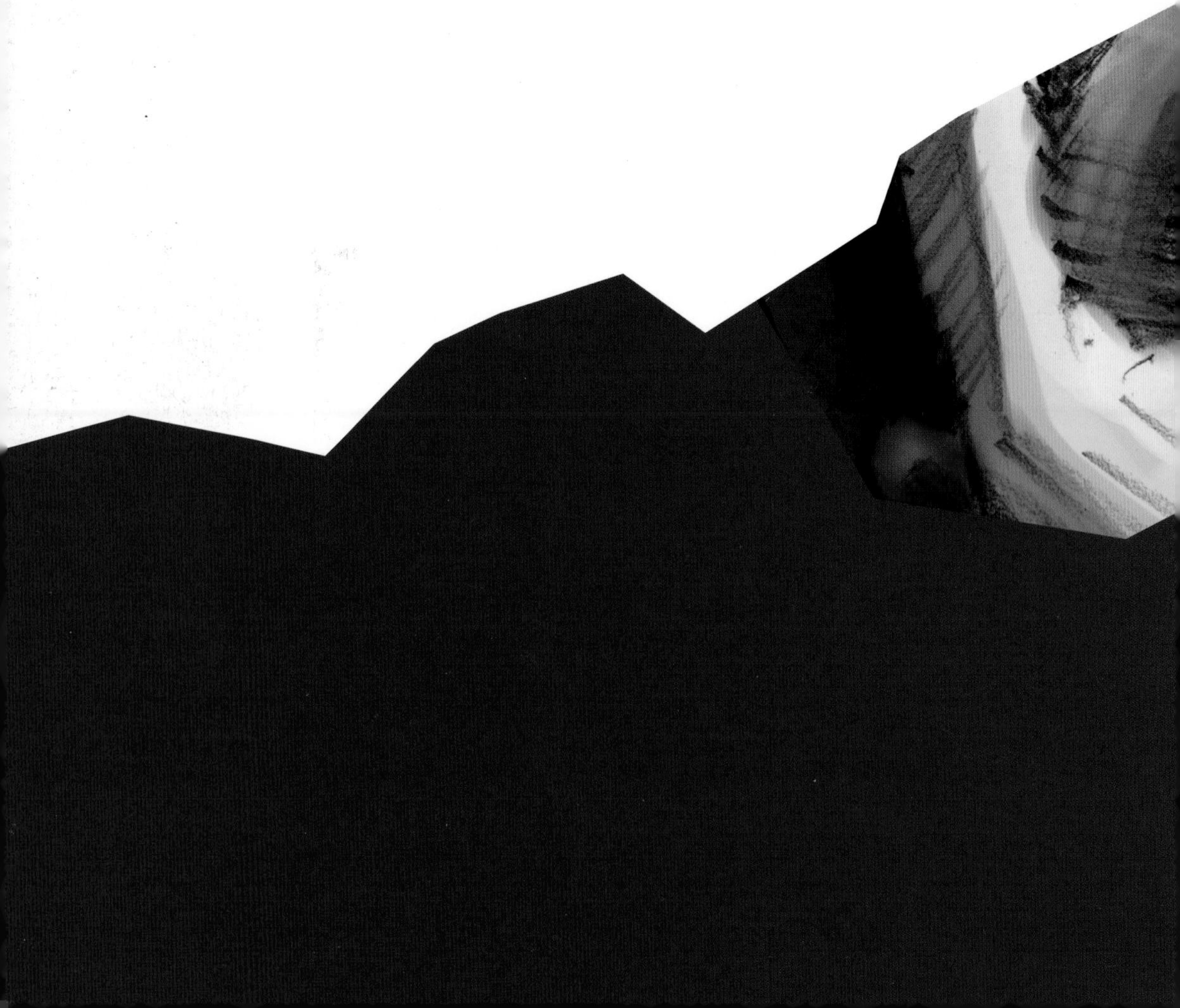

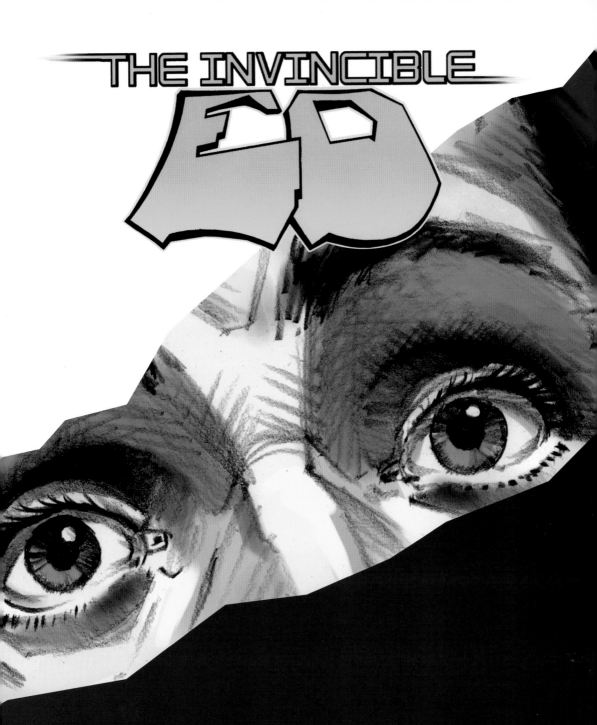

THE INVINCIBLE ED

created by

RYAN WOODWARD

DARK HORSE BOOKS™

designer
LANI SCHREIBSTEIN

art director
LIA RIBACCHI

publisher
MIKE RICHARDSON

RYAN WOODWARD'S THE INVINCIBLE ED

Dark Horse Books
A division of Dark Horse Comics, Inc.
10956 SE Main Street
Milwaukie, OR 97222

www.darkhorse.com
An original publication of Summertime Comics
www.summertimebooks.com

First edition: May 2004
ISBN: 1-59307-194-9

10 9 8 7 6 5 4 3 2 1

Printed in China

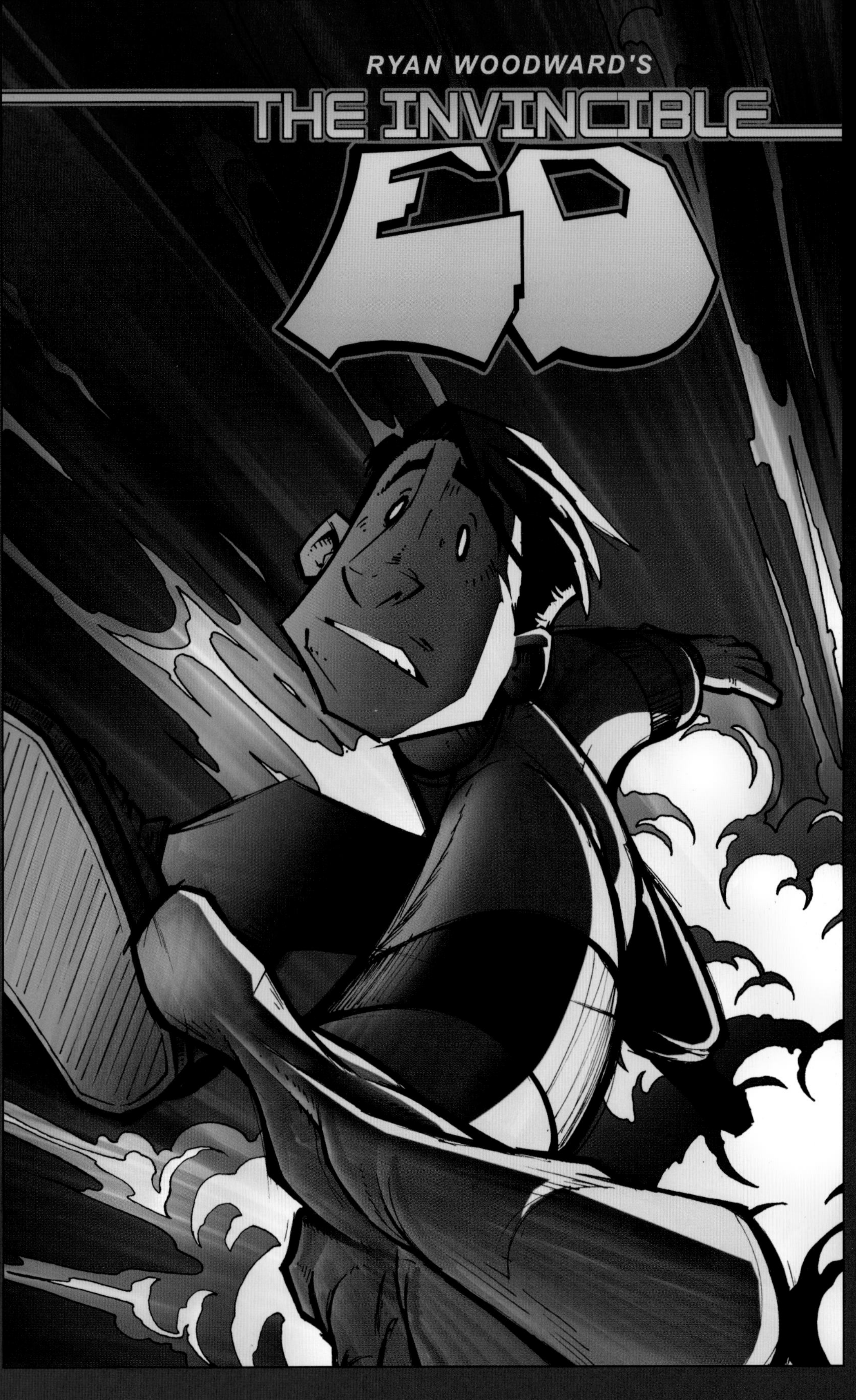
RYAN WOODWARD'S
THE INVINCIBLE
ED

written and illustrated
RYAN WOODWARD

comic fonts
NATE PIEKOS

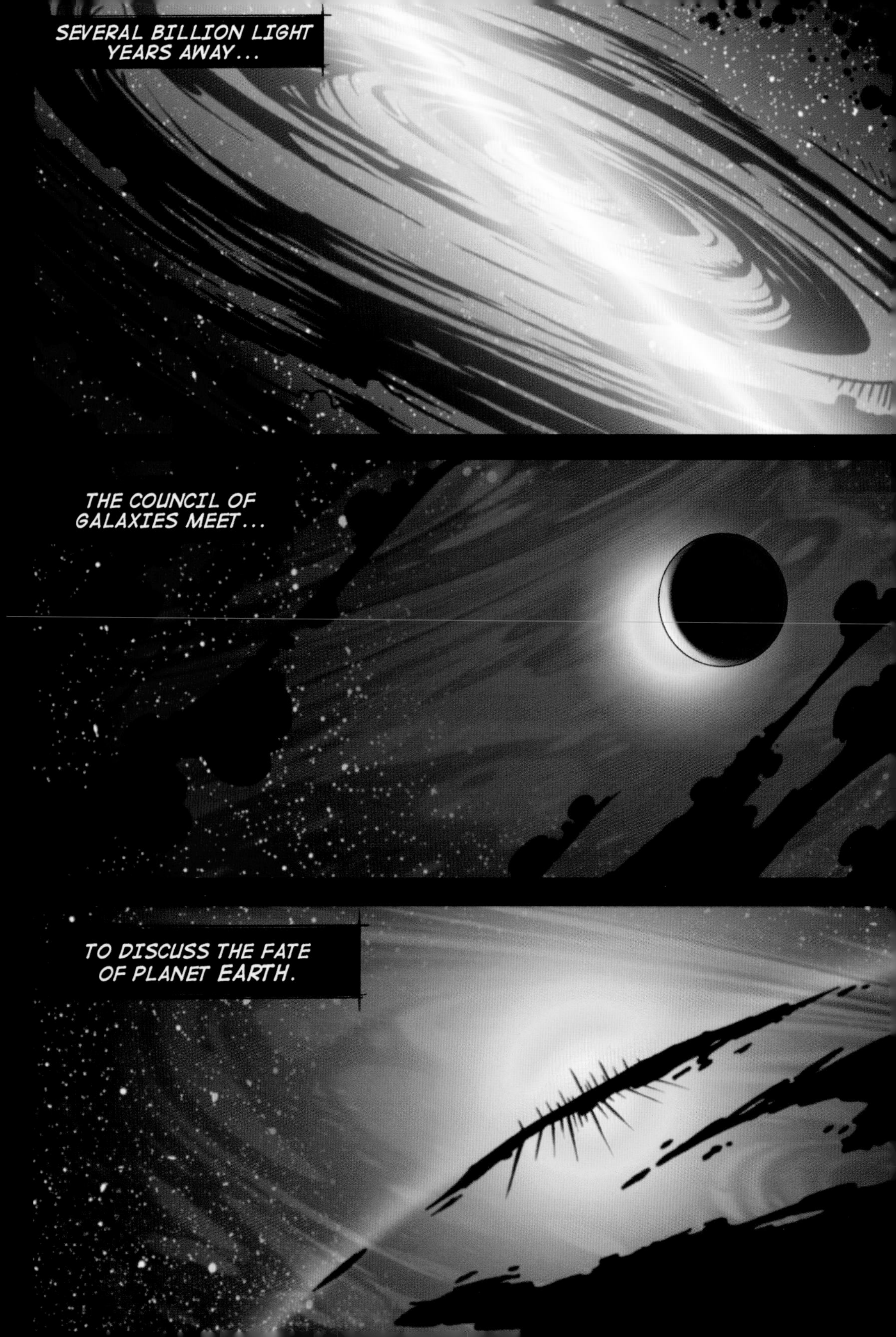
SEVERAL BILLION LIGHT YEARS AWAY...
THE COUNCIL OF GALAXIES MEET...
TO DISCUSS THE FATE OF PLANET EARTH.

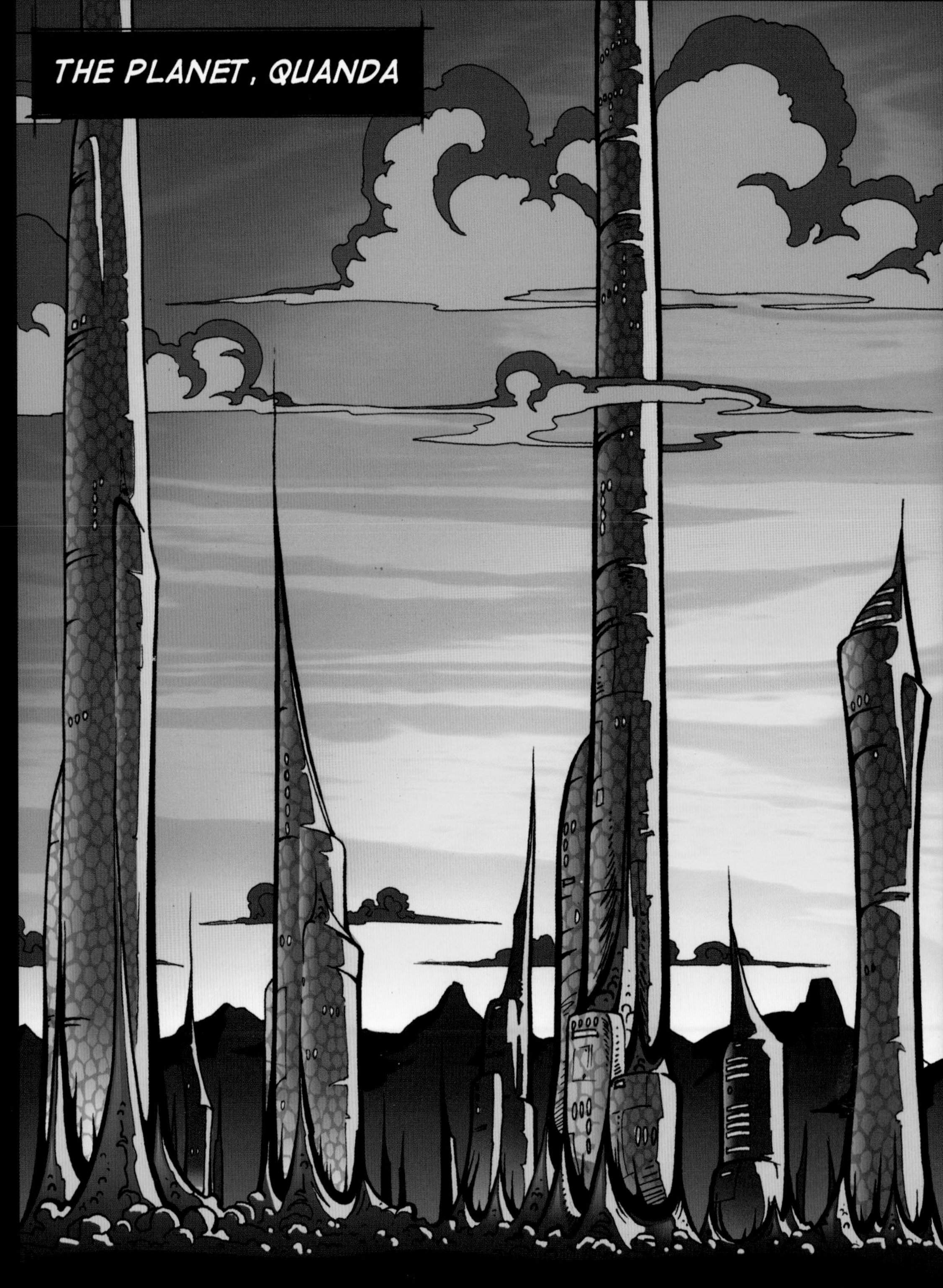
THE PLANET, QUANDA

QUANDA IS THE CENTRAL UNIVERSAL PLANET WHERE THE GRAND COUNCIL MEETS TO DISCUSS THE PROBLEMATIC COURSES OF PLANETS. INTERVENTION IS RARELY THE CASE

HOWEVER,

EARTH IS FACING A CRISIS. CRIME IS ON THE RISE. BASIC HUMAN KINDNESS IS MORE SCARCE THAN EVER BEFORE. THE COUNCIL CONSIDERS INTERVENTION.

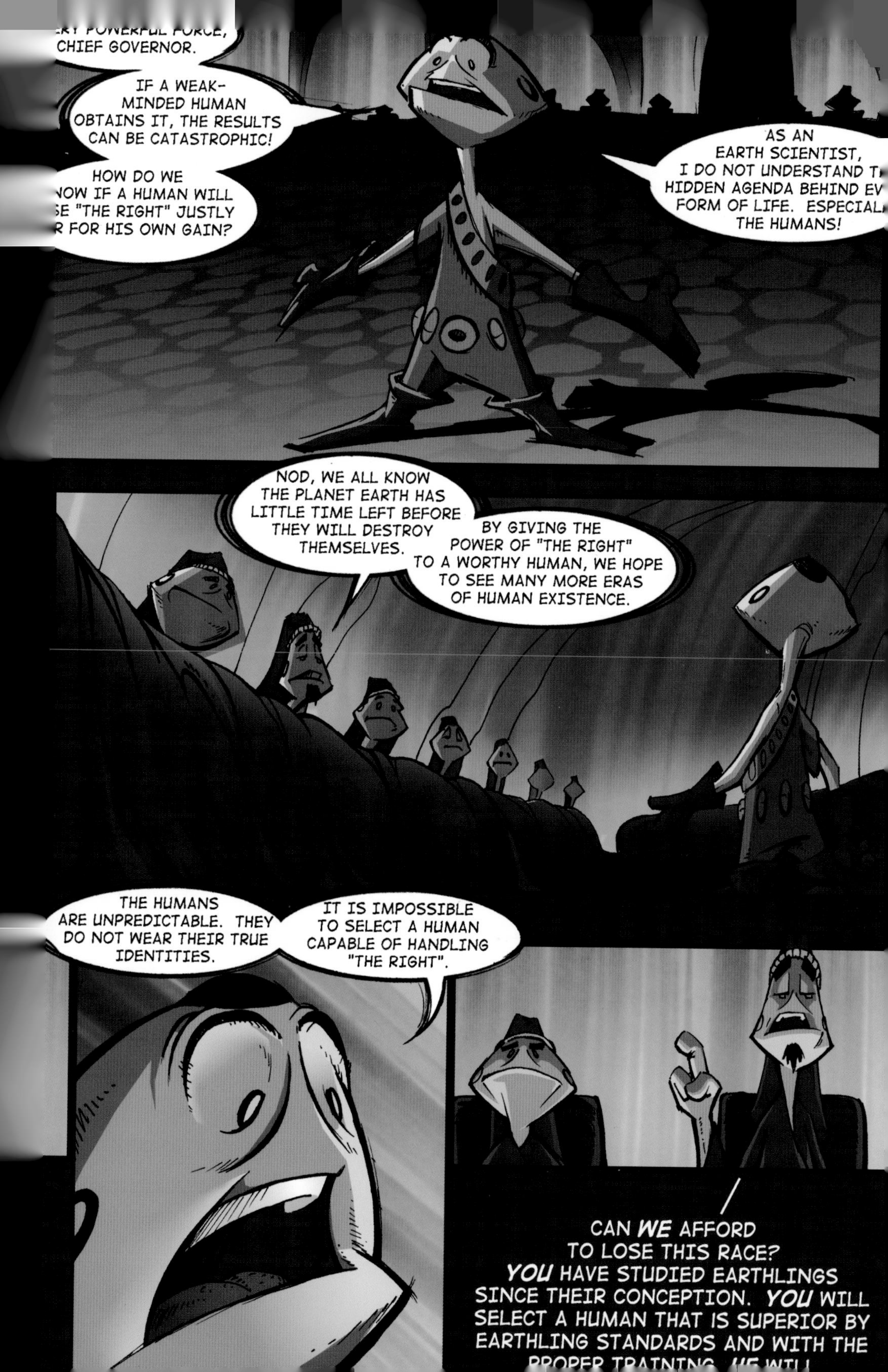

CHIEF GOVERNOR.
IF A WEAK-MINDED HUMAN OBTAINS IT, THE RESULTS CAN BE CATASTROPHIC!
HOW DO WE NOW IF A HUMAN WILL SE "THE RIGHT" JUSTLY R FOR HIS OWN GAIN?
AS AN EARTH SCIENTIST, I DO NOT UNDERSTAND T HIDDEN AGENDA BEHIND EV FORM OF LIFE. ESPECIAL THE HUMANS!
NOD, WE ALL KNOW THE PLANET EARTH HAS LITTLE TIME LEFT BEFORE THEY WILL DESTROY THEMSELVES.
BY GIVING THE POWER OF "THE RIGHT" TO A WORTHY HUMAN, WE HOPE TO SEE MANY MORE ERAS OF HUMAN EXISTENCE.
THE HUMANS ARE UNPREDICTABLE. THEY DO NOT WEAR THEIR TRUE IDENTITIES.
IT IS IMPOSSIBLE TO SELECT A HUMAN CAPABLE OF HANDLING "THE RIGHT".
CAN WE AFFORD TO LOSE THIS RACE? YOU HAVE STUDIED EARTHLINGS SINCE THEIR CONCEPTION. YOU WILL SELECT A HUMAN THAT IS SUPERIOR BY EARTHLING STANDARDS AND WITH THE

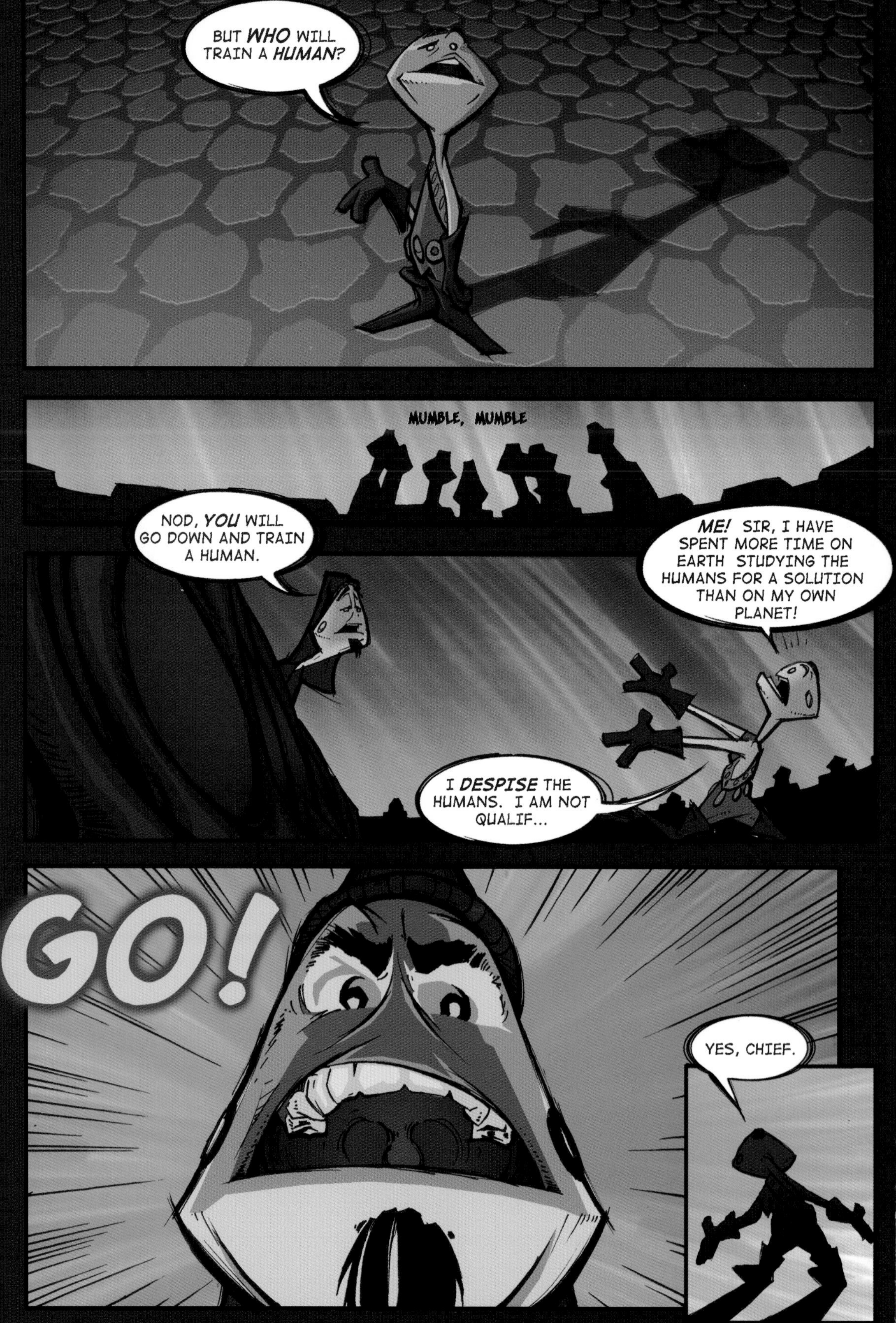

BUT WHO WILL TRAIN A HUMAN?
MUMBLE, MUMBLE
NOD, YOU WILL GO DOWN AND TRAIN A HUMAN.
ME! SIR, I HAVE SPENT MORE TIME ON EARTH STUDYING THE HUMANS FOR A SOLUTION THAN ON MY OWN PLANET!
I DESPISE THE HUMANS. I AM NOT QUALIF...
GO!
YES, CHIEF.

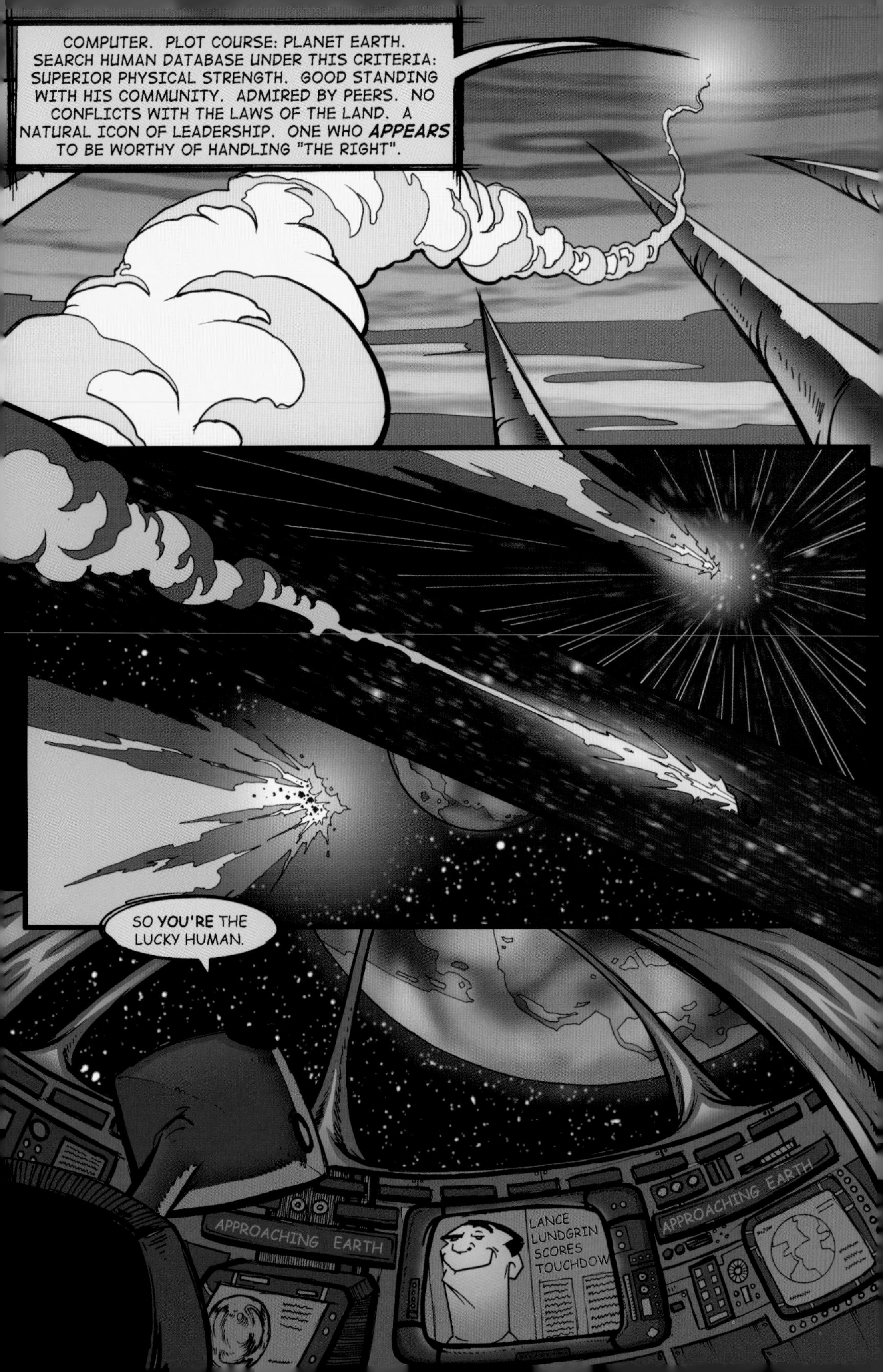

COMPUTER. PLOT COURSE: PLANET EARTH. SEARCH HUMAN DATABASE UNDER THIS CRITERIA: SUPERIOR PHYSICAL STRENGTH. GOOD STANDING WITH HIS COMMUNITY. ADMIRED BY PEERS. NO CONFLICTS WITH THE LAWS OF THE LAND. A NATURAL ICON OF LEADERSHIP. ONE WHO *APPEARS* TO BE WORTHY OF HANDLING "THE RIGHT".
SO **YOU'RE** THE LUCKY HUMAN.
APPROACHING EARTH
LANCE LUNDGRIN SCORES TOUCHDOW
APPROACHING EARTH

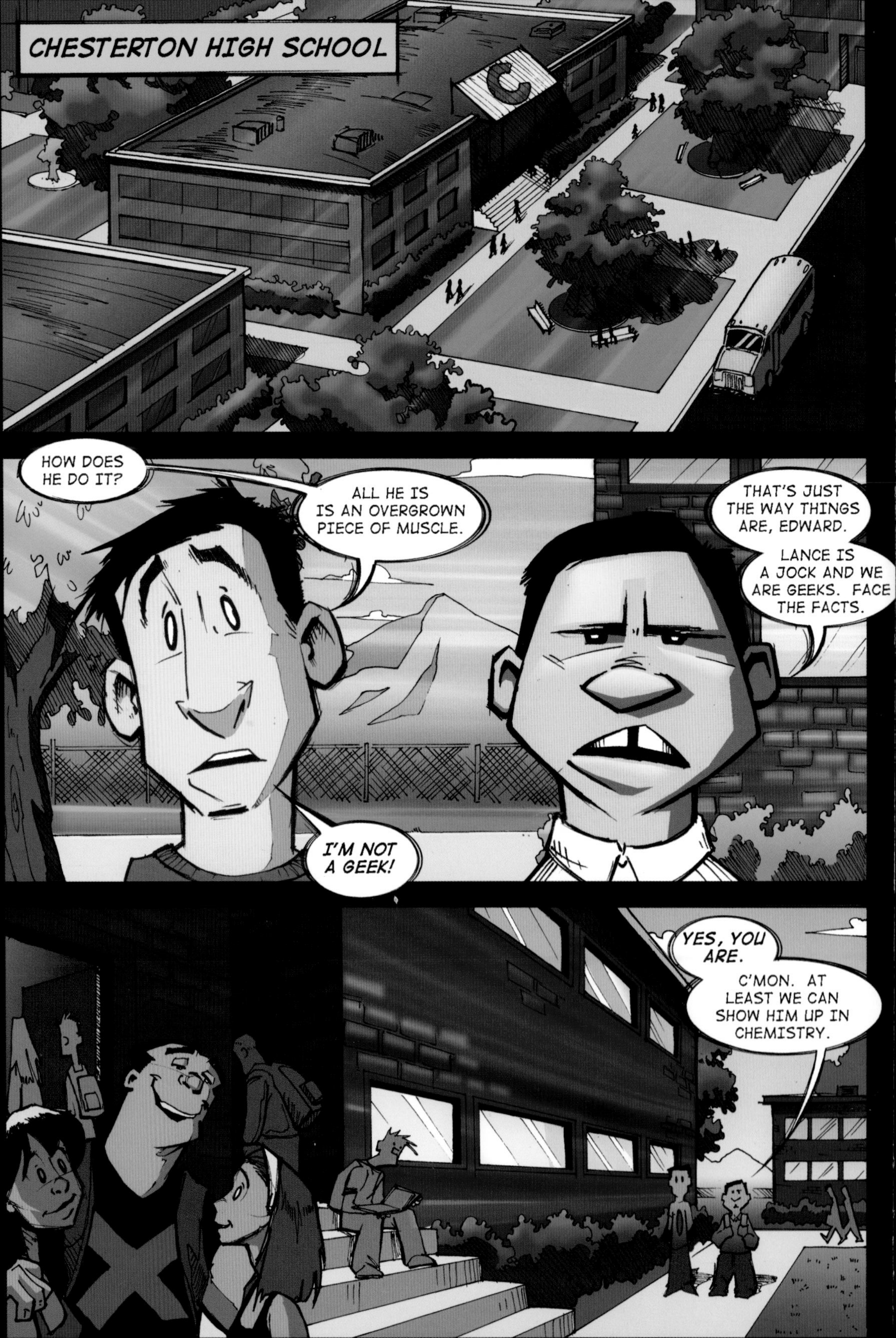
CHESTERTON HIGH SCHOOL
HOW DOES HE DO IT?
ALL HE IS IS AN OVERGROWN PIECE OF MUSCLE.
THAT'S JUST THE WAY THINGS ARE, EDWARD.
LANCE IS A JOCK AND WE ARE GEEKS. FACE THE FACTS.
I'M NOT A GEEK!
YES, YOU ARE.
C'MON. AT LEAST WE CAN SHOW HIM UP IN CHEMISTRY.

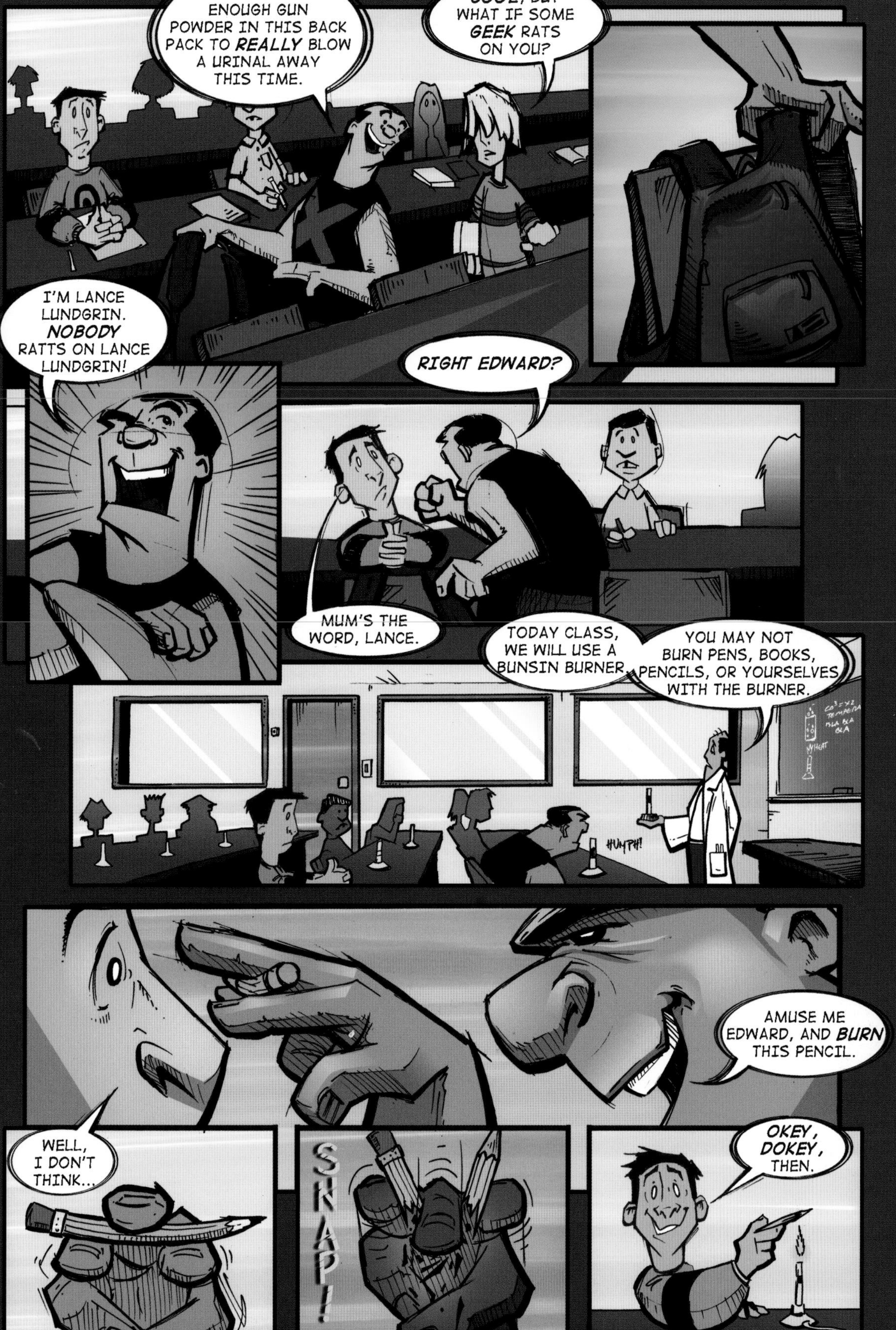

I'VE GOT ENOUGH GUN POWDER IN THIS BACK PACK TO REALLY BLOW A URINAL AWAY THIS TIME.
COOL, BUT WHAT IF SOME GEEK RATS ON YOU?
I'M LANCE LUNDGRIN. NOBODY RATTS ON LANCE LUNDGRIN!
RIGHT EDWARD?
MUM'S THE WORD, LANCE.
TODAY CLASS, WE WILL USE A BUNSIN BURNER.
YOU MAY NOT BURN PENS, BOOKS, PENCILS, OR YOURSELVES WITH THE BURNER.
HUMPH!
AMUSE ME EDWARD, AND BURN THIS PENCIL.
WELL, I DON'T THINK...
SNAP!
OKEY, DOKEY, THEN.

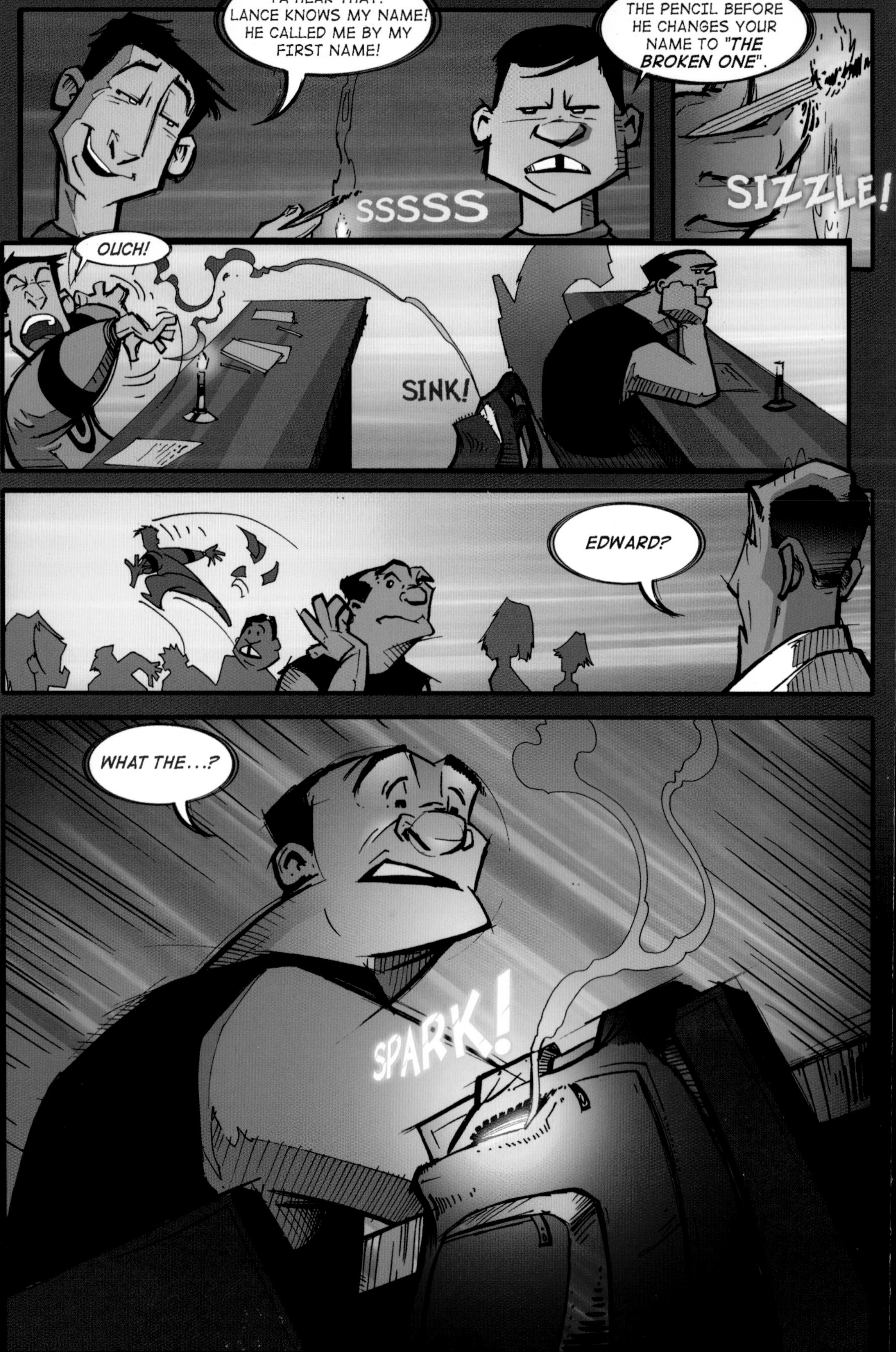
YA HEAR THAT? LANCE KNOWS MY NAME! HE CALLED ME BY MY FIRST NAME!
SSSSS
JUST BURN THE PENCIL BEFORE HE CHANGES YOUR NAME TO "THE BROKEN ONE".
SIZZLE!
OUCH!
SINK!
EDWARD?
WHAT THE...?
SPARK!

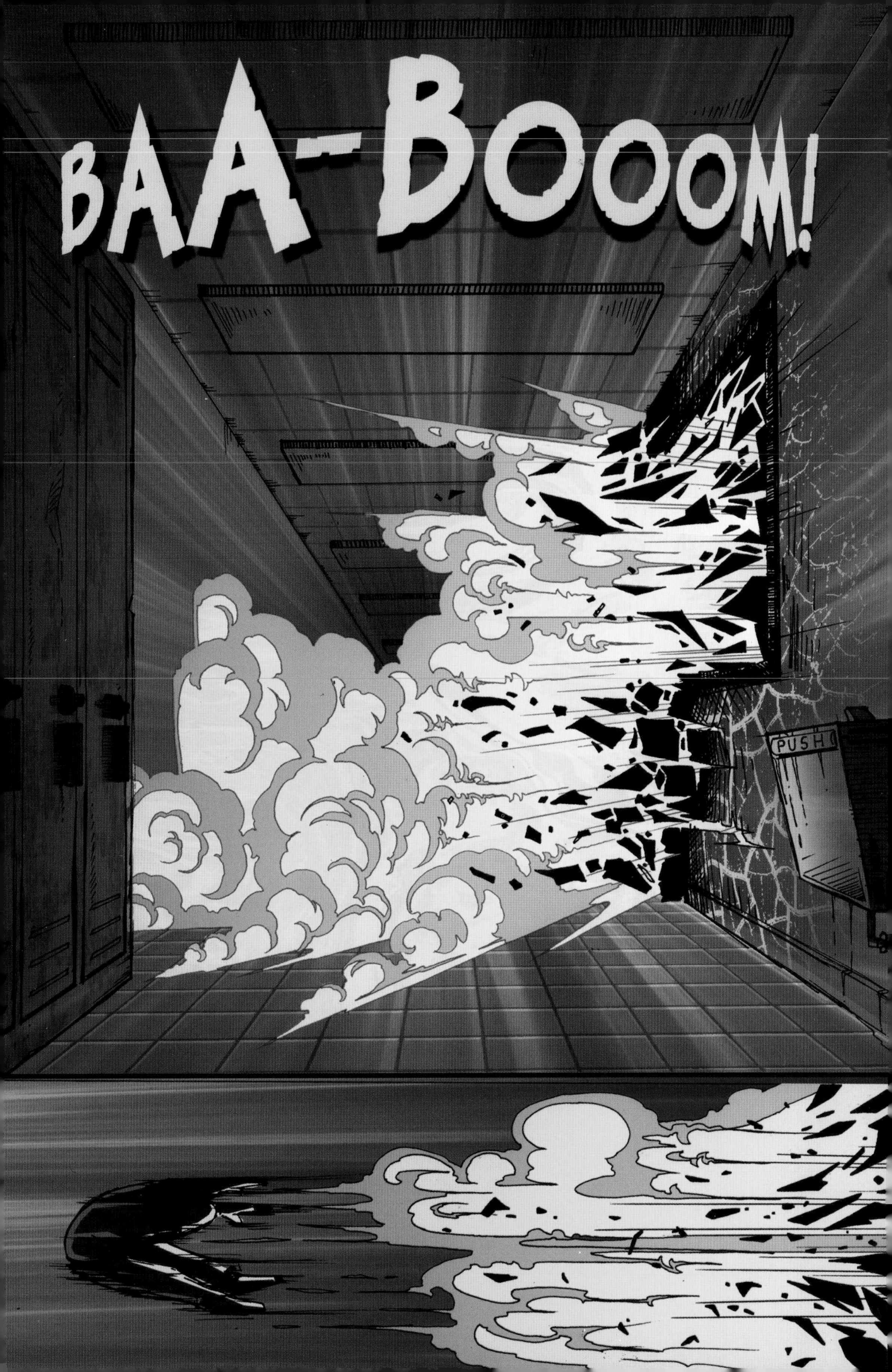
BAA-BOOOM!
PUSH

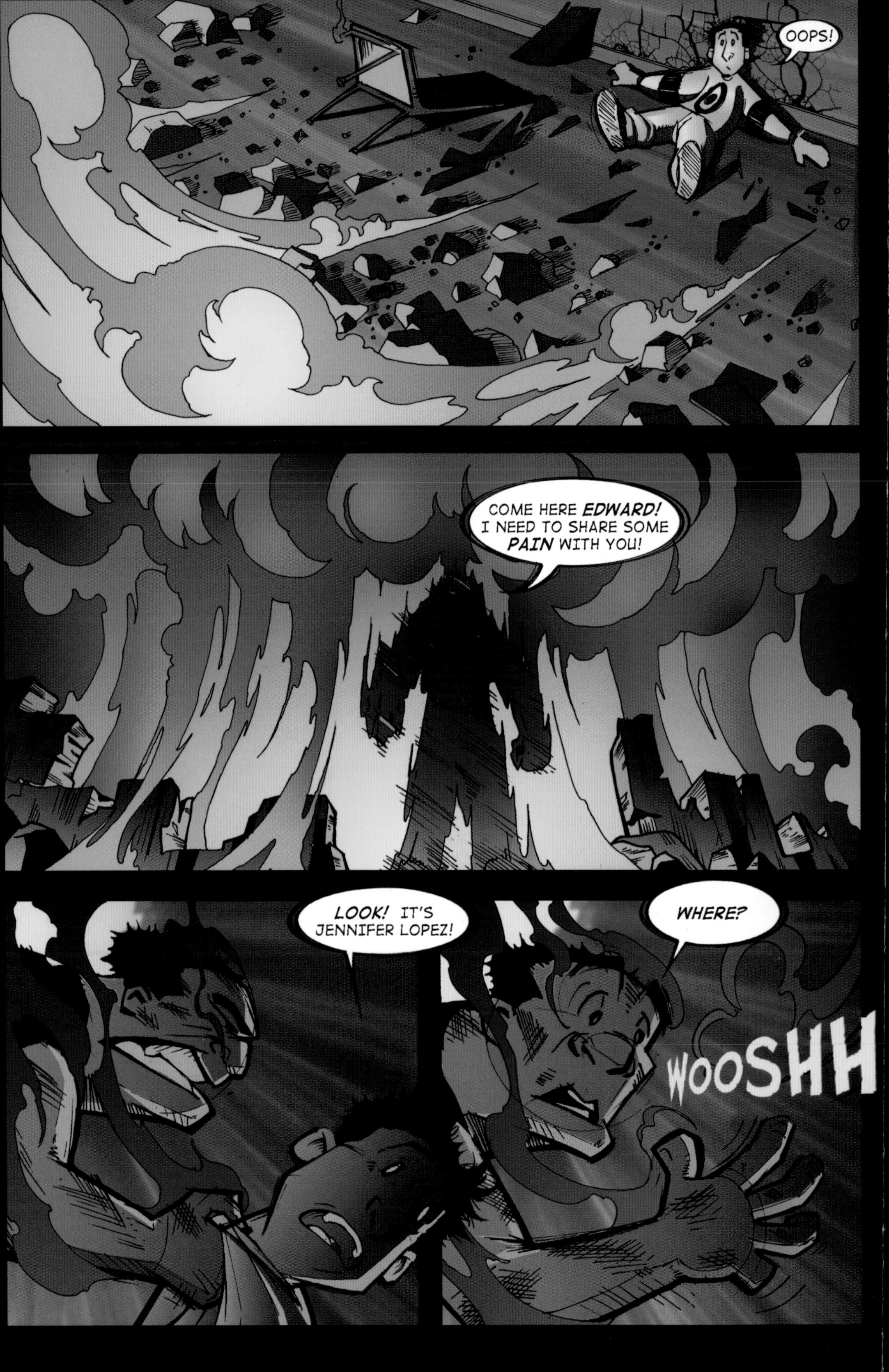
OOPS!
COME HERE EDWARD! I NEED TO SHARE SOME PAIN WITH YOU!
LOOK! IT'S JENNIFER LOPEZ!
WHERE?
WOOSHH

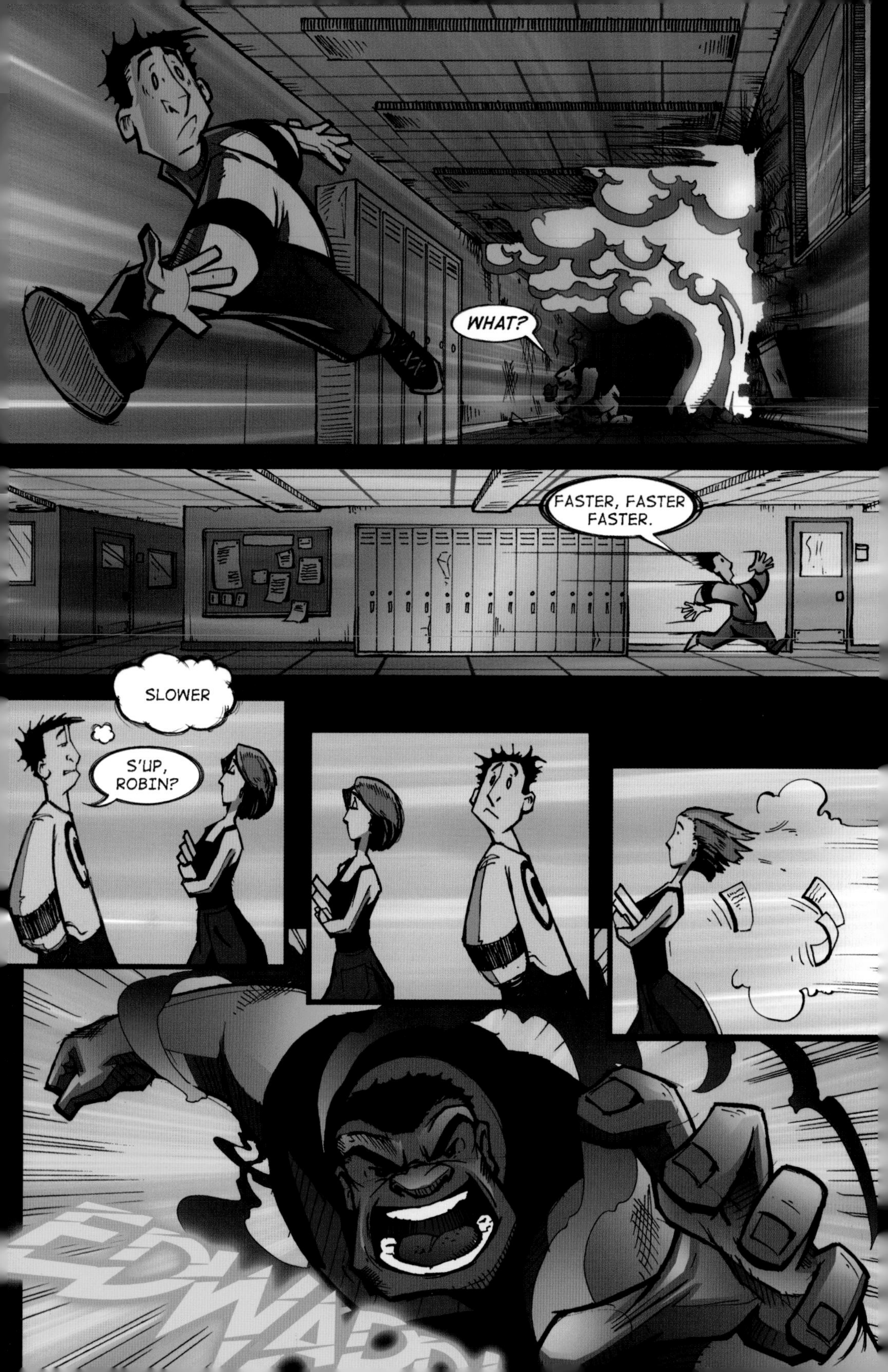

WHAT?
FASTER, FASTER
FASTER.
SLOWER
S'UP, ROBIN?

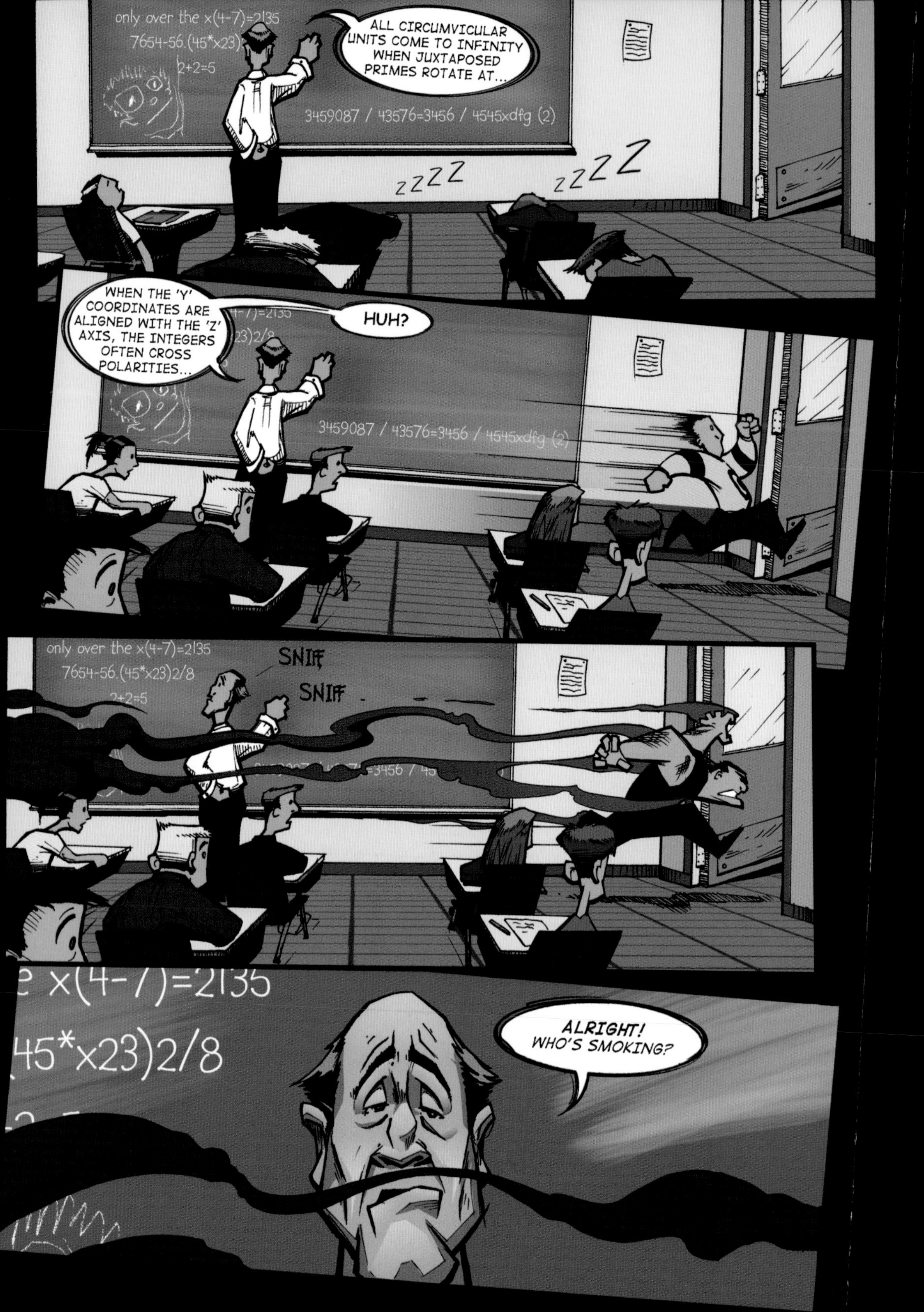
only over the x(4-7)=2135
7654-56.(45*x23)
2+2=5
ALL CIRCUMVICULAR UNITS COME TO INFINITY WHEN JUXTAPOSED PRIMES ROTATE AT...
3459087 / 43576=3456 / 4545xdfg (2)
zzZZ
zzZZ
WHEN THE 'Y' COORDINATES ARE ALIGNED WITH THE 'Z' AXIS, THE INTEGERS OFTEN CROSS POLARITIES...
HUH?
SNIFF
SNIFF
ALRIGHT! WHO'S SMOKING?

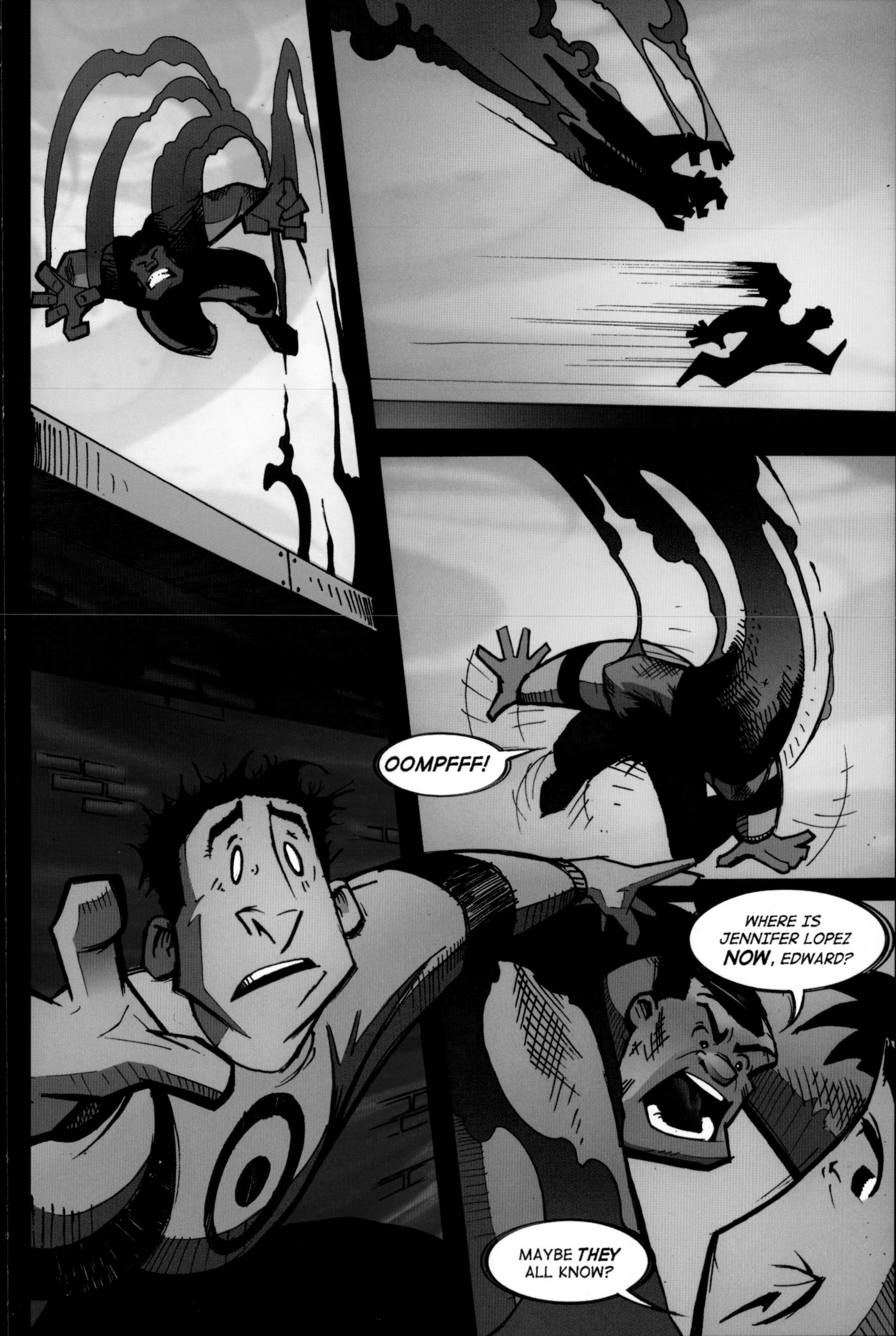
OOMPFFF!
WHERE IS JENNIFER LOPEZ NOW, EDWARD?
MAYBE THEY ALL KNOW?

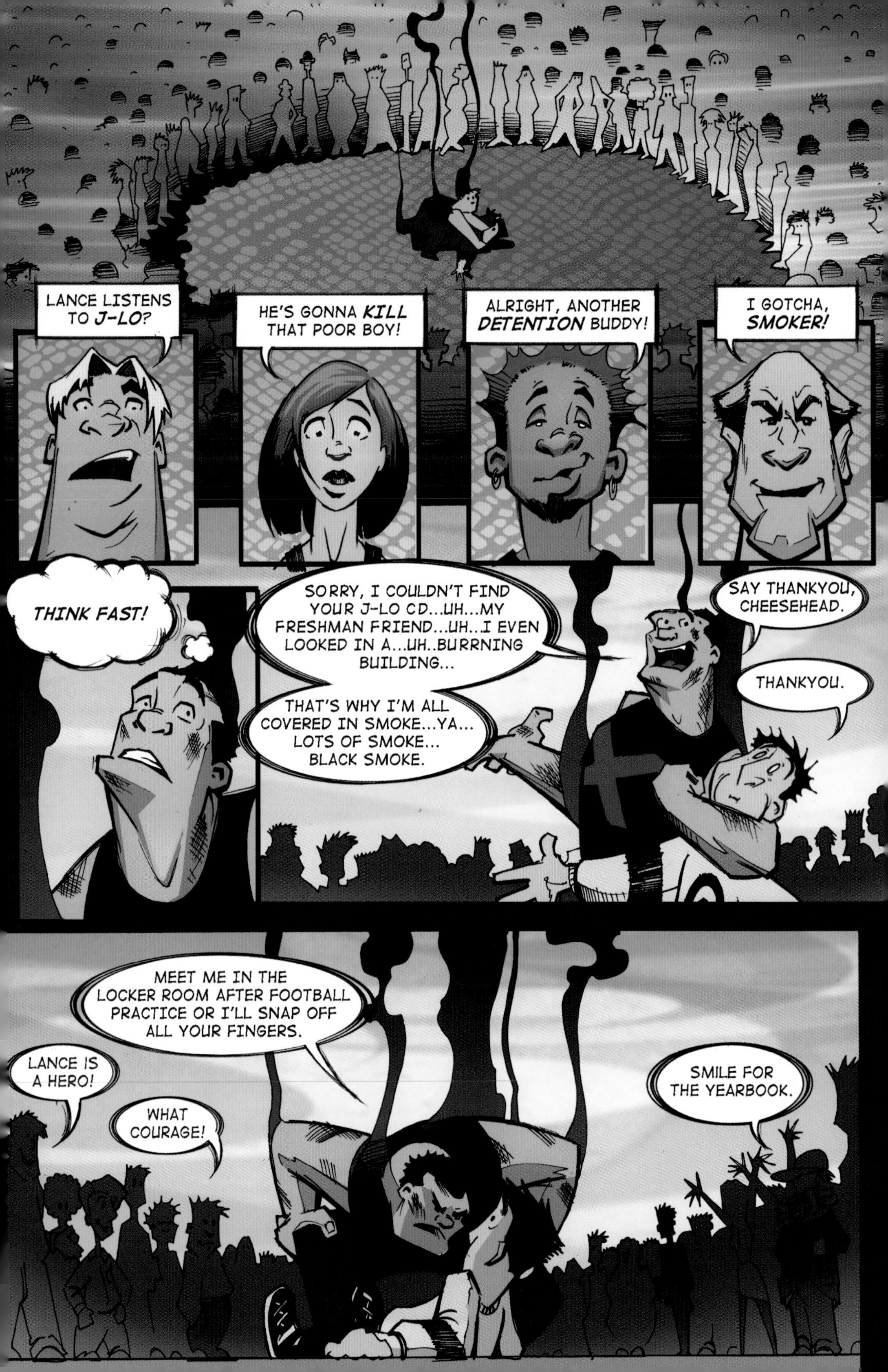
LANCE LISTENS TO J-LO?
HE'S GONNA KILL THAT POOR BOY!
ALRIGHT, ANOTHER DETENTION BUDDY!
I GOTCHA, SMOKER!
THINK FAST!
SORRY, I COULDN'T FIND YOUR J-LO CD...UH...MY FRESHMAN FRIEND...UH...I EVEN LOOKED IN A...UH..BURRNING BUILDING...
THAT'S WHY I'M ALL COVERED IN SMOKE...YA... LOTS OF SMOKE... BLACK SMOKE.
SAY THANKYOU, CHEESEHEAD.
THANKYOU.
MEET ME IN THE LOCKER ROOM AFTER FOOTBALL PRACTICE OR I'LL SNAP OFF ALL YOUR FINGERS.
LANCE IS A HERO!
WHAT COURAGE!
SMILE FOR THE YEARBOOK.

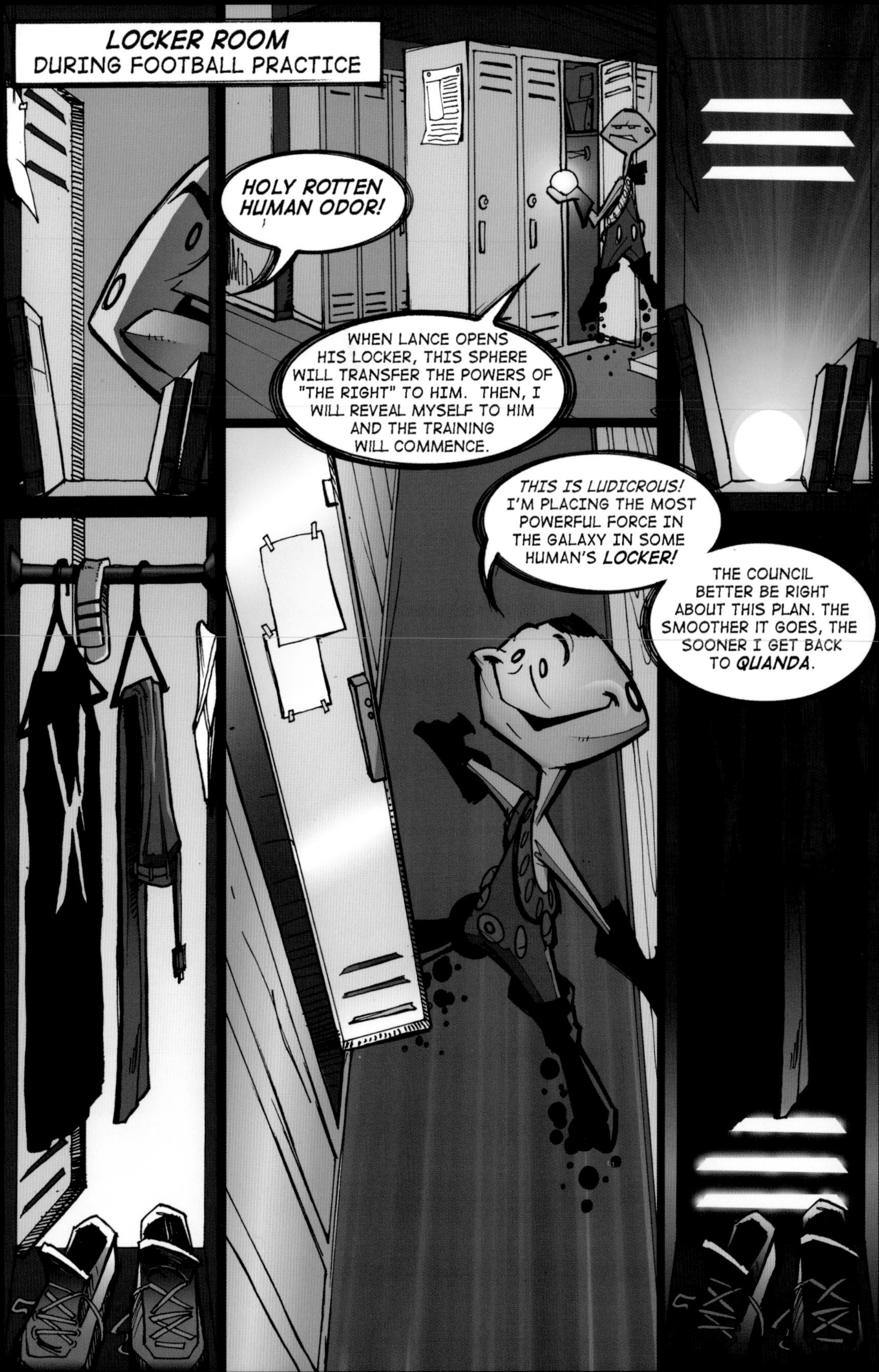
LOCKER ROOM
DURING FOOTBALL PRACTICE
HOLY ROTTEN HUMAN ODOR!
WHEN LANCE OPENS HIS LOCKER, THIS SPHERE WILL TRANSFER THE POWERS OF "THE RIGHT" TO HIM. THEN, I WILL REVEAL MYSELF TO HIM AND THE TRAINING WILL COMMENCE.
THIS IS LUDICROUS! I'M PLACING THE MOST POWERFUL FORCE IN THE GALAXY IN SOME HUMAN'S LOCKER!
THE COUNCIL BETTER BE RIGHT ABOUT THIS PLAN. THE SMOOTHER IT GOES, THE SOONER I GET BACK TO QUANDA.

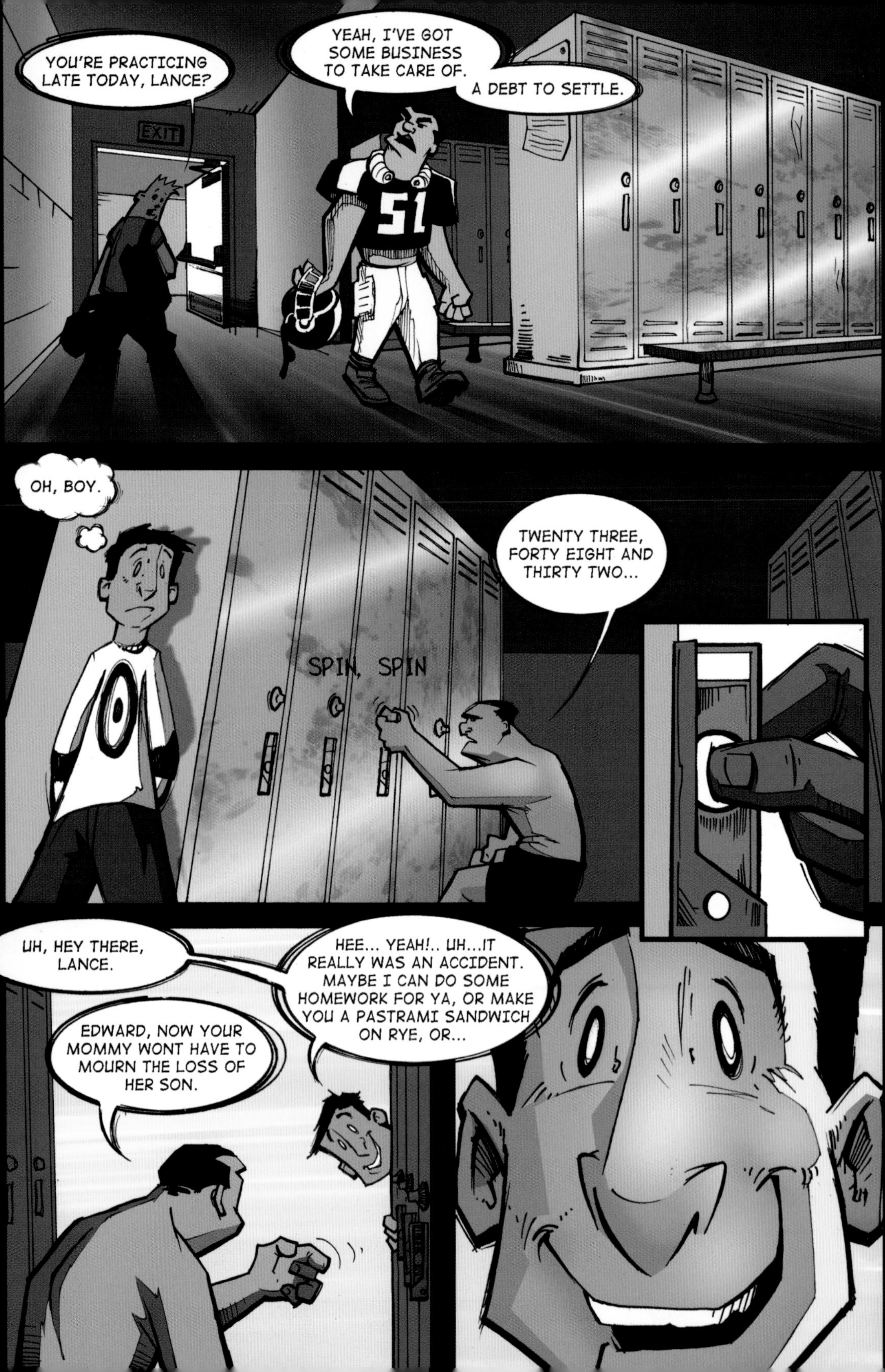
YOU'RE PRACTICING LATE TODAY, LANCE?
YEAH, I'VE GOT SOME BUSINESS TO TAKE CARE OF.
A DEBT TO SETTLE.
EXIT
51
OH, BOY.
TWENTY THREE, FORTY EIGHT AND THIRTY TWO...
SPIN, SPIN
UH, HEY THERE, LANCE.
HEE... YEAH!.. UH...IT REALLY WAS AN ACCIDENT. MAYBE I CAN DO SOME HOMEWORK FOR YA, OR MAKE YOU A PASTRAMI SANDWICH ON RYE, OR...
EDWARD, NOW YOUR MOMMY WONT HAVE TO MOURN THE LOSS OF HER SON.

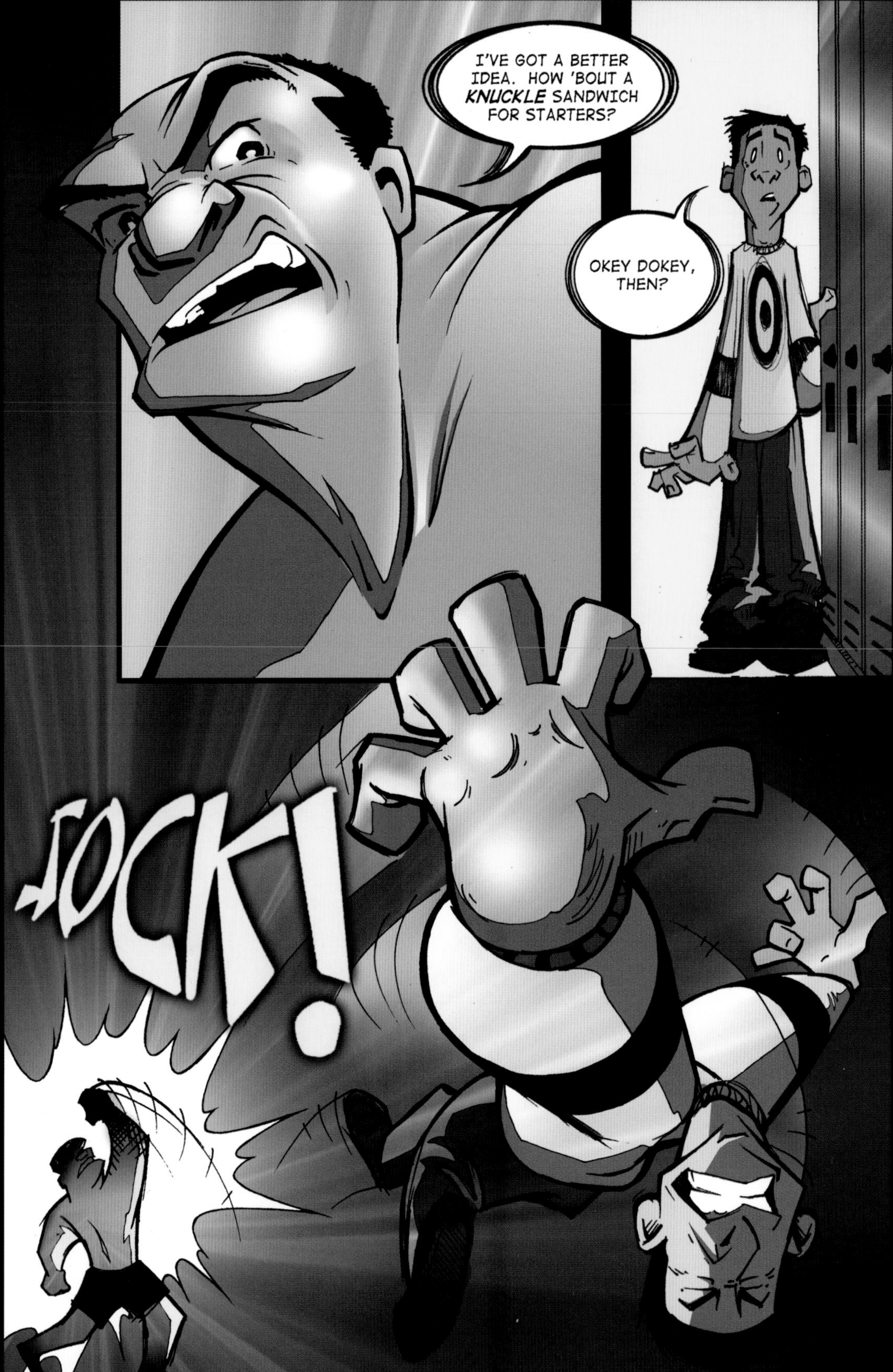
I'VE GOT A BETTER IDEA. HOW 'BOUT A KNUCKLE SANDWICH FOR STARTERS?
OKEY DOKEY, THEN?
SOCK!

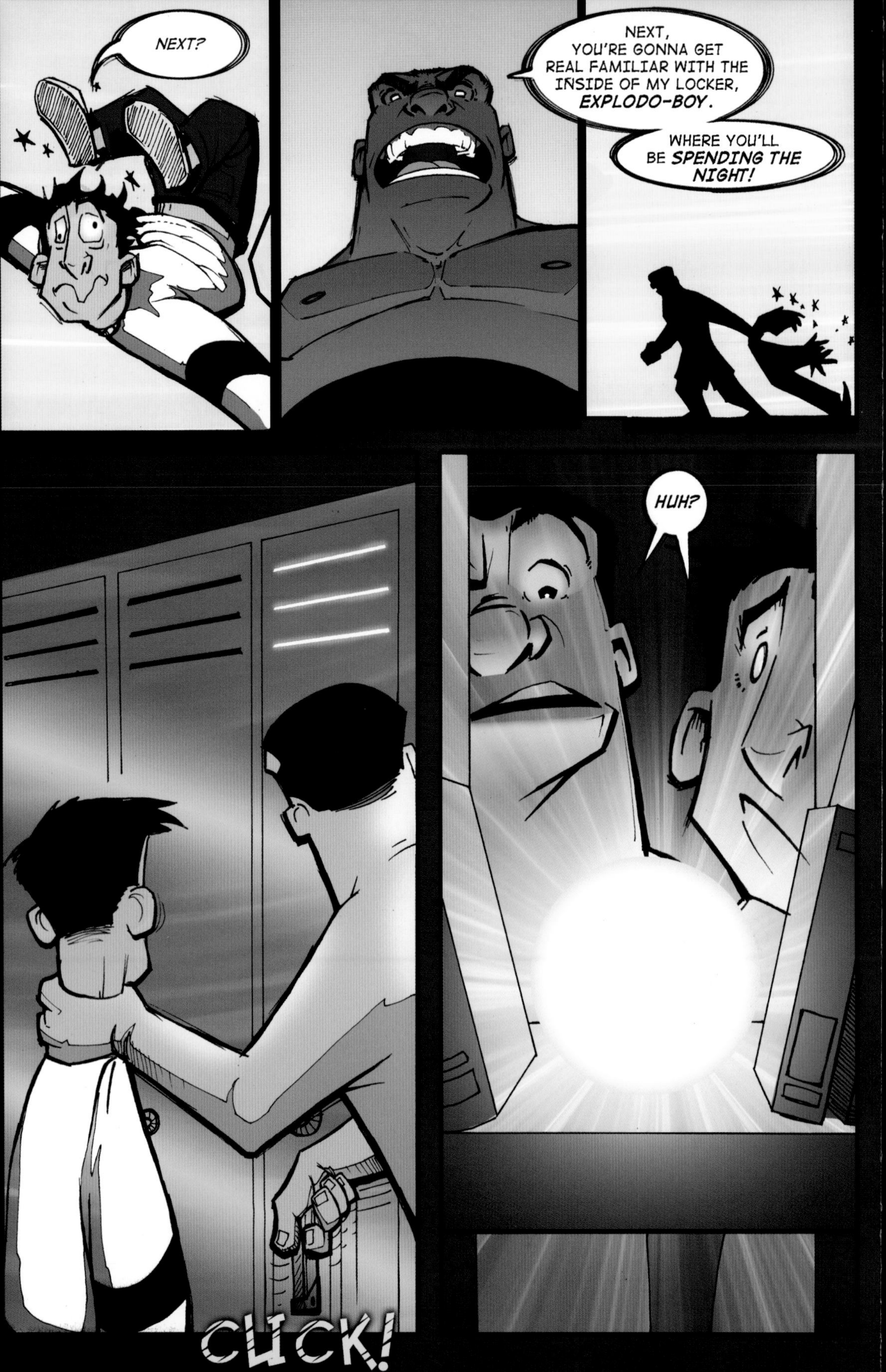
NEXT?
NEXT, YOU'RE GONNA GET REAL FAMILIAR WITH THE INSIDE OF MY LOCKER, EXPLODO-BOY.
WHERE YOU'LL BE SPENDING THE NIGHT!
CLICK!
HUH?

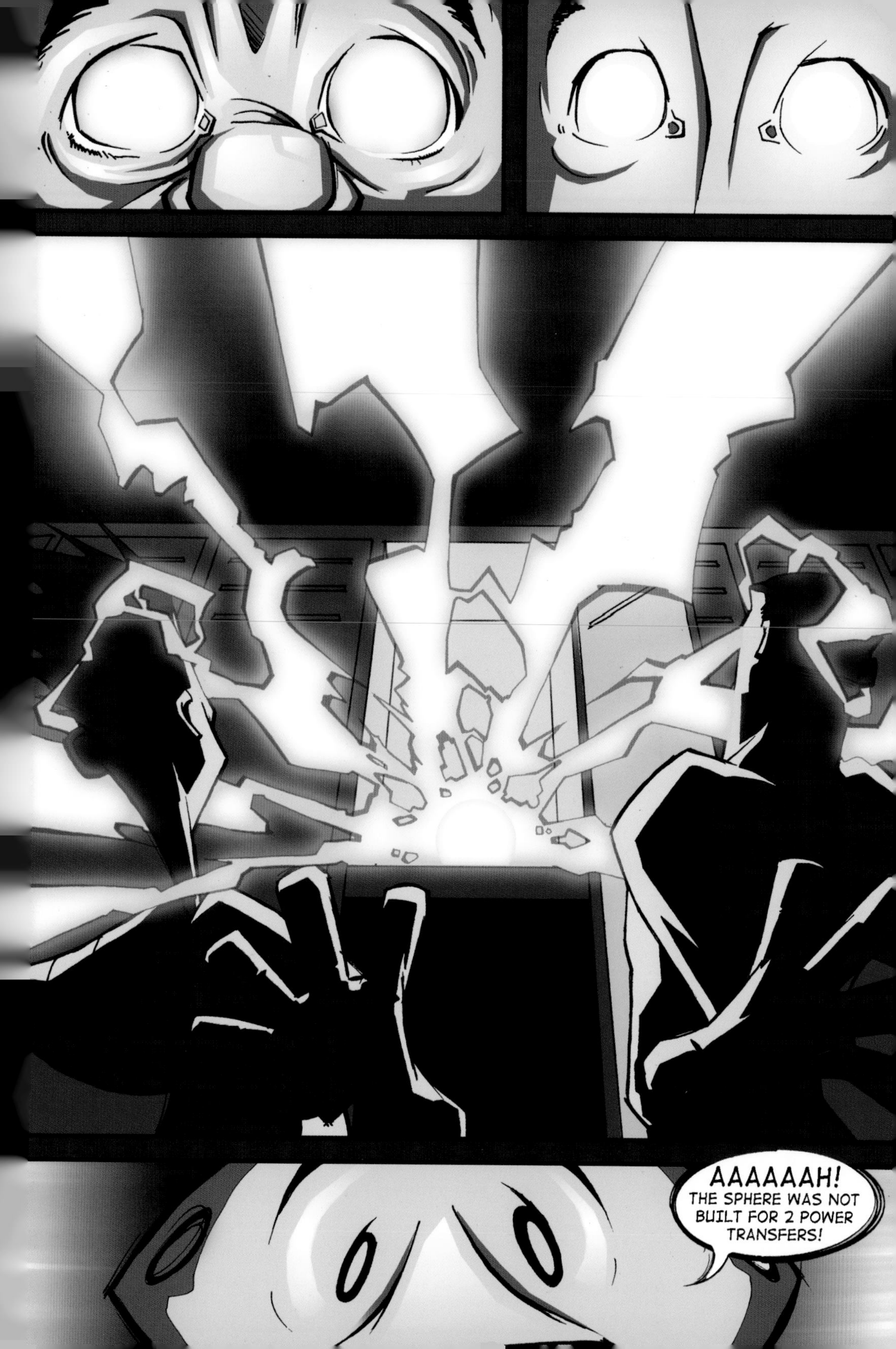
AAAAAAH! THE SPHERE WAS NOT BUILT FOR 2 POWER TRANSFERS!

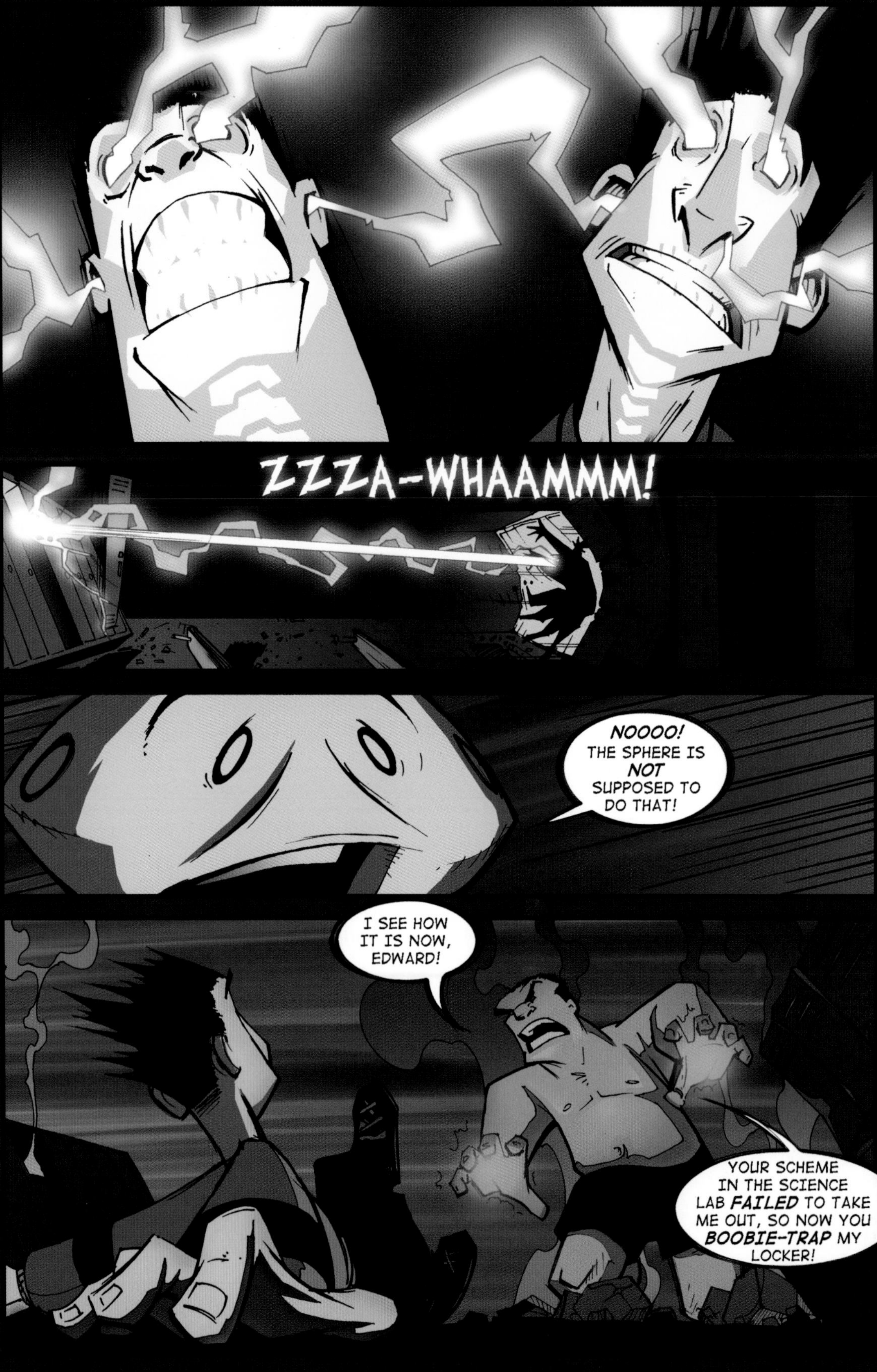
ZZZA-WHAAMMM!
NOOOO! THE SPHERE IS NOT SUPPOSED TO DO THAT!
I SEE HOW IT IS NOW, EDWARD!
YOUR SCHEME IN THE SCIENCE LAB FAILED TO TAKE ME OUT, SO NOW YOU BOOBIE-TRAP MY LOCKER!

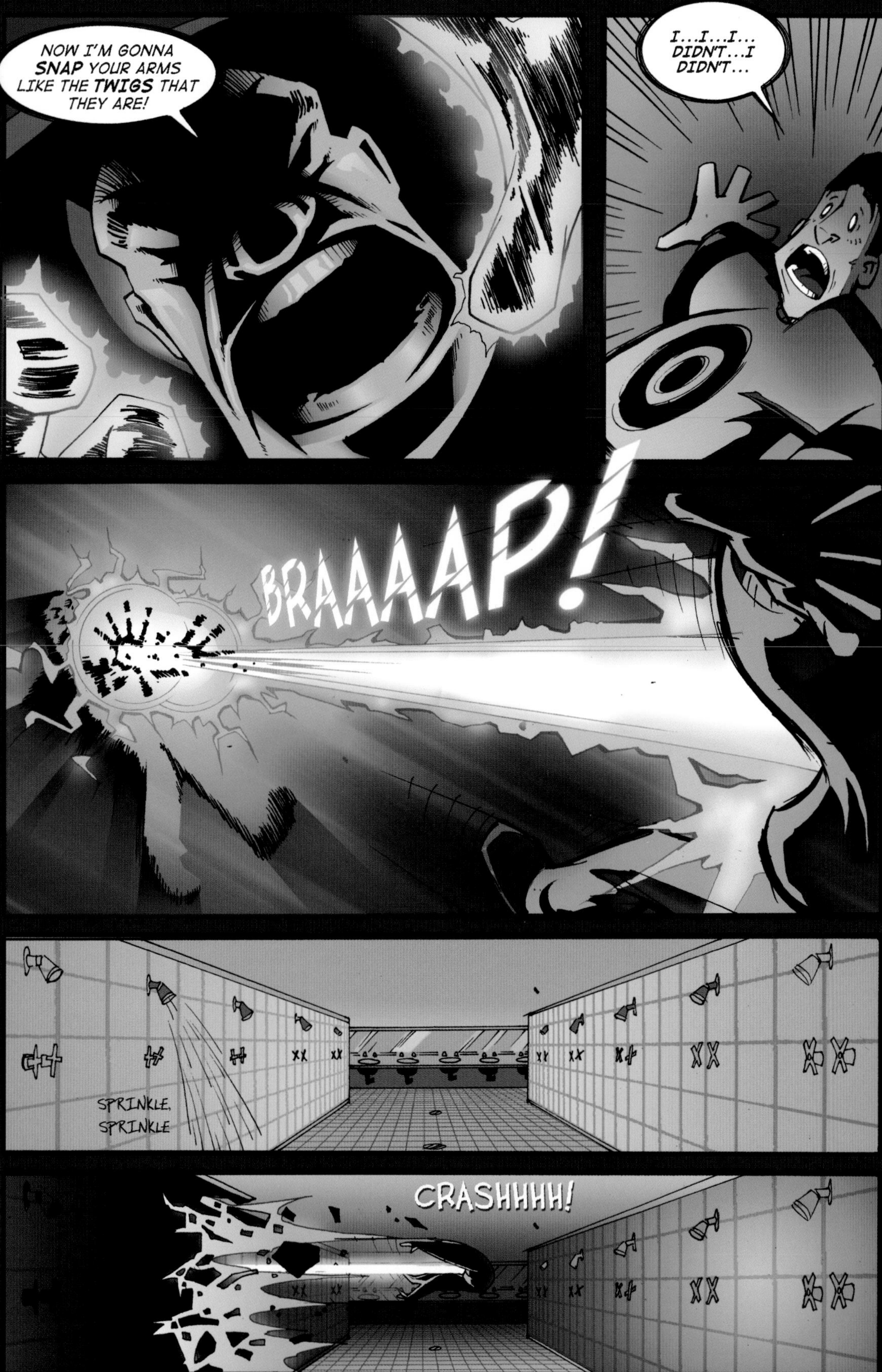
NOW I'M GONNA SNAP YOUR ARMS LIKE THE TWIGS THAT THEY ARE!
I...I...I... DIDN'T...I DIDN'T...
BRAAAAP!
SPRINKLE, SPRINKLE
CRASHHHH!

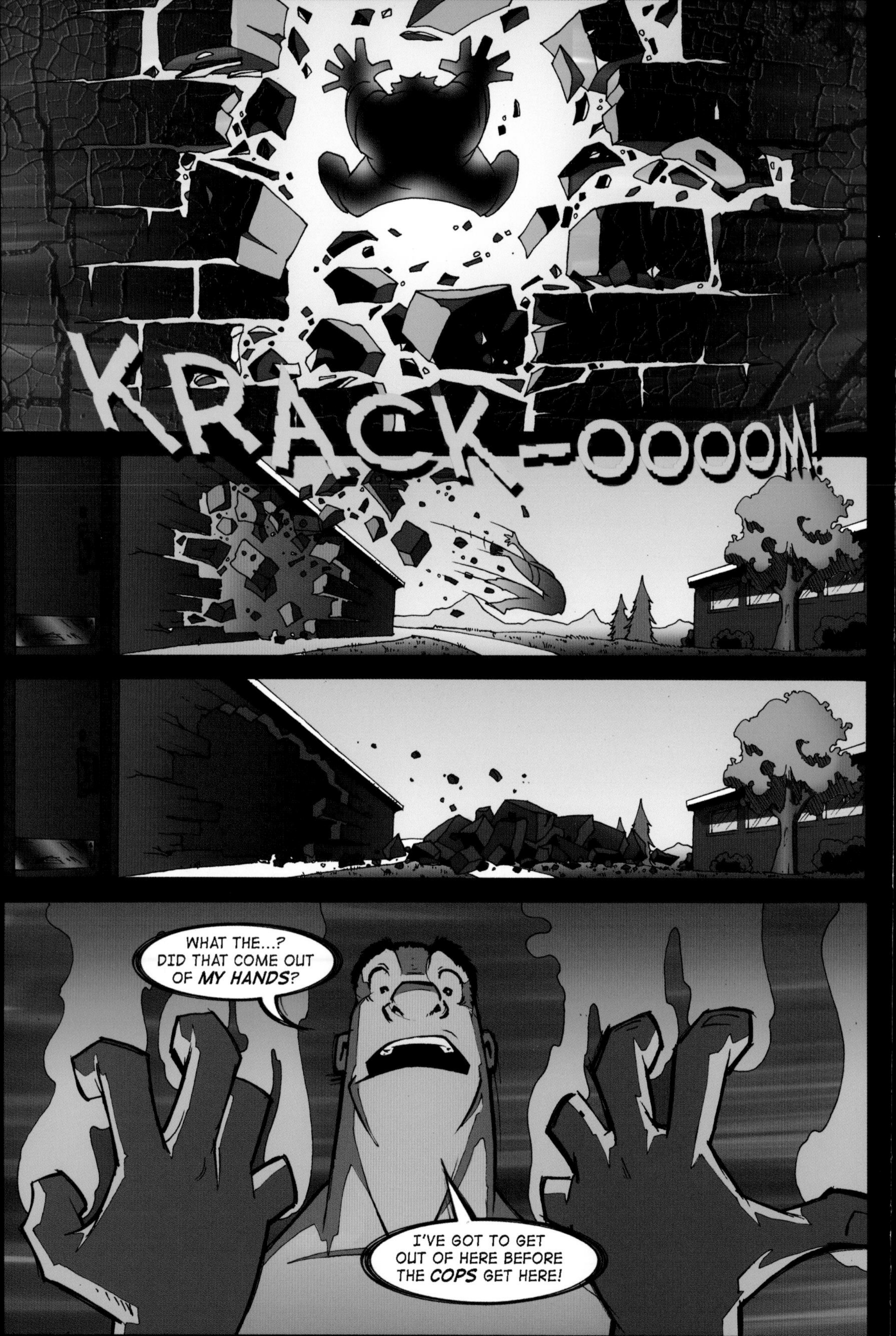
KRACK-OOOOM!
WHAT THE...? DID THAT COME OUT OF MY HANDS?
I'VE GOT TO GET OUT OF HERE BEFORE THE COPS GET HERE!

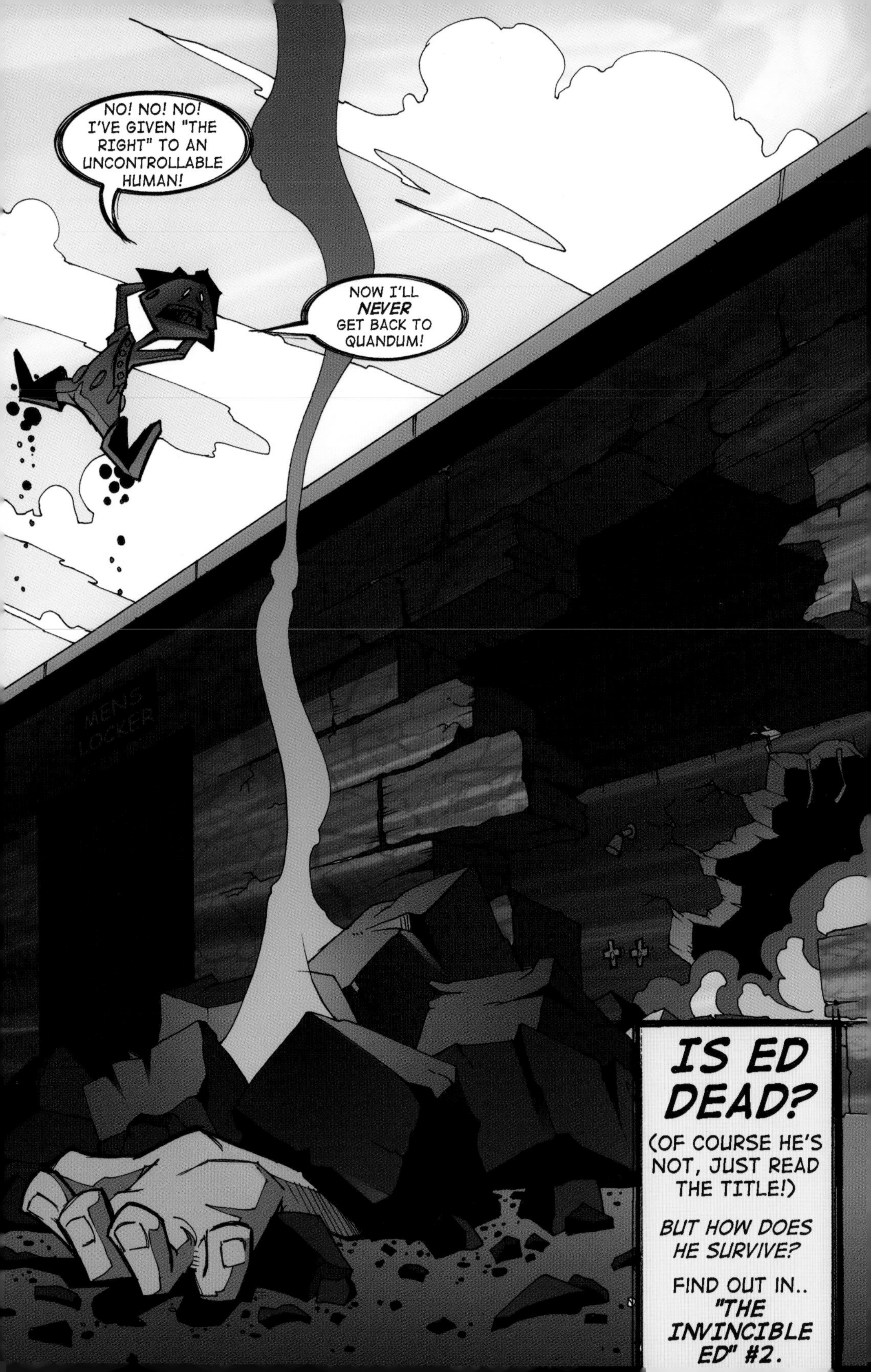
NO! NO! NO! I'VE GIVEN "THE RIGHT" TO AN UNCONTROLLABLE HUMAN!
NOW I'LL ***NEVER*** GET BACK TO QUANDUM!
MENS LOCKER
IS ED DEAD?
(OF COURSE HE'S NOT, JUST READ THE TITLE!)
BUT HOW DOES HE SURVIVE?
FIND OUT IN.. "THE INVINCIBLE ED" #2.

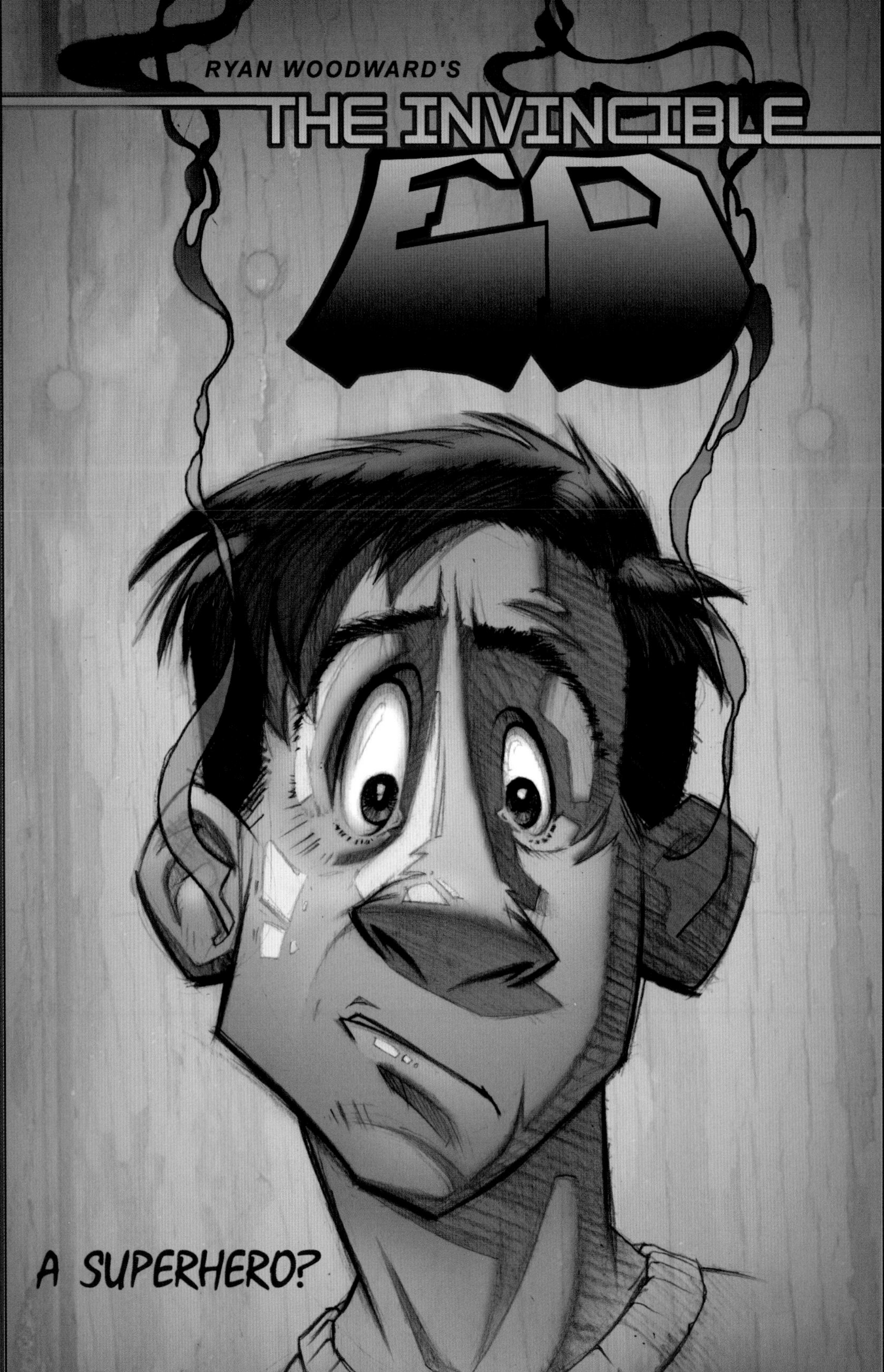
RYAN WOODWARD'S
THE INVINCIBLE
ED
A SUPERHERO?

written and penciled
RYAN WOODWARD

colors
MIKE GARCIA

comic fonts
NATE PIEKOS

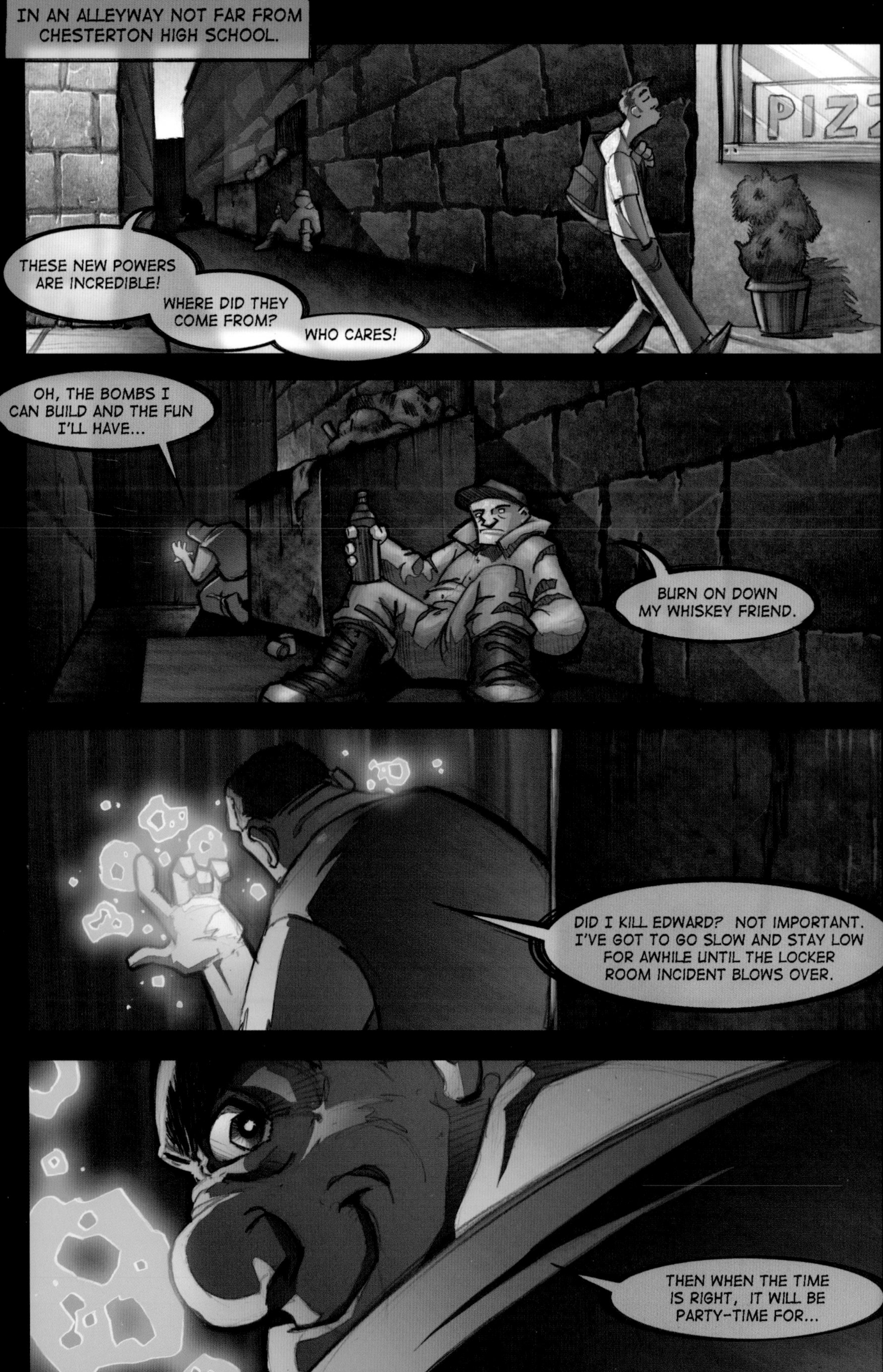
IN AN ALLEYWAY NOT FAR FROM CHESTERTON HIGH SCHOOL.
PIZZ
THESE NEW POWERS ARE INCREDIBLE!
WHERE DID THEY COME FROM?
WHO CARES!
OH, THE BOMBS I CAN BUILD AND THE FUN I'LL HAVE...
BURN ON DOWN MY WHISKEY FRIEND.
DID I KILL EDWARD? NOT IMPORTANT. I'VE GOT TO GO SLOW AND STAY LOW FOR AWHILE UNTIL THE LOCKER ROOM INCIDENT BLOWS OVER.
THEN WHEN THE TIME IS RIGHT, IT WILL BE PARTY-TIME FOR...

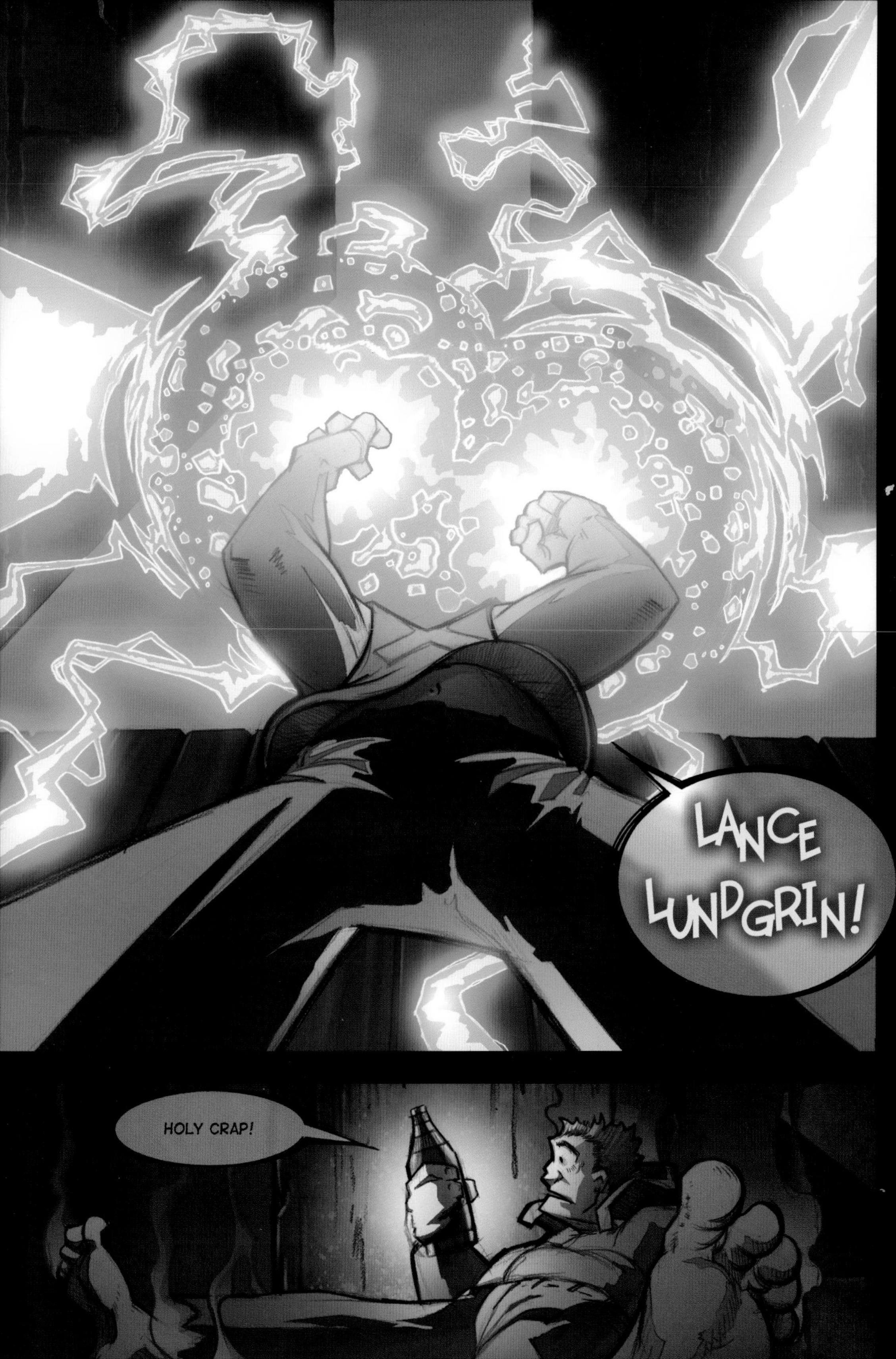
LANCE LUNDGRIN!
HOLY CRAP!

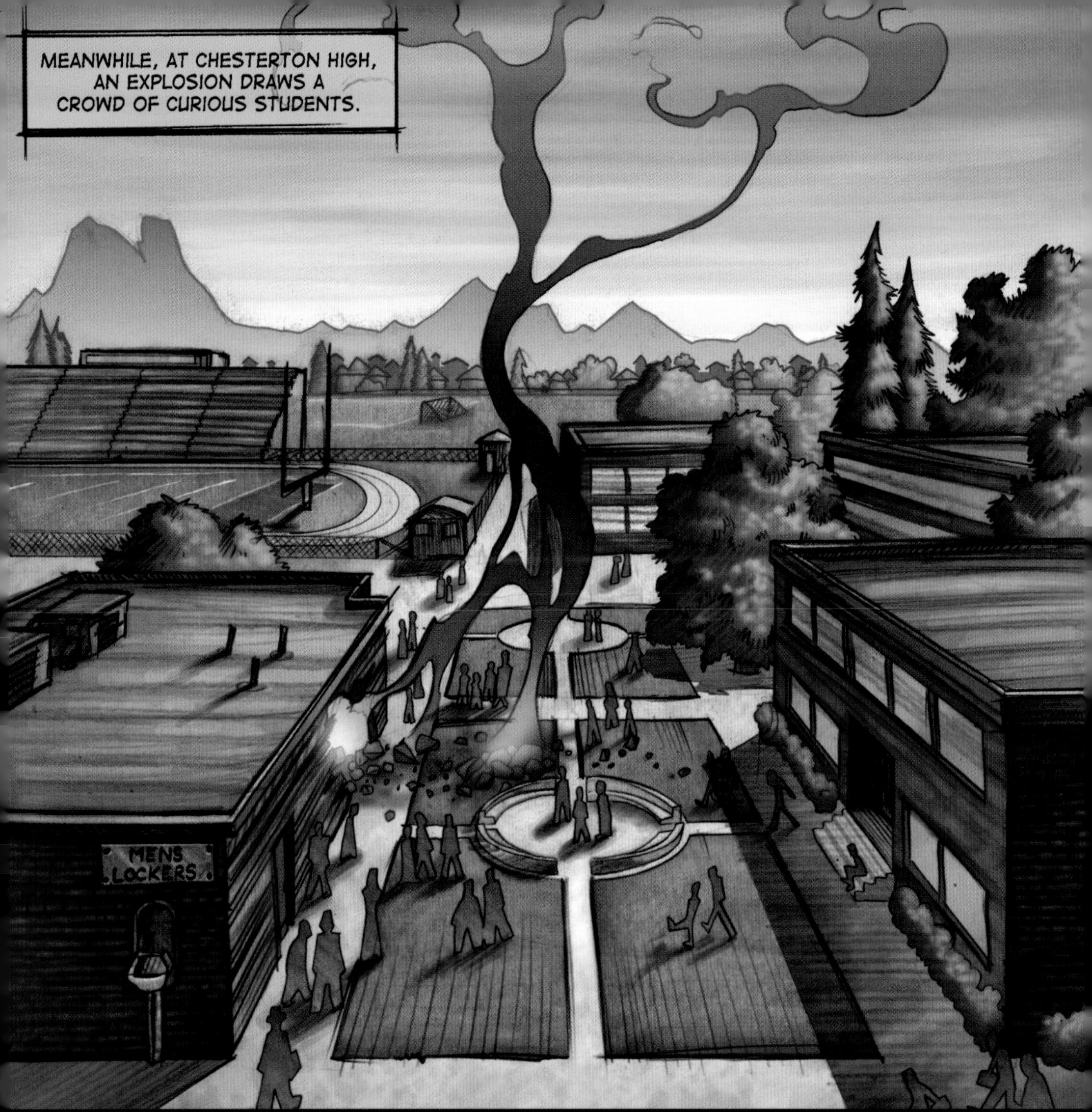
MEANWHILE, AT CHESTERTON HIGH, AN EXPLOSION DRAWS A CROWD OF CURIOUS STUDENTS.
MENS LOCKERS

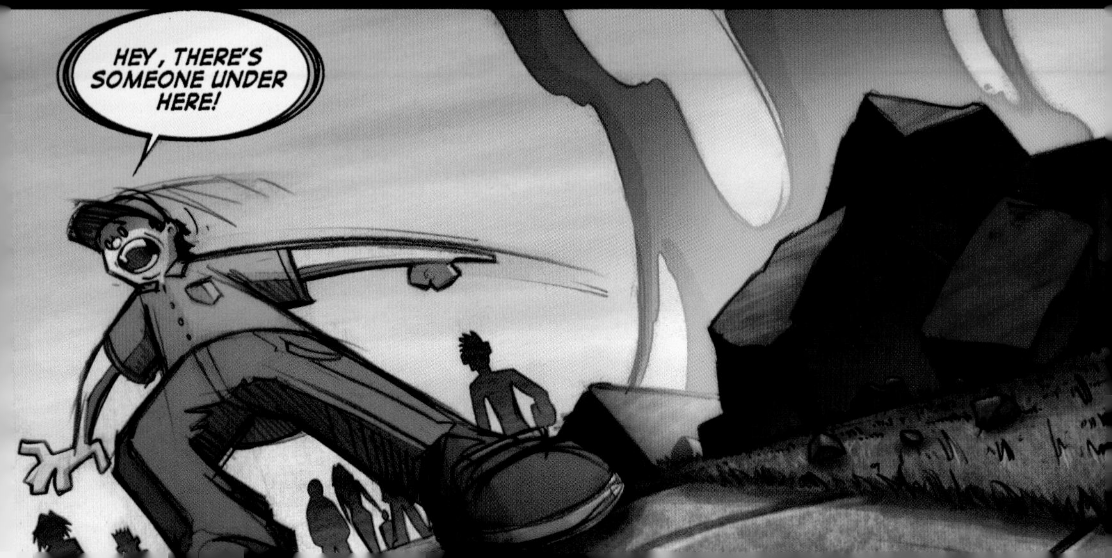
HEY, THERE'S SOMEONE UNDER HERE!

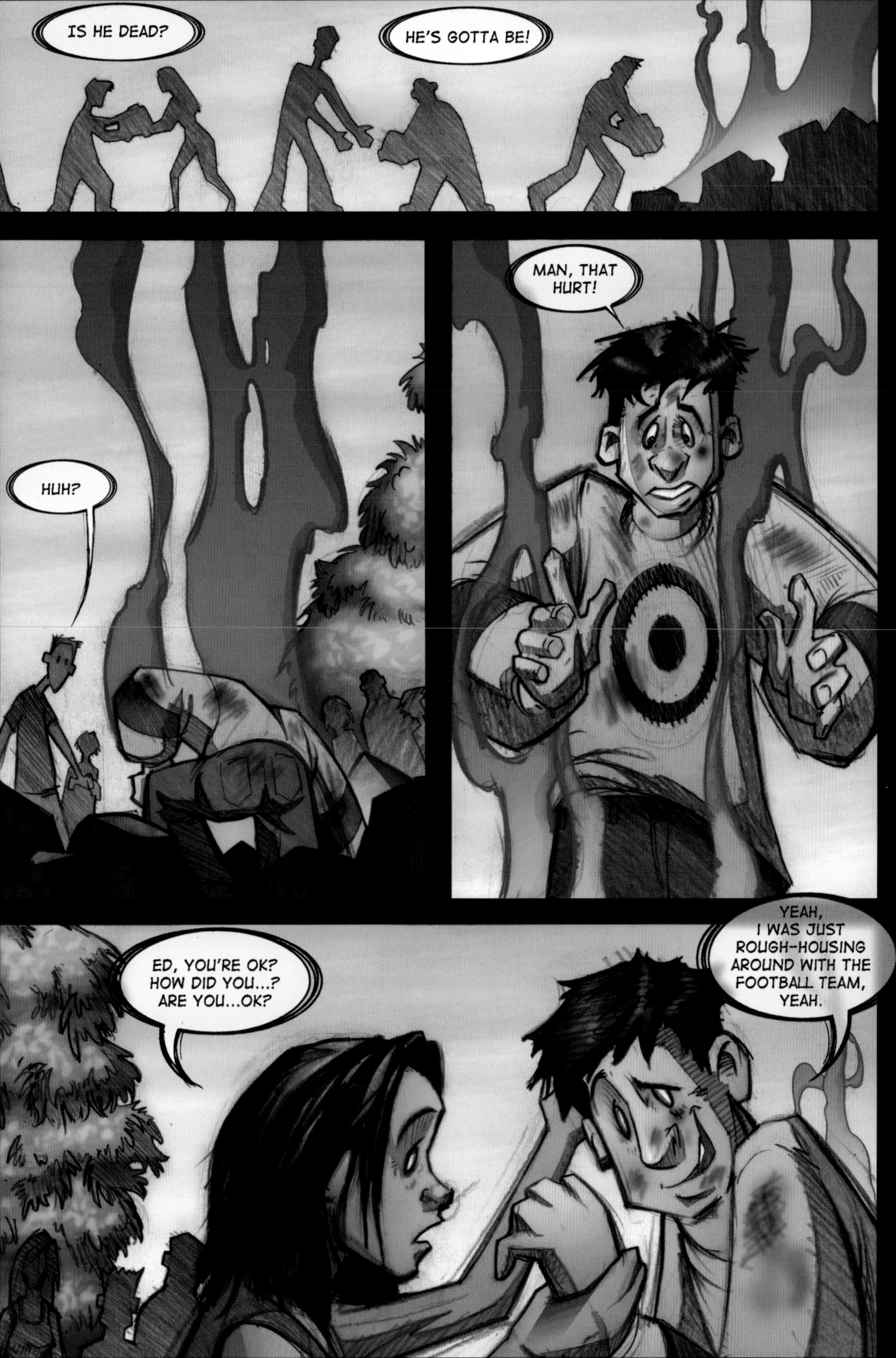
IS HE DEAD?
HE'S GOTTA BE!
HUH?
MAN, THAT HURT!
ED, YOU'RE OK? HOW DID YOU...? ARE YOU...OK?
YEAH, I WAS JUST ROUGH-HOUSING AROUND WITH THE FOOTBALL TEAM, YEAH.

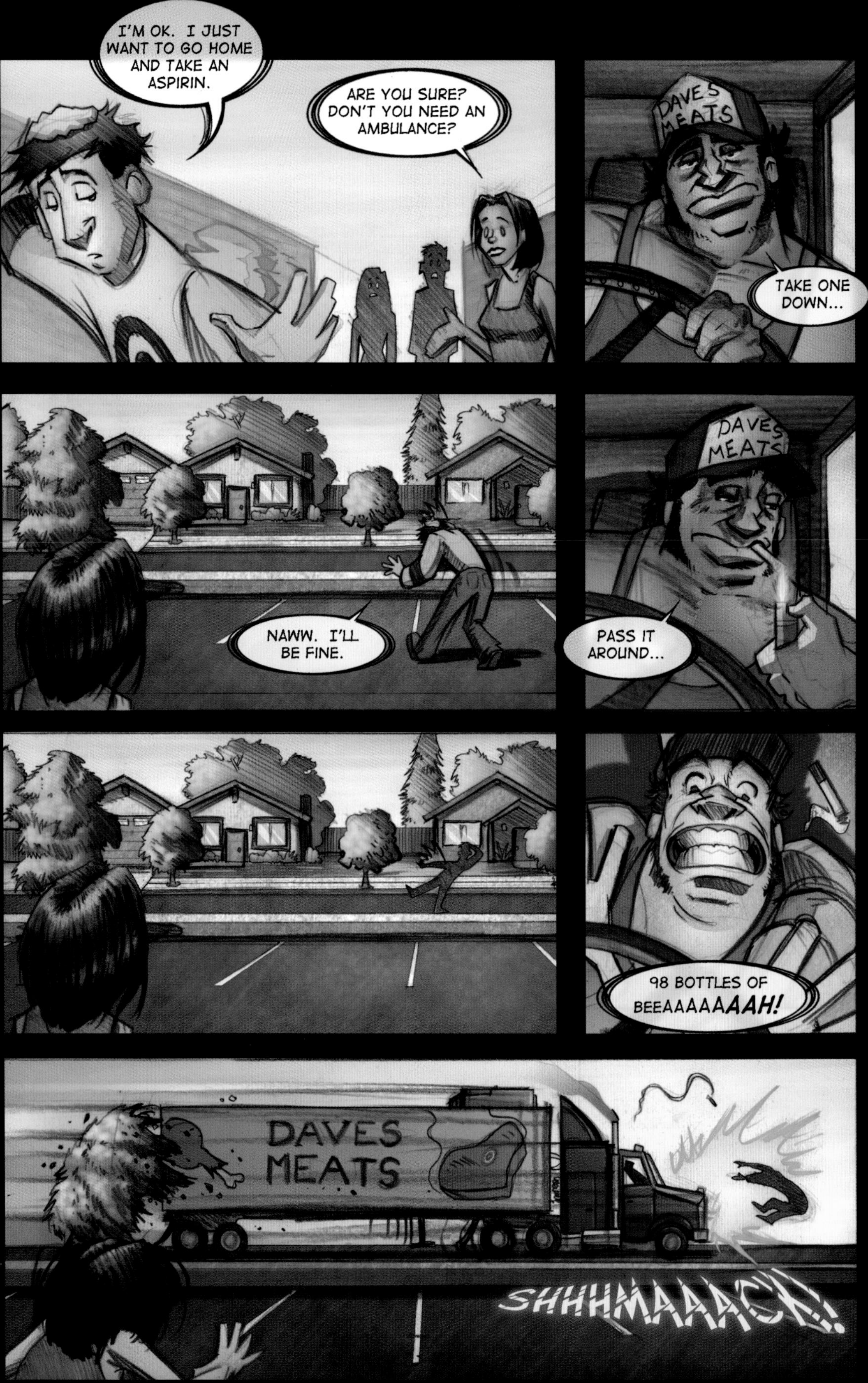
I'M OK. I JUST WANT TO GO HOME AND TAKE AN ASPIRIN.
ARE YOU SURE? DON'T YOU NEED AN AMBULANCE?
DAVES MEATS
TAKE ONE DOWN...
NAWW. I'LL BE FINE.
DAVES MEATS
PASS IT AROUND...
98 BOTTLES OF BEEAAAAAAAH!
DAVES MEATS
SHHHMAAACK!!

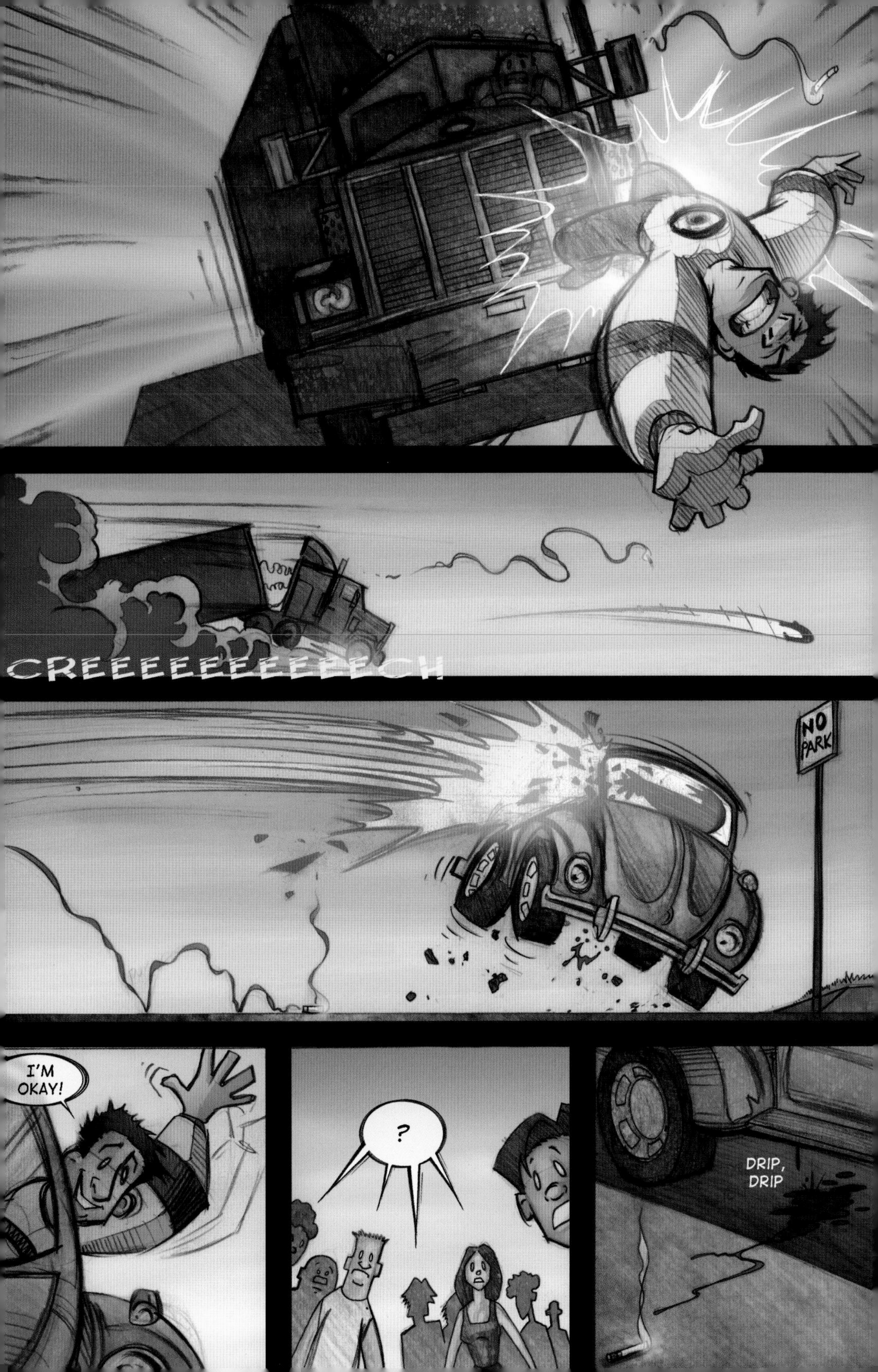
CREEEEEEEEEEEECH
NO PARK
I'M OKAY!
?
DRIP, DRIP

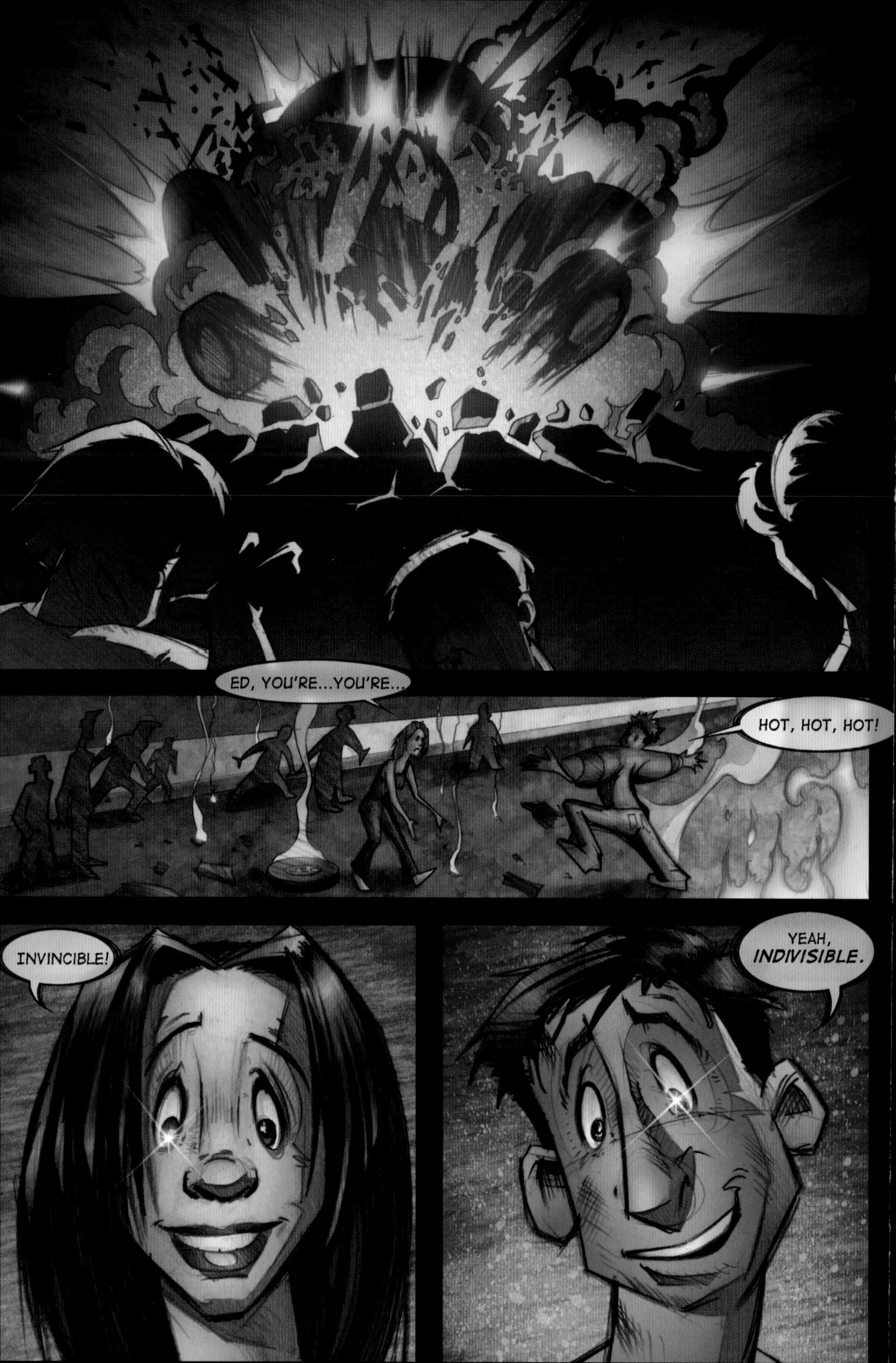
ED, YOU'RE...YOU'RE...
HOT, HOT, HOT!
INVINCIBLE!
YEAH, INDIVISIBLE.

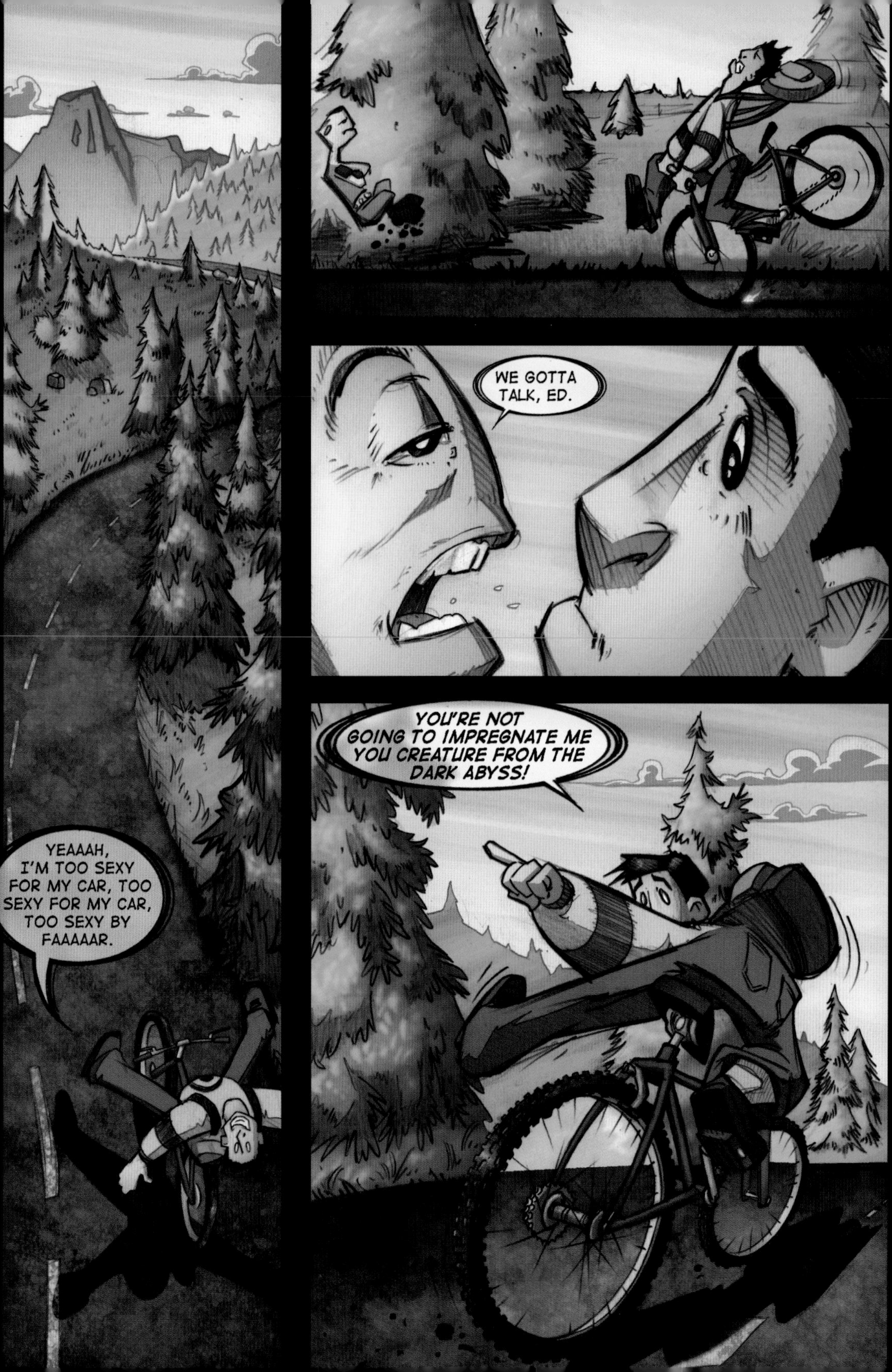
YEAAAH, I'M TOO SEXY FOR MY CAR, TOO SEXY FOR MY CAR, TOO SEXY BY FAAAAAR.
WE GOTTA TALK, ED.
YOU'RE NOT GOING TO IMPREGNATE ME YOU CREATURE FROM THE DARK ABYSS!

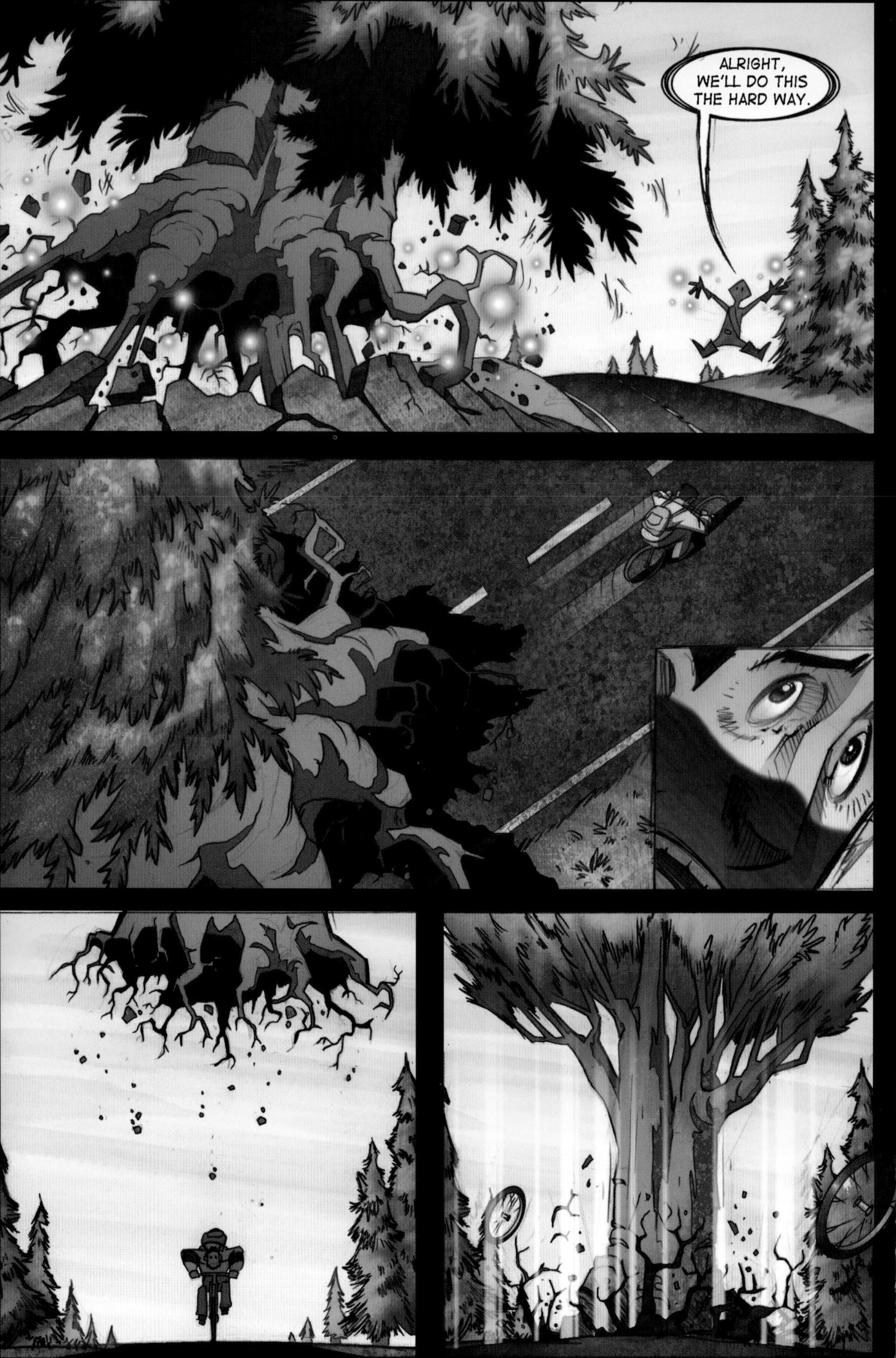
ALRIGHT, WE'LL DO THIS THE HARD WAY.

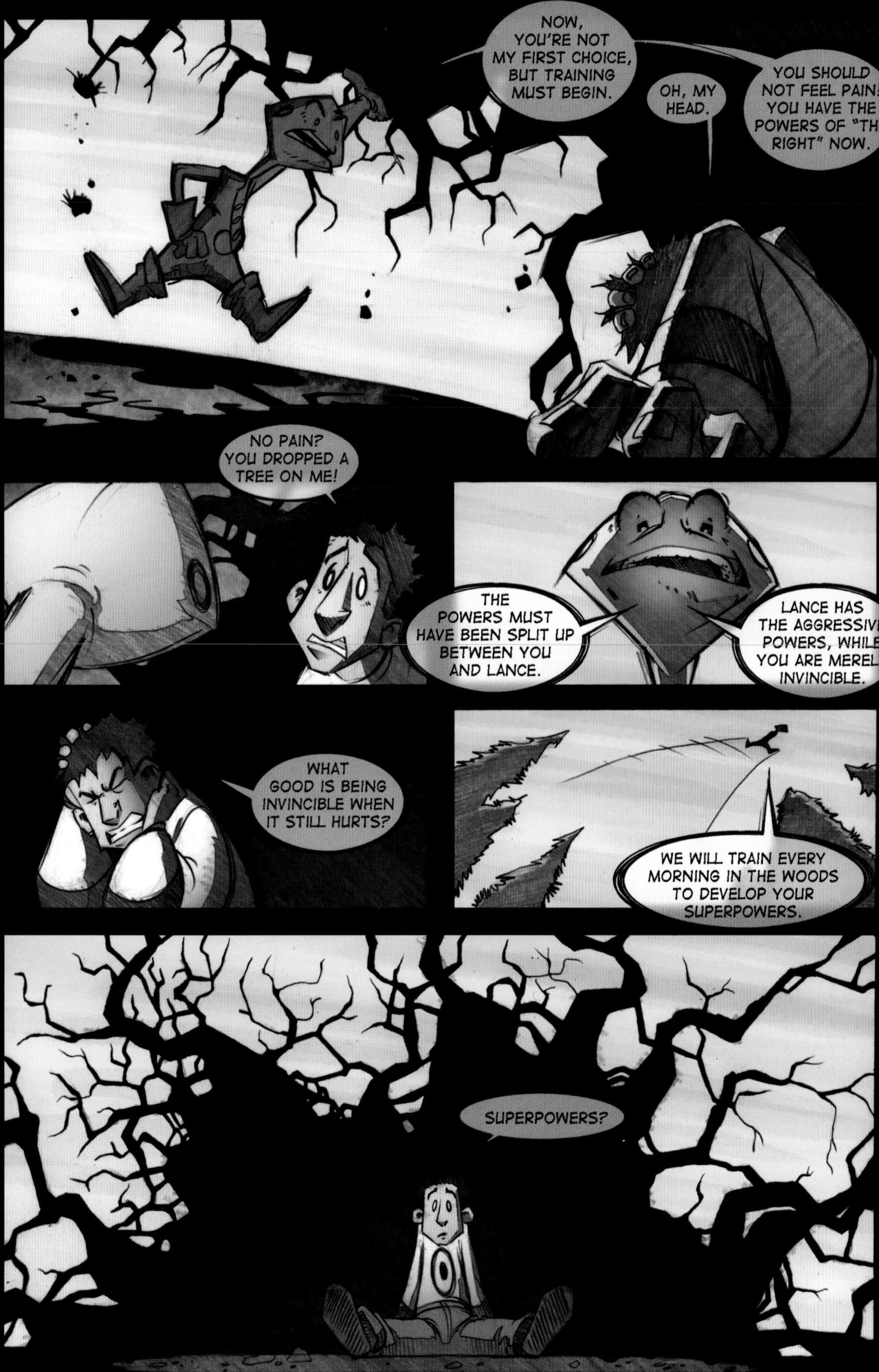
NOW, YOU'RE NOT MY FIRST CHOICE, BUT TRAINING MUST BEGIN.
OH, MY HEAD.
YOU SHOULD NOT FEEL PAIN! YOU HAVE THE POWERS OF "THE RIGHT" NOW.
NO PAIN? YOU DROPPED A TREE ON ME!
THE POWERS MUST HAVE BEEN SPLIT UP BETWEEN YOU AND LANCE.
LANCE HAS THE AGGRESSIVE POWERS, WHILE YOU ARE MERELY INVINCIBLE.
WHAT GOOD IS BEING INVINCIBLE WHEN IT STILL HURTS?
WE WILL TRAIN EVERY MORNING IN THE WOODS TO DEVELOP YOUR SUPERPOWERS.
SUPERPOWERS?

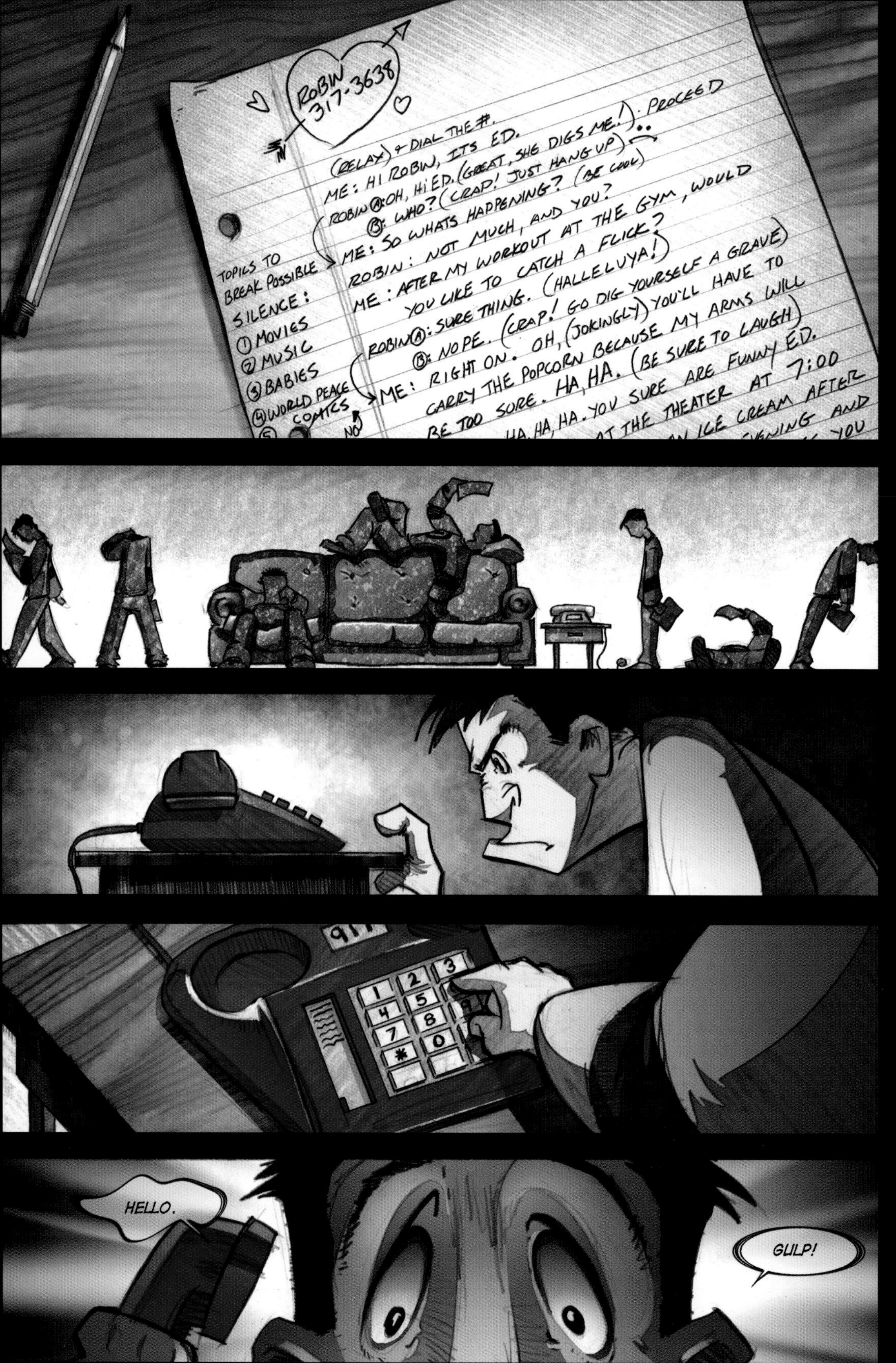
ROBIN 317-3638
(RELAX) & DIAL THE #.
ME: HI ROBIN, ITS ED.
ROBIN Ⓐ: OH, Hi ED. (GREAT, SHE DIGS ME!). PROCEED
Ⓑ: WHO? (CRAP! JUST HANG UP)
ME: SO WHATS HAPPENING? (BE COOL)
ROBIN: NOT MUCH, AND YOU?
ME: AFTER MY WORKOUT AT THE GYM, WOULD YOU LIKE TO CATCH A FLICK?
ROBIN Ⓐ: SURE THING. (HALLELUYA!)
Ⓑ: NOPE. (CRAP! GO DIG YOURSELF A GRAVE)
ME: RIGHT ON. OH, (JOKINGLY) YOU'LL HAVE TO CARRY THE POPCORN BECAUSE MY ARMS WILL BE TOO SORE. HA, HA. (BE SURE TO LAUGH)
HA, HA, HA. YOU SURE ARE FUNNY ED.
TOPICS TO BREAK POSSIBLE SILENCE:
① MOVIES
② MUSIC
③ BABIES
④ WORLD PEACE
COMICS NO
HELLO.
GULP!

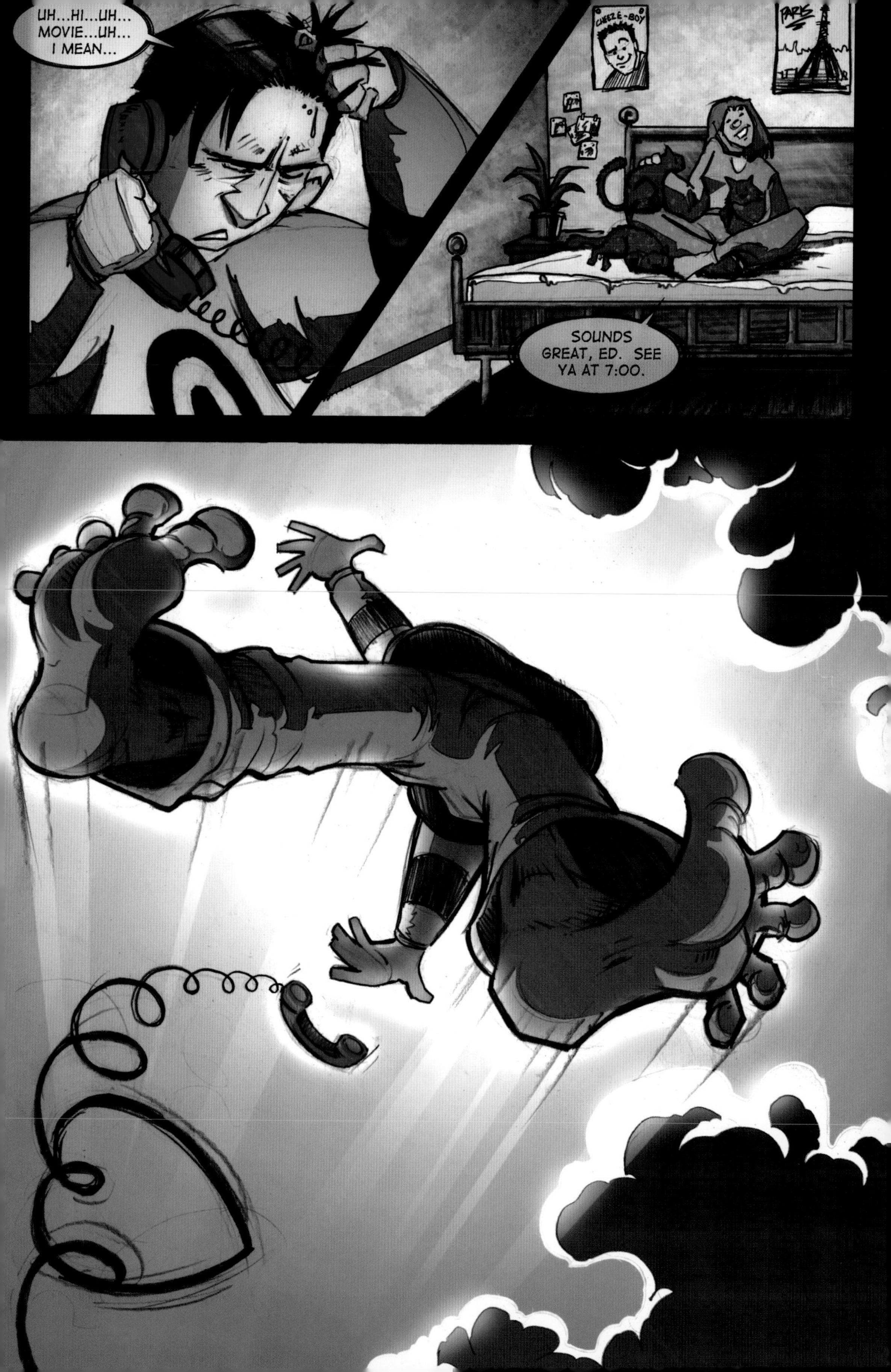
UH...HI...UH...
MOVIE...UH...
I MEAN...
CHEEZE-BOY
PARIS
SOUNDS
GREAT, ED. SEE
YA AT 7:00.

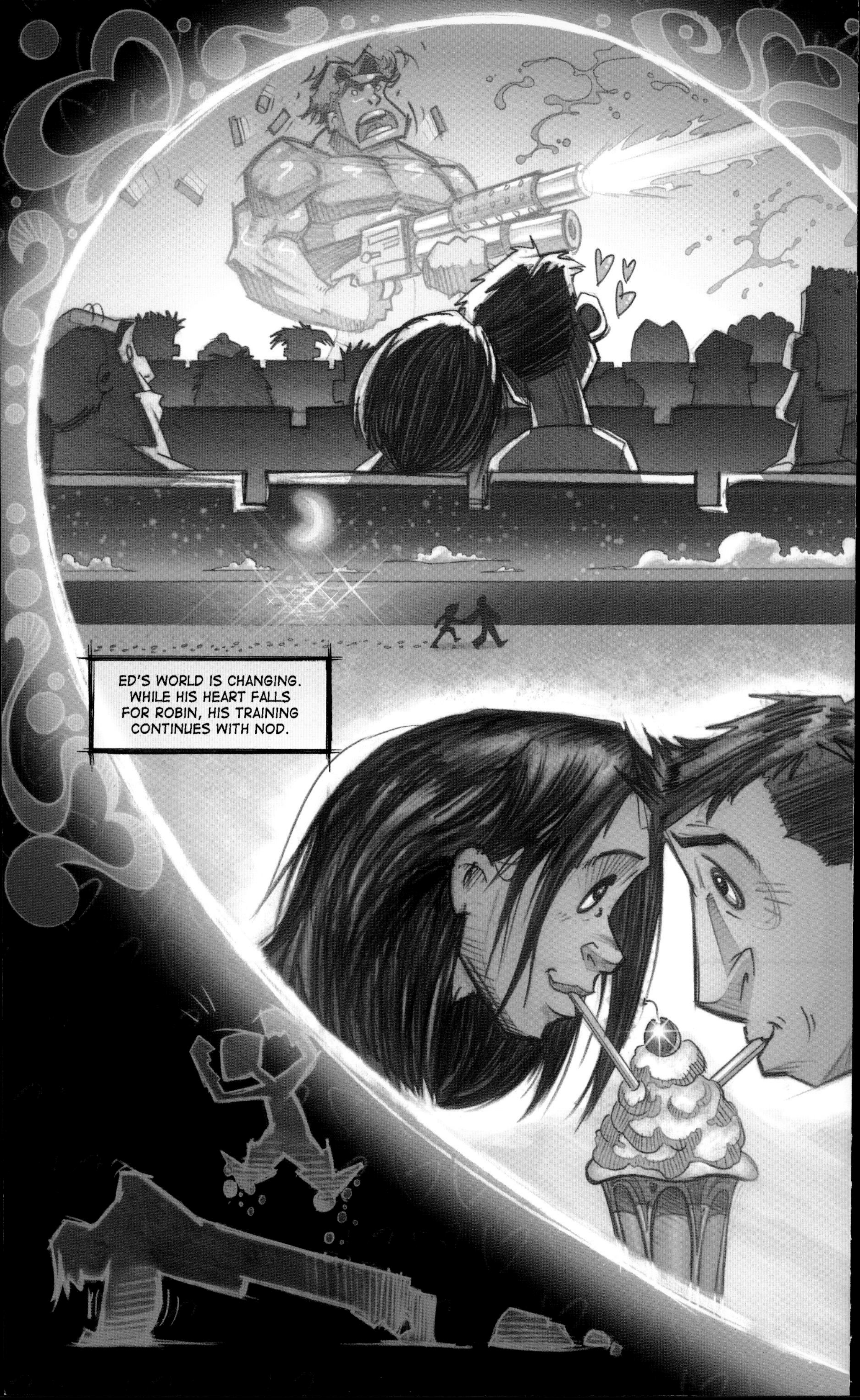
ED'S WORLD IS CHANGING. WHILE HIS HEART FALLS FOR ROBIN, HIS TRAINING CONTINUES WITH NOD.

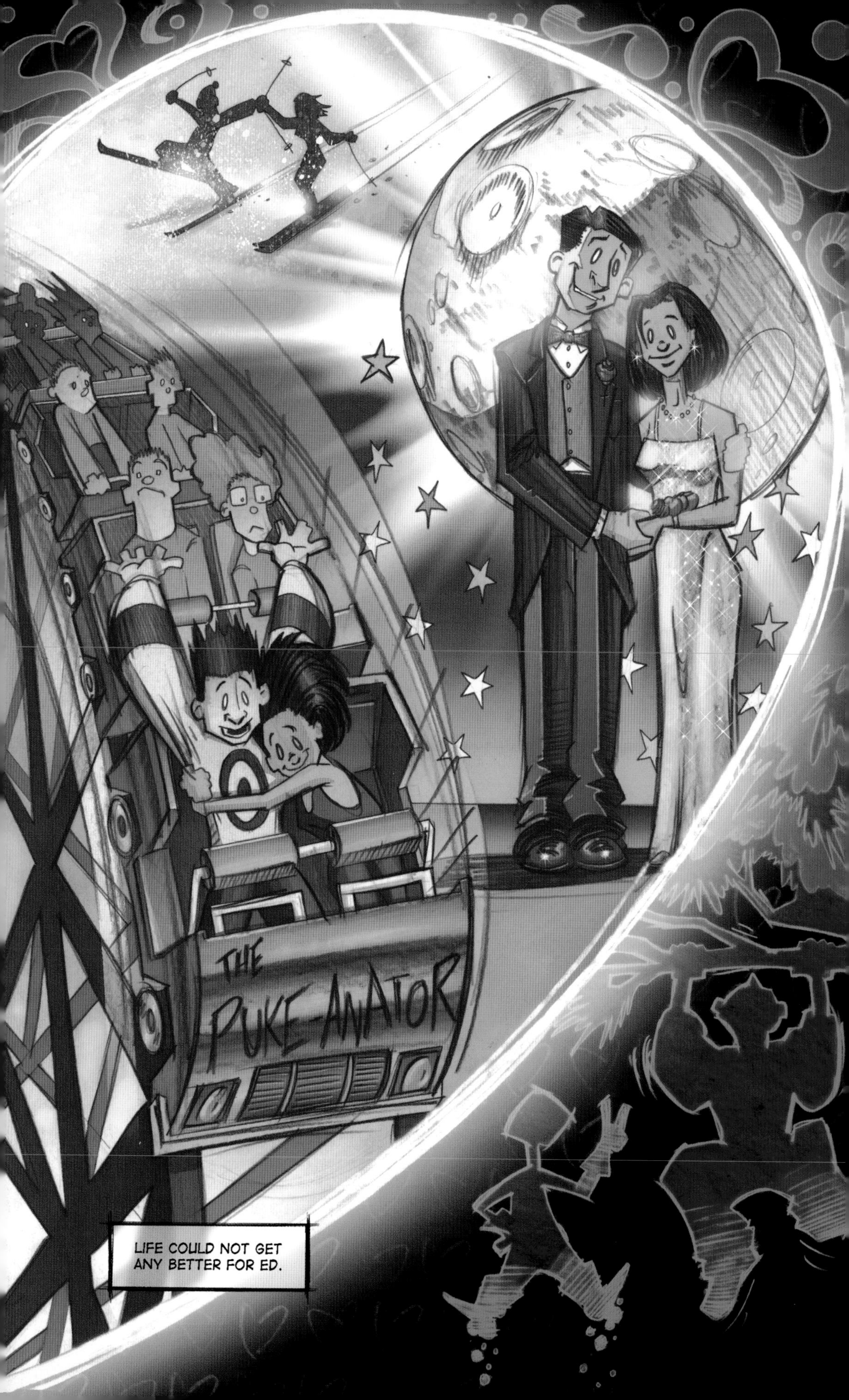
THE PUKE-ANATOR
LIFE COULD NOT GET ANY BETTER FOR ED.

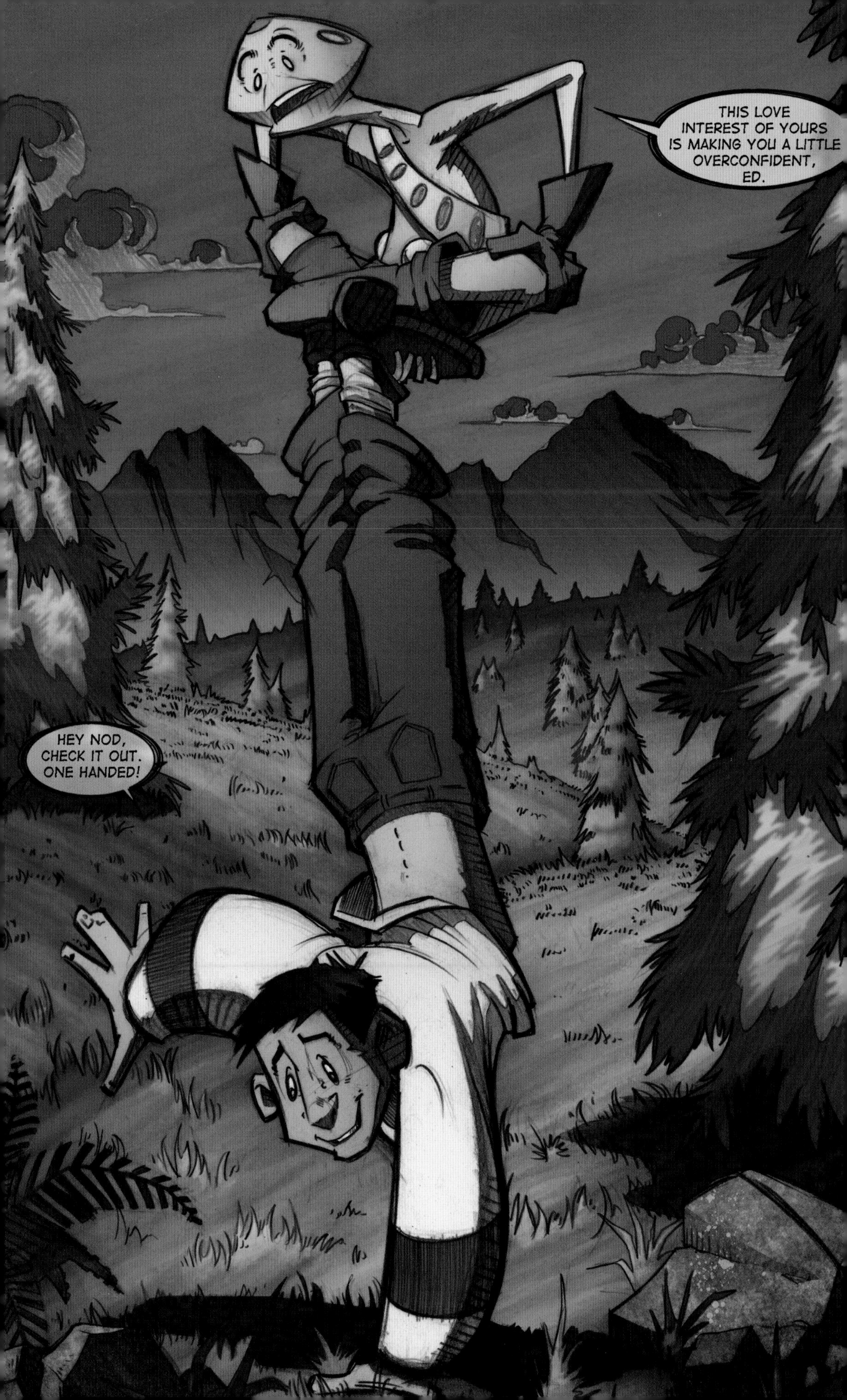
THIS LOVE INTEREST OF YOURS IS MAKING YOU A LITTLE OVERCONFIDENT, ED.
HEY NOD, CHECK IT OUT. ONE HANDED!

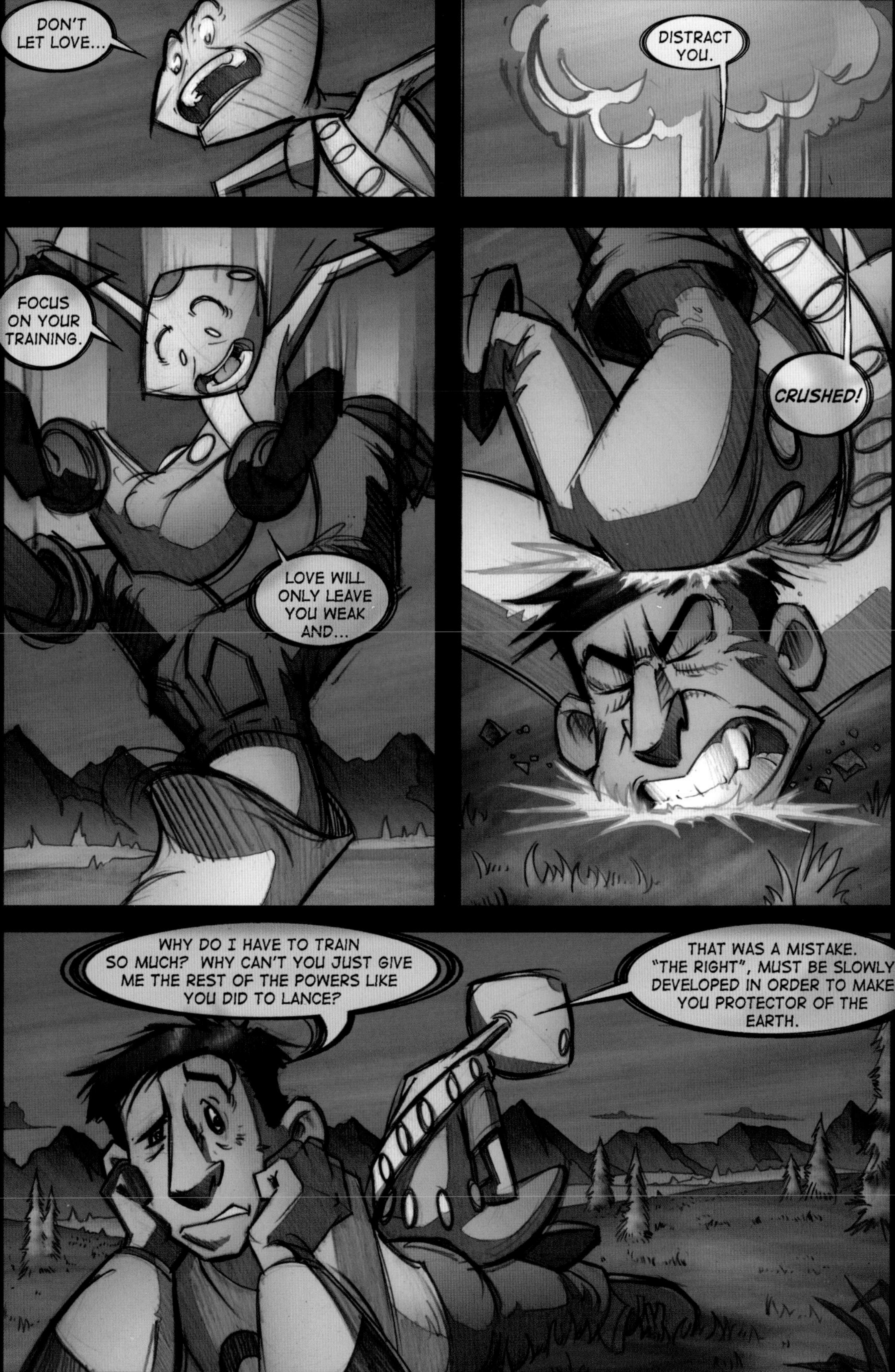
DON'T LET LOVE...
DISTRACT YOU.
FOCUS ON YOUR TRAINING.
LOVE WILL ONLY LEAVE YOU WEAK AND...
CRUSHED!
WHY DO I HAVE TO TRAIN SO MUCH? WHY CAN'T YOU JUST GIVE ME THE REST OF THE POWERS LIKE YOU DID TO LANCE?
THAT WAS A MISTAKE. "THE RIGHT", MUST BE SLOWLY DEVELOPED IN ORDER TO MAKE YOU PROTECTOR OF THE EARTH.

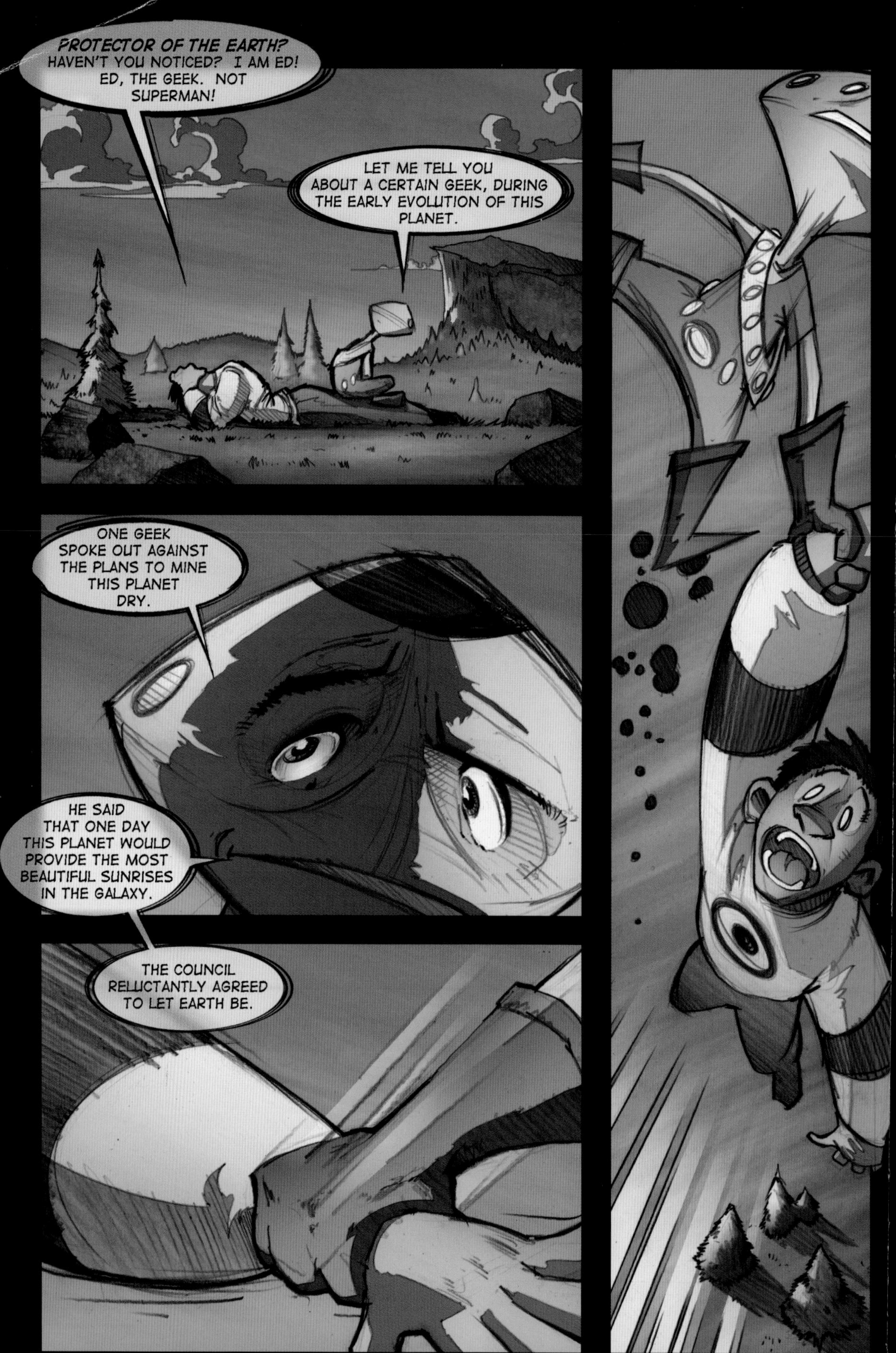
PROTECTOR OF THE EARTH? HAVEN'T YOU NOTICED? I AM ED! ED, THE GEEK. NOT SUPERMAN!
LET ME TELL YOU ABOUT A CERTAIN GEEK, DURING THE EARLY EVOLUTION OF THIS PLANET.
ONE GEEK SPOKE OUT AGAINST THE PLANS TO MINE THIS PLANET DRY.
HE SAID THAT ONE DAY THIS PLANET WOULD PROVIDE THE MOST BEAUTIFUL SUNRISES IN THE GALAXY.
THE COUNCIL RELUCTANTLY AGREED TO LET EARTH BE.

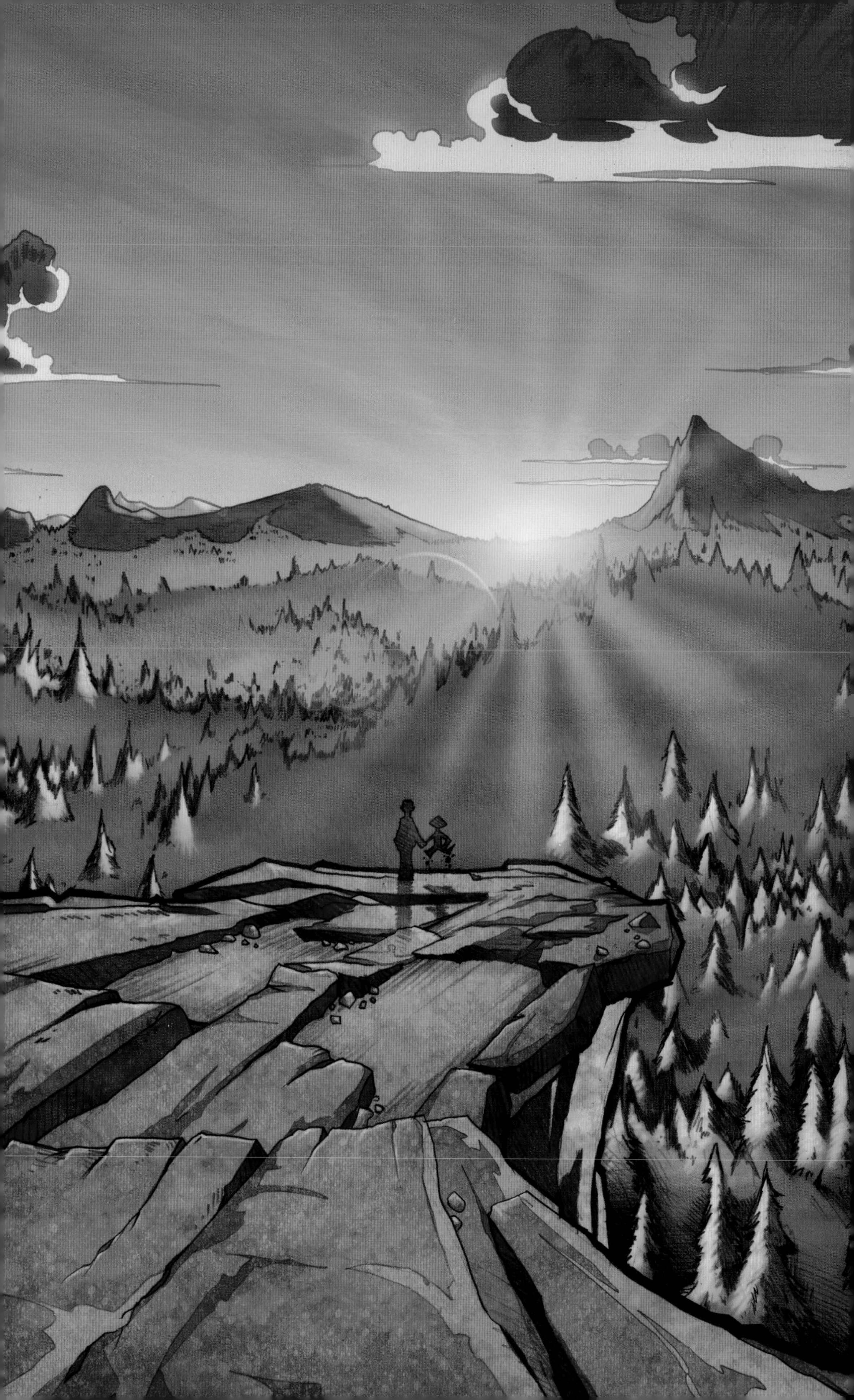

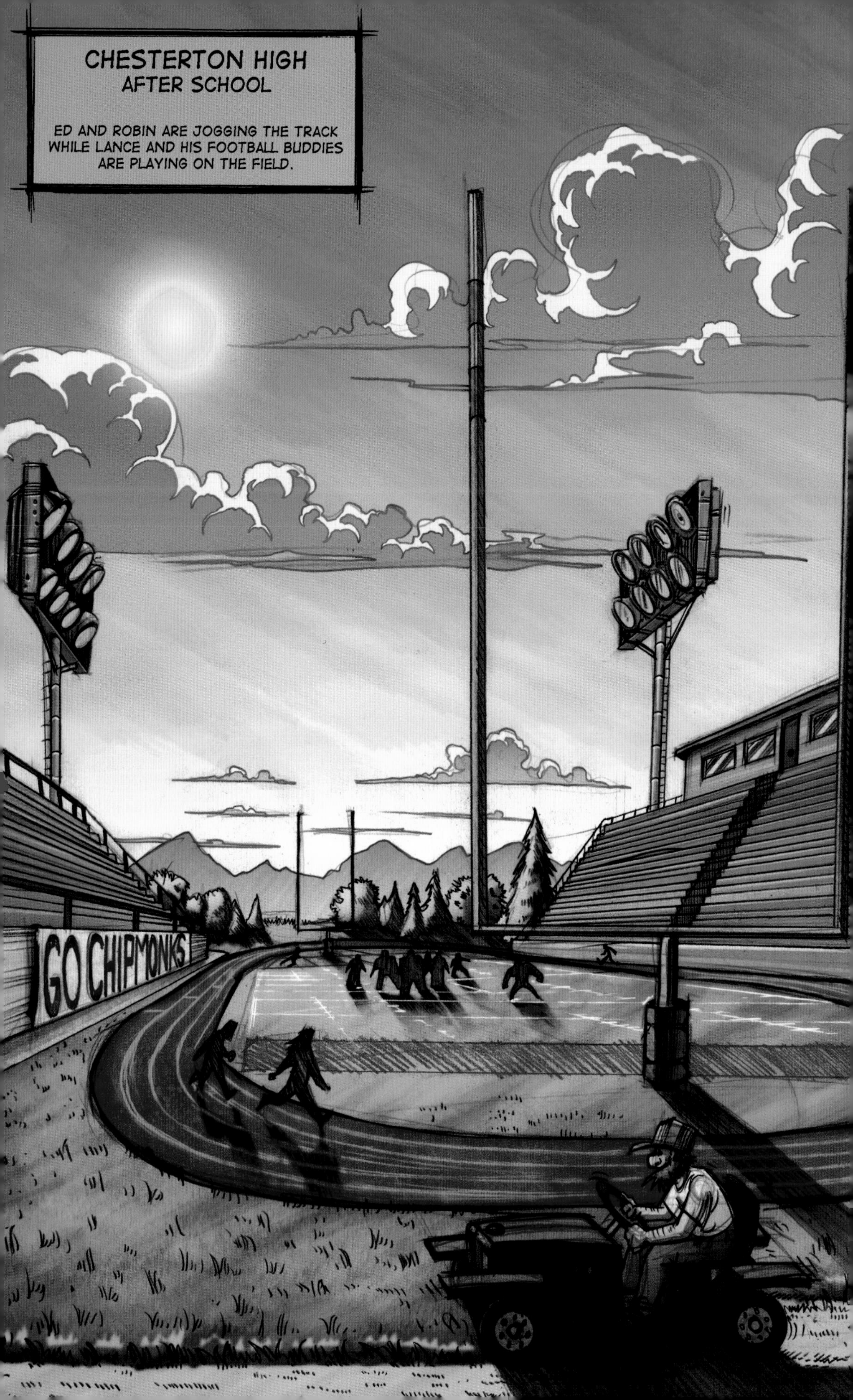
CHESTERTON HIGH
AFTER SCHOOL
ED AND ROBIN ARE JOGGING THE TRACK WHILE LANCE AND HIS FOOTBALL BUDDIES ARE PLAYING ON THE FIELD.
GO CHIPMONKS

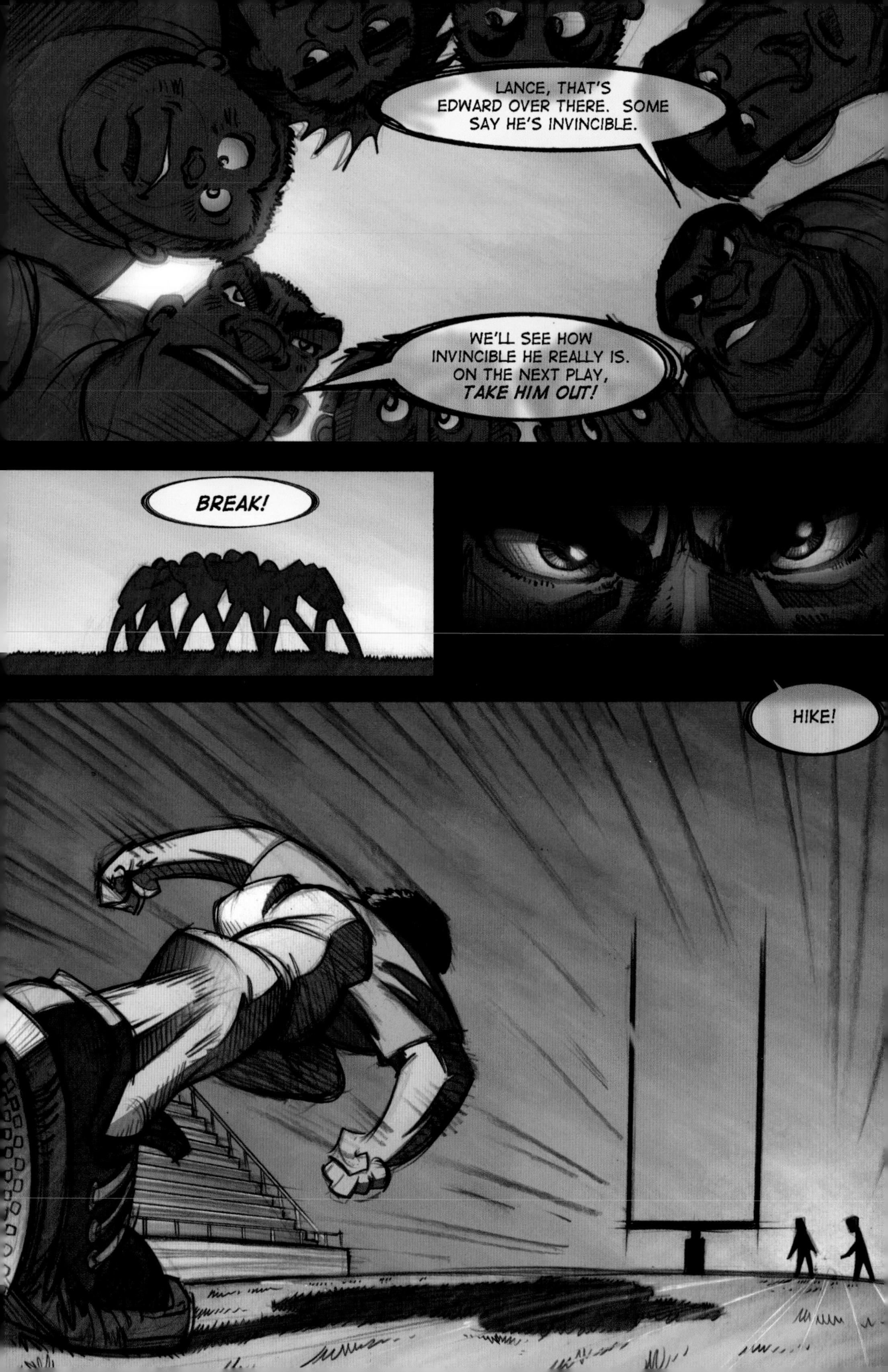
LANCE, THAT'S EDWARD OVER THERE. SOME SAY HE'S INVINCIBLE.
WE'LL SEE HOW INVINCIBLE HE REALLY IS. ON THE NEXT PLAY, *TAKE HIM OUT!*
BREAK!
HIKE!

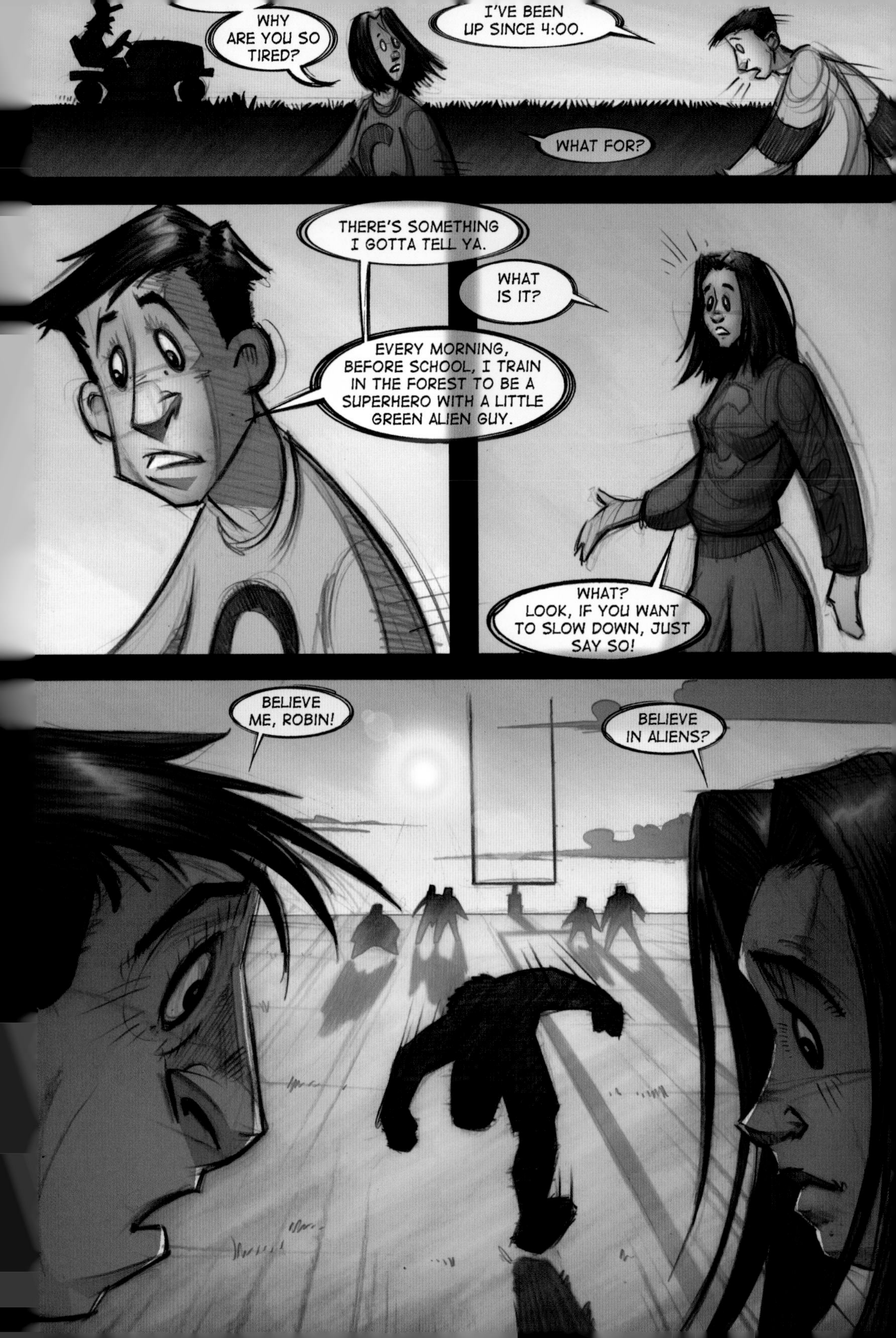
WHY ARE YOU SO TIRED?
I'VE BEEN UP SINCE 4:00.
WHAT FOR?
THERE'S SOMETHING I GOTTA TELL YA.
WHAT IS IT?
EVERY MORNING, BEFORE SCHOOL, I TRAIN IN THE FOREST TO BE A SUPERHERO WITH A LITTLE GREEN ALIEN GUY.
WHAT? LOOK, IF YOU WANT TO SLOW DOWN, JUST SAY SO!
BELIEVE ME, ROBIN!
BELIEVE IN ALIENS?

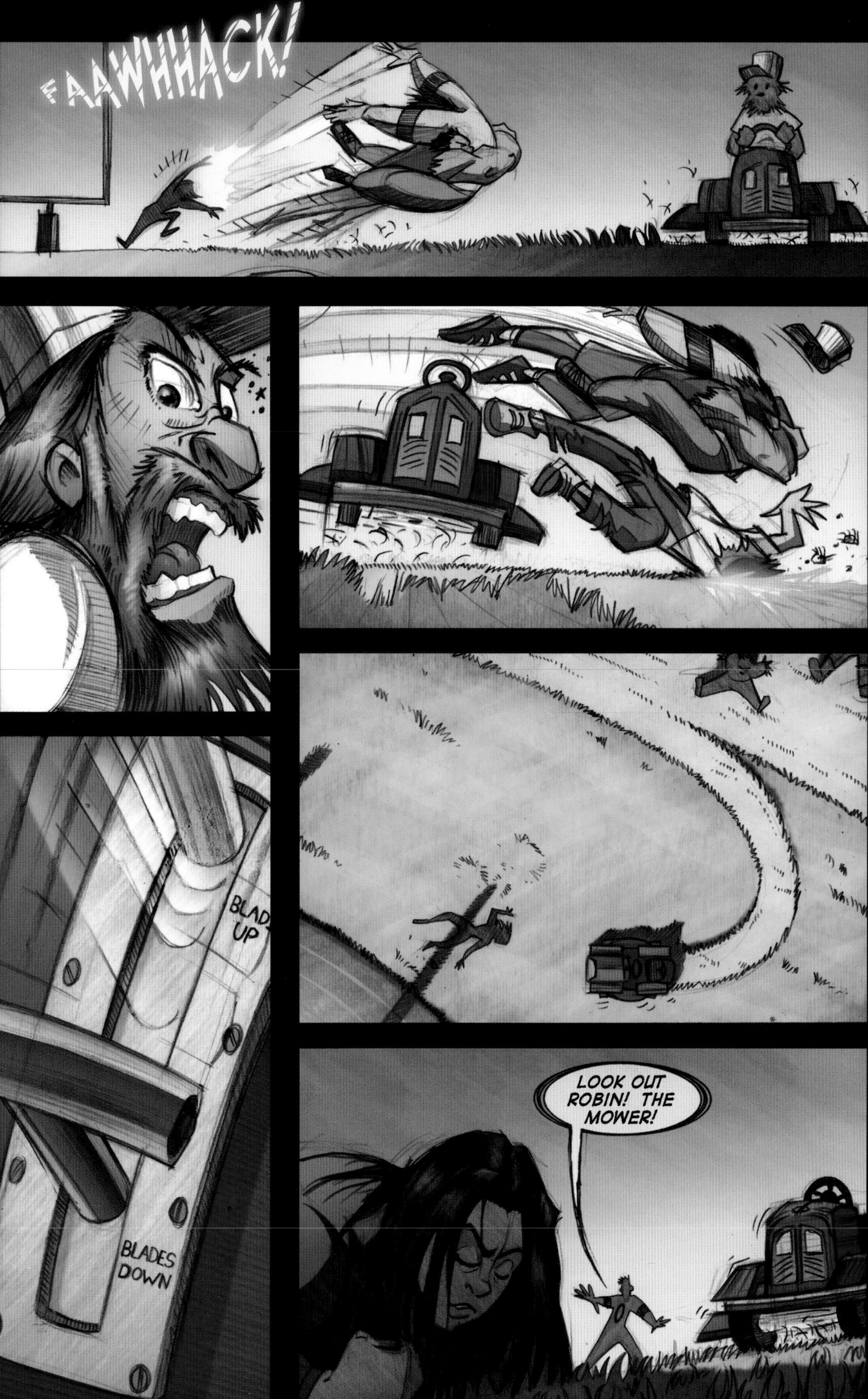
FAAWHHACK!
BLADES UP
BLADES DOWN
LOOK OUT ROBIN! THE MOWER!

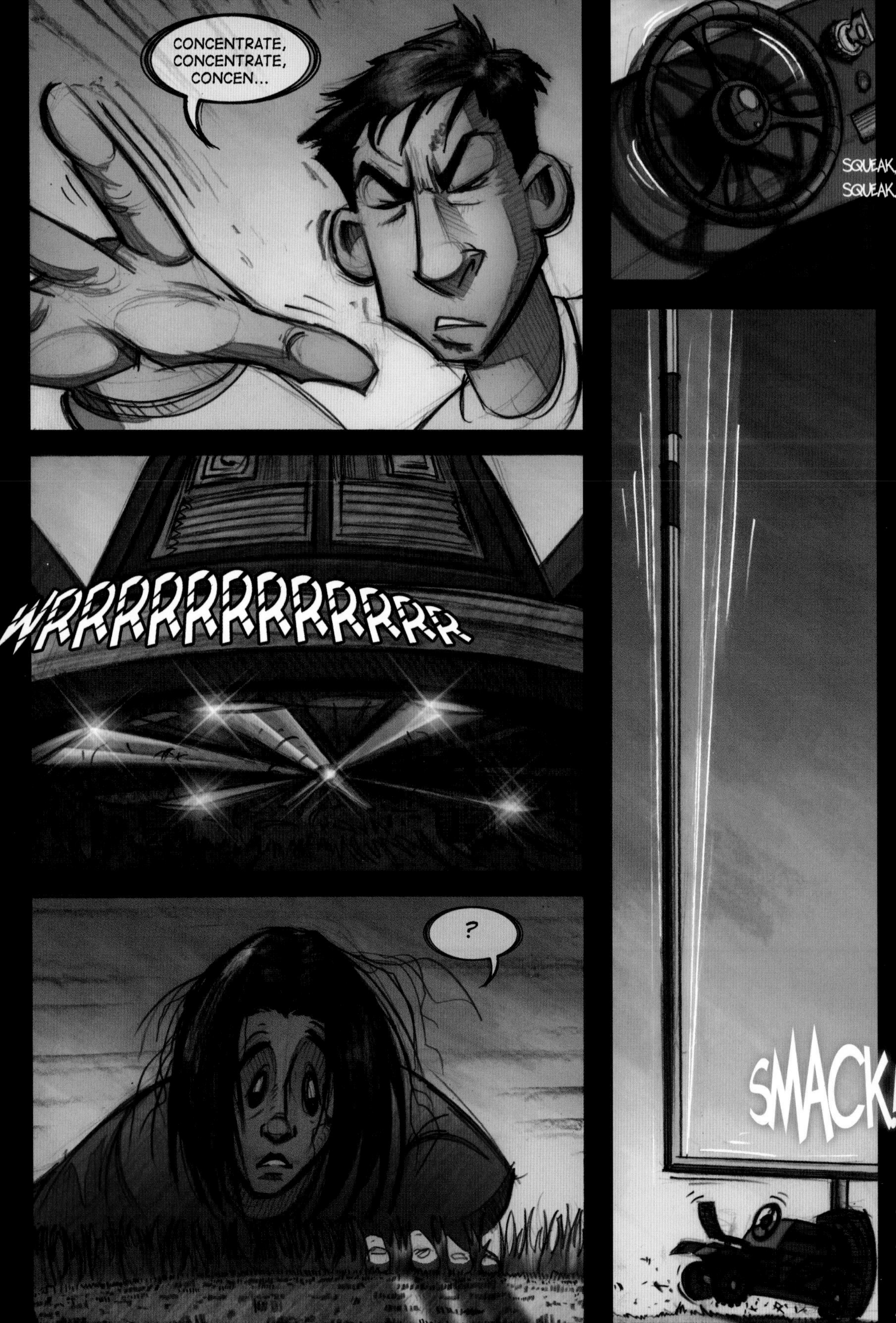
CONCENTRATE, CONCENTRATE, CONCEN...
SQUEAK, SQUEAK,
WRRRRRRRRRRRRRRR
?
SMACK!

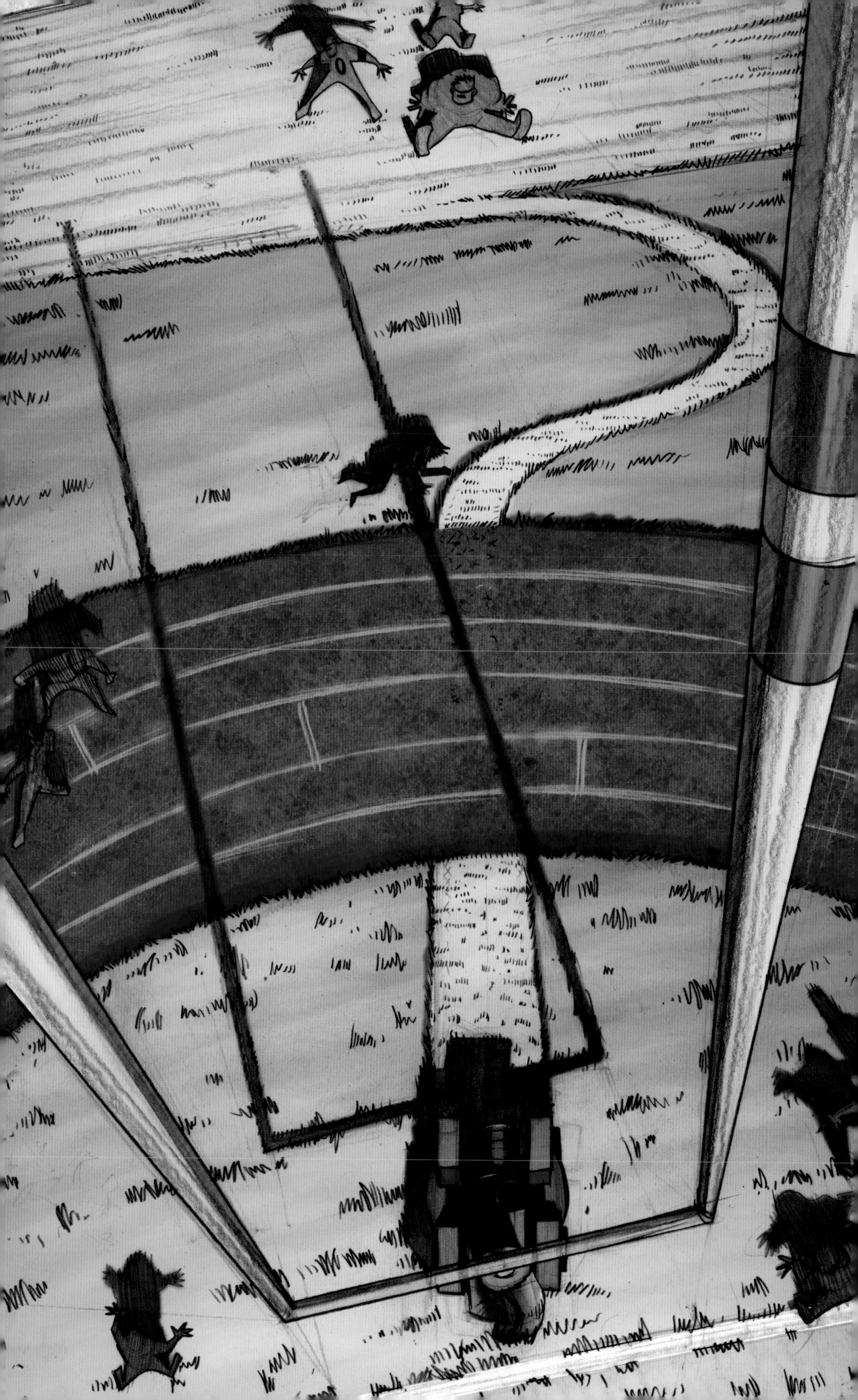

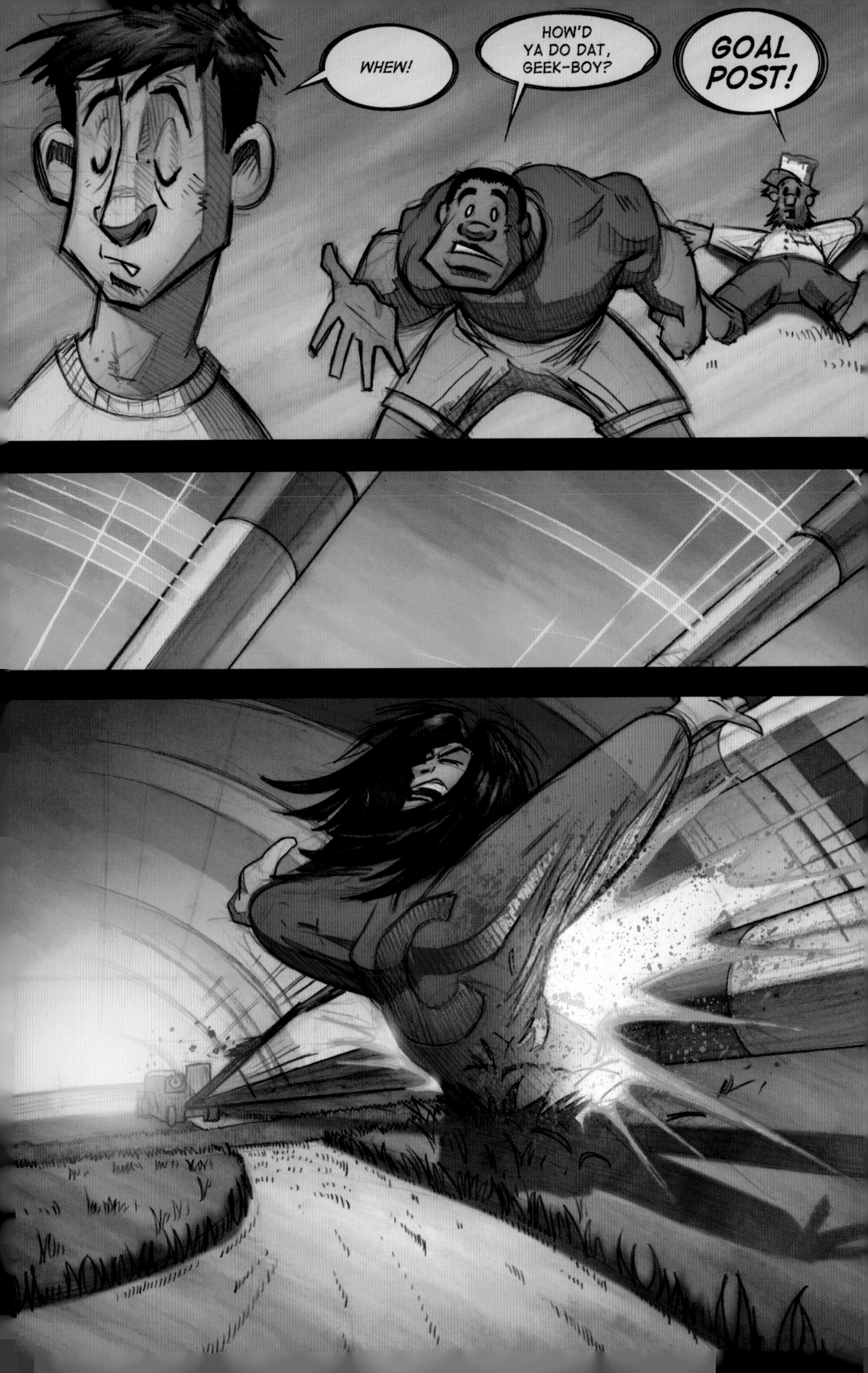
WHEW!
HOW'D YA DO DAT, GEEK-BOY?
GOAL POST!

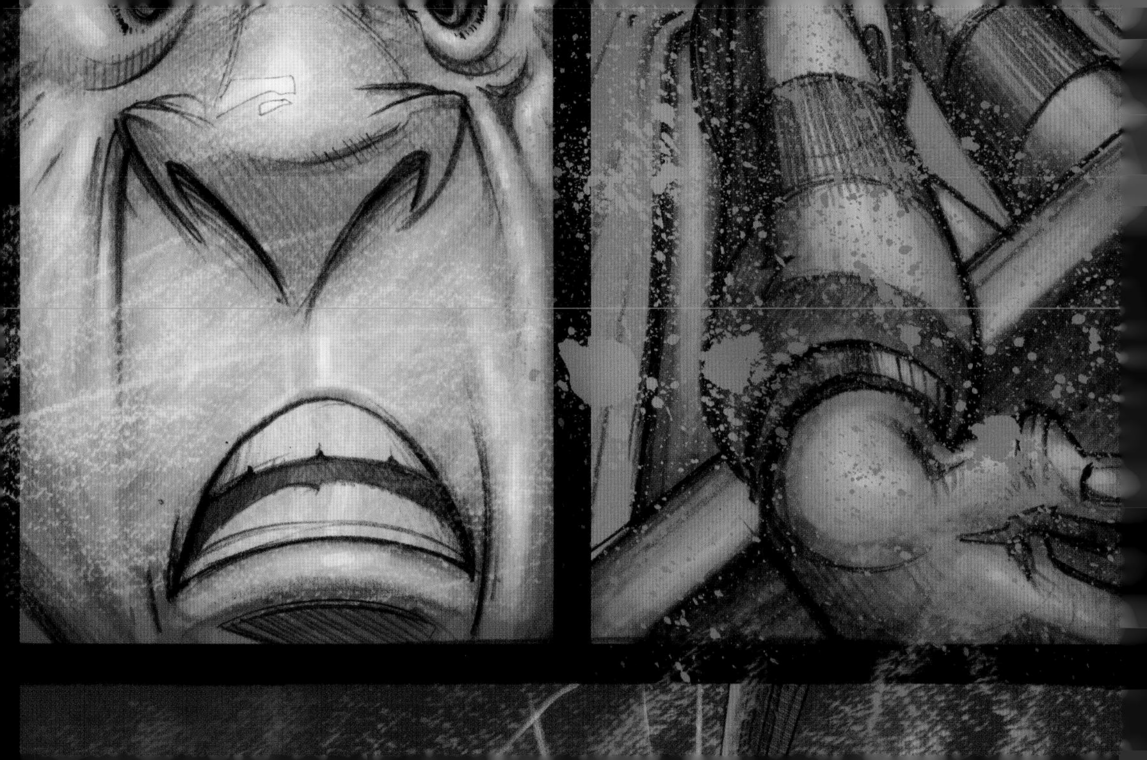

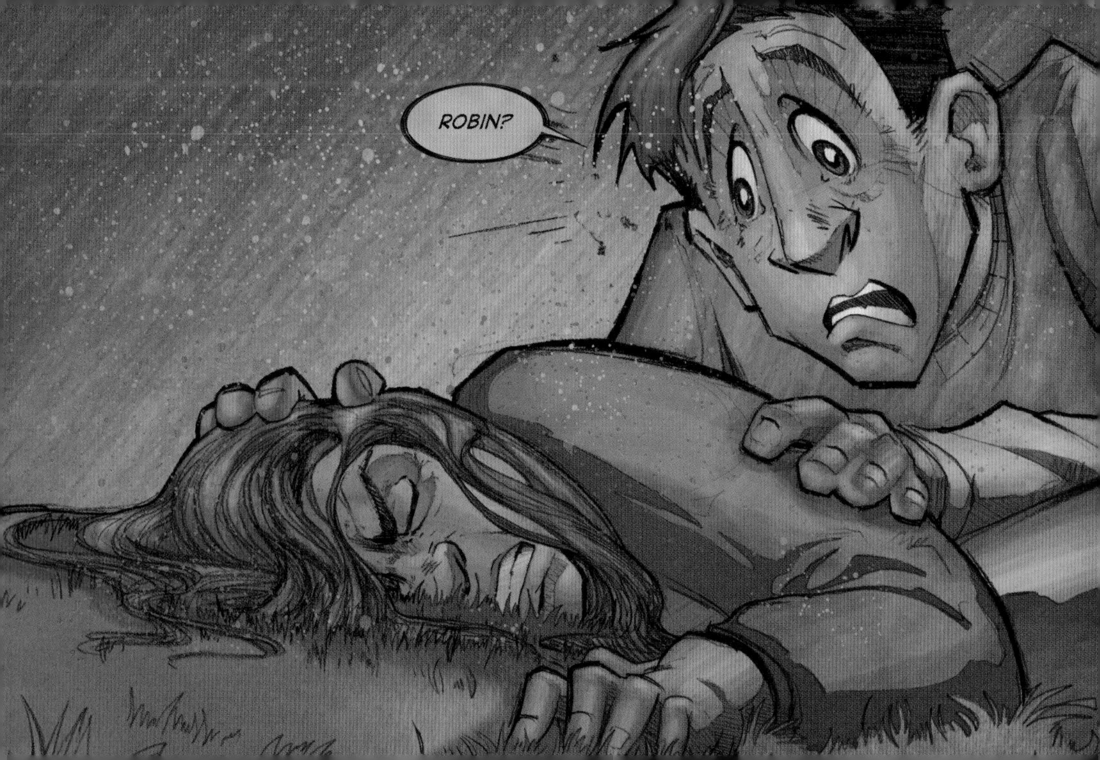
ROBIN?

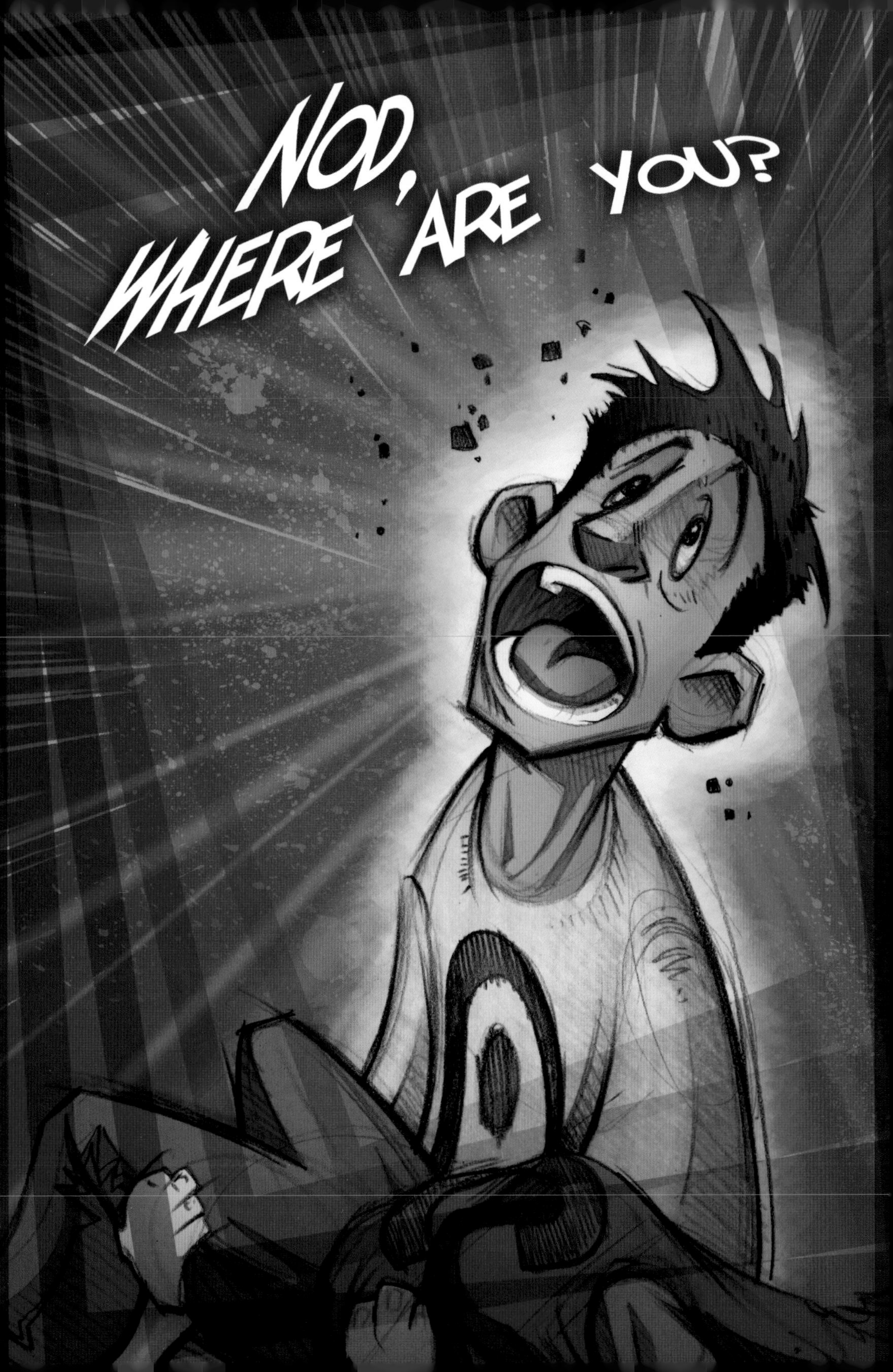
NOD, WHERE ARE YOU?

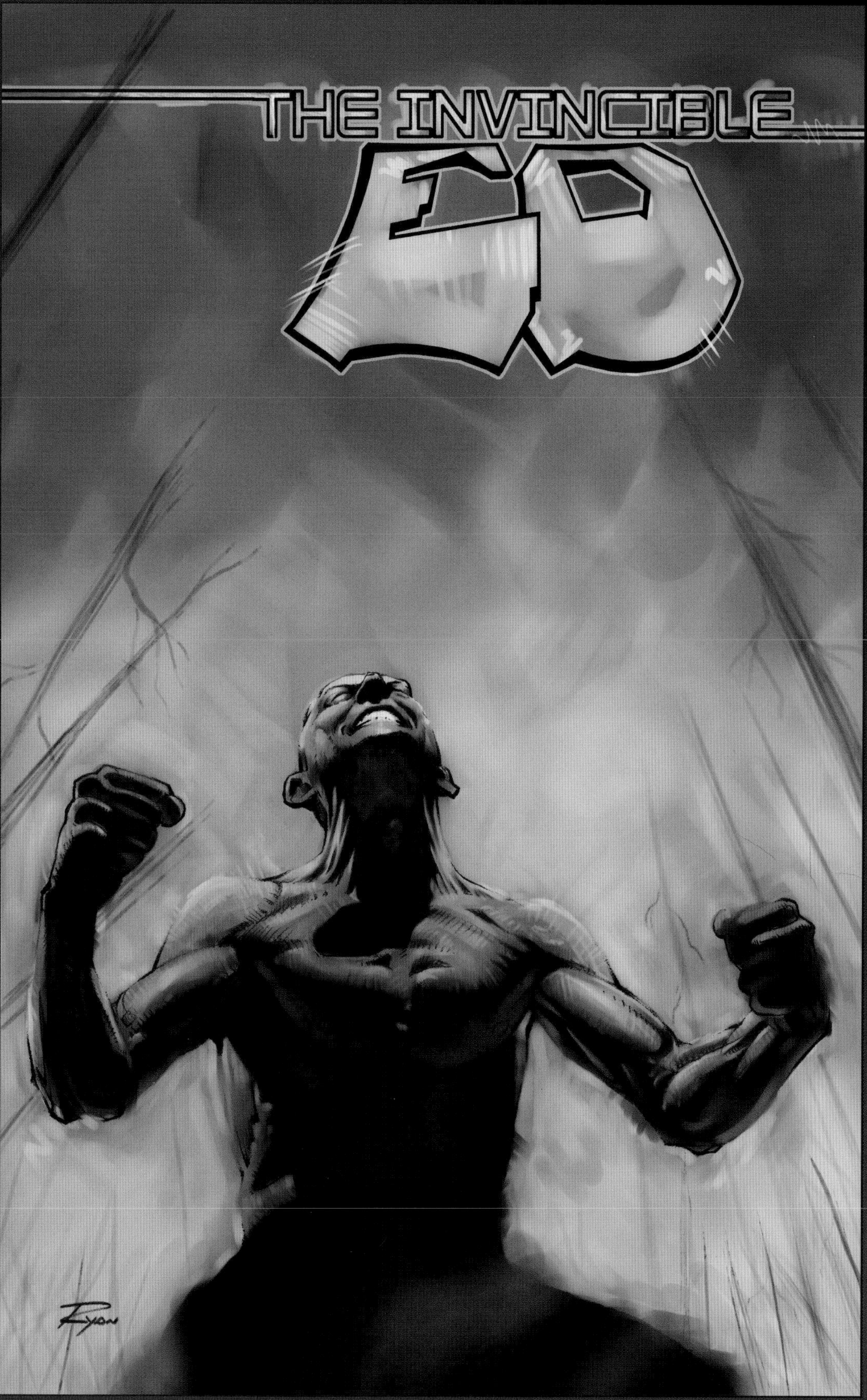
THE INVINCIBLE
ED
Ryan

written and illustrated
RYAN WOODWARD

comic fonts
NATE PIEKOS

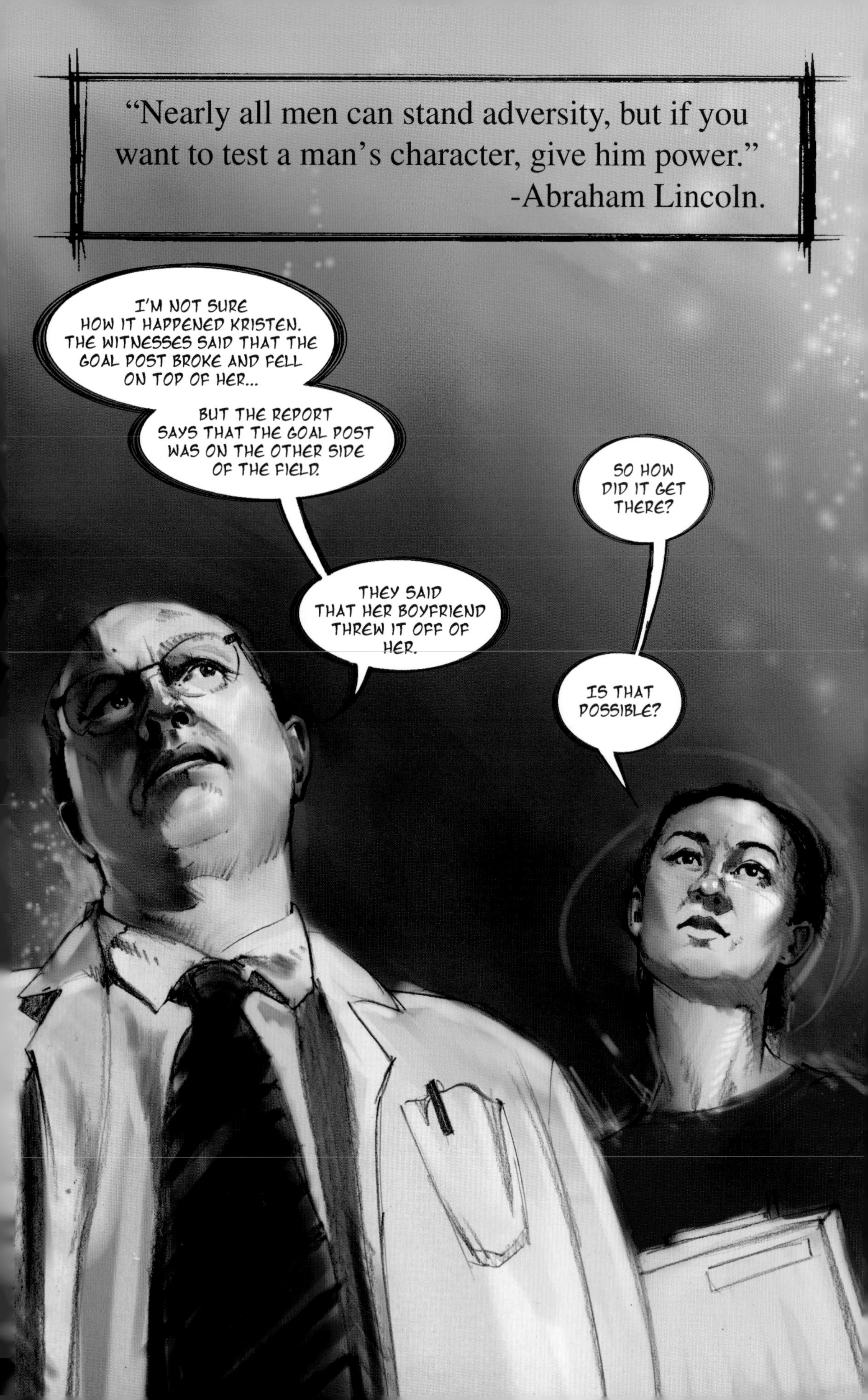
"Nearly all men can stand adversity, but if you want to test a man's character, give him power."
-Abraham Lincoln.
I'M NOT SURE HOW IT HAPPENED KRISTEN. THE WITNESSES SAID THAT THE GOAL POST BROKE AND FELL ON TOP OF HER...
BUT THE REPORT SAYS THAT THE GOAL POST WAS ON THE OTHER SIDE OF THE FIELD.
SO HOW DID IT GET THERE?
THEY SAID THAT HER BOYFRIEND THREW IT OFF OF HER.
IS THAT POSSIBLE?

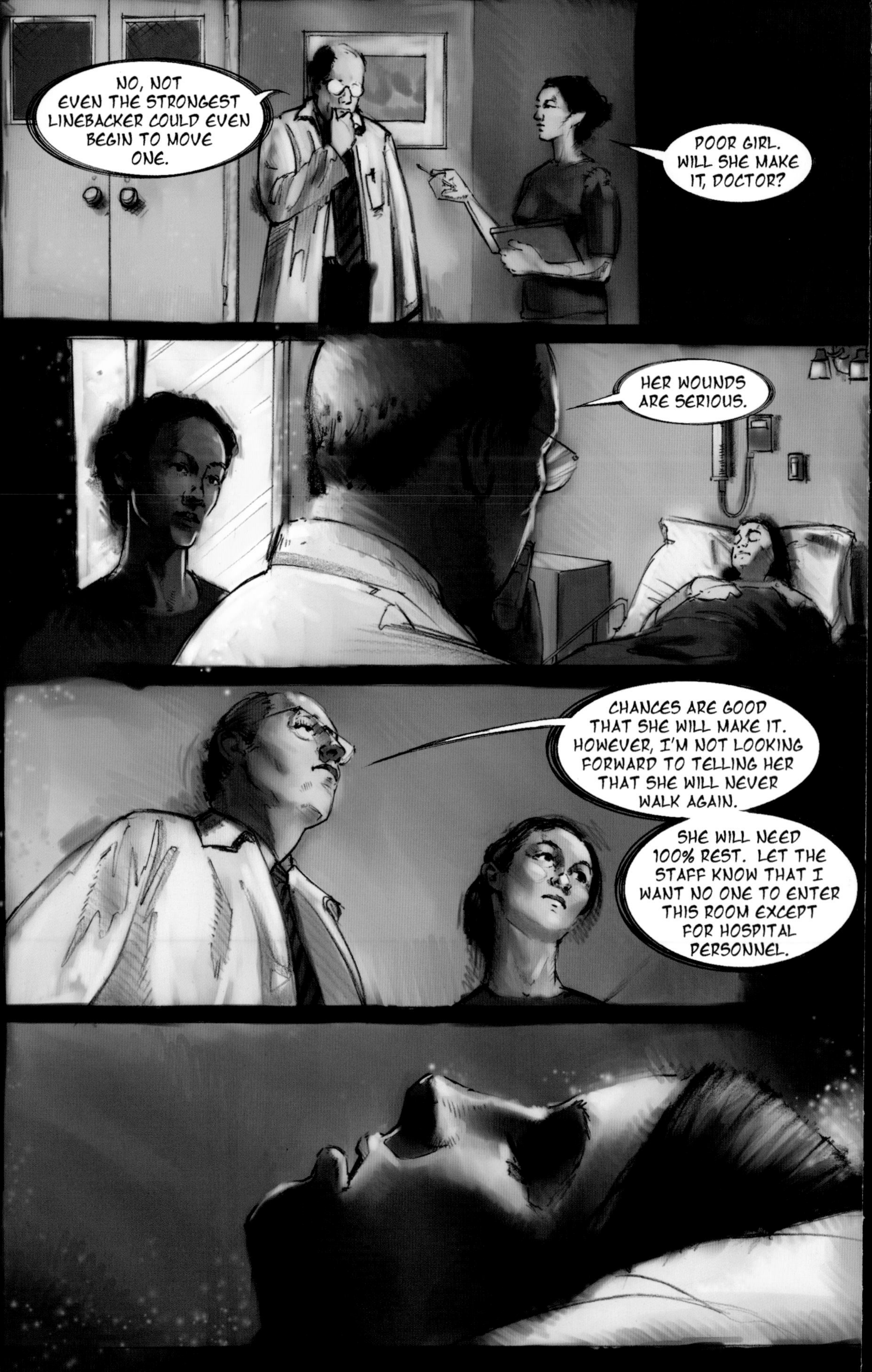
NO, NOT EVEN THE STRONGEST LINEBACKER COULD EVEN BEGIN TO MOVE ONE.
POOR GIRL. WILL SHE MAKE IT, DOCTOR?
HER WOUNDS ARE SERIOUS.
CHANCES ARE GOOD THAT SHE WILL MAKE IT. HOWEVER, I'M NOT LOOKING FORWARD TO TELLING HER THAT SHE WILL NEVER WALK AGAIN.
SHE WILL NEED 100% REST. LET THE STAFF KNOW THAT I WANT NO ONE TO ENTER THIS ROOM EXCEPT FOR HOSPITAL PERSONNEL.

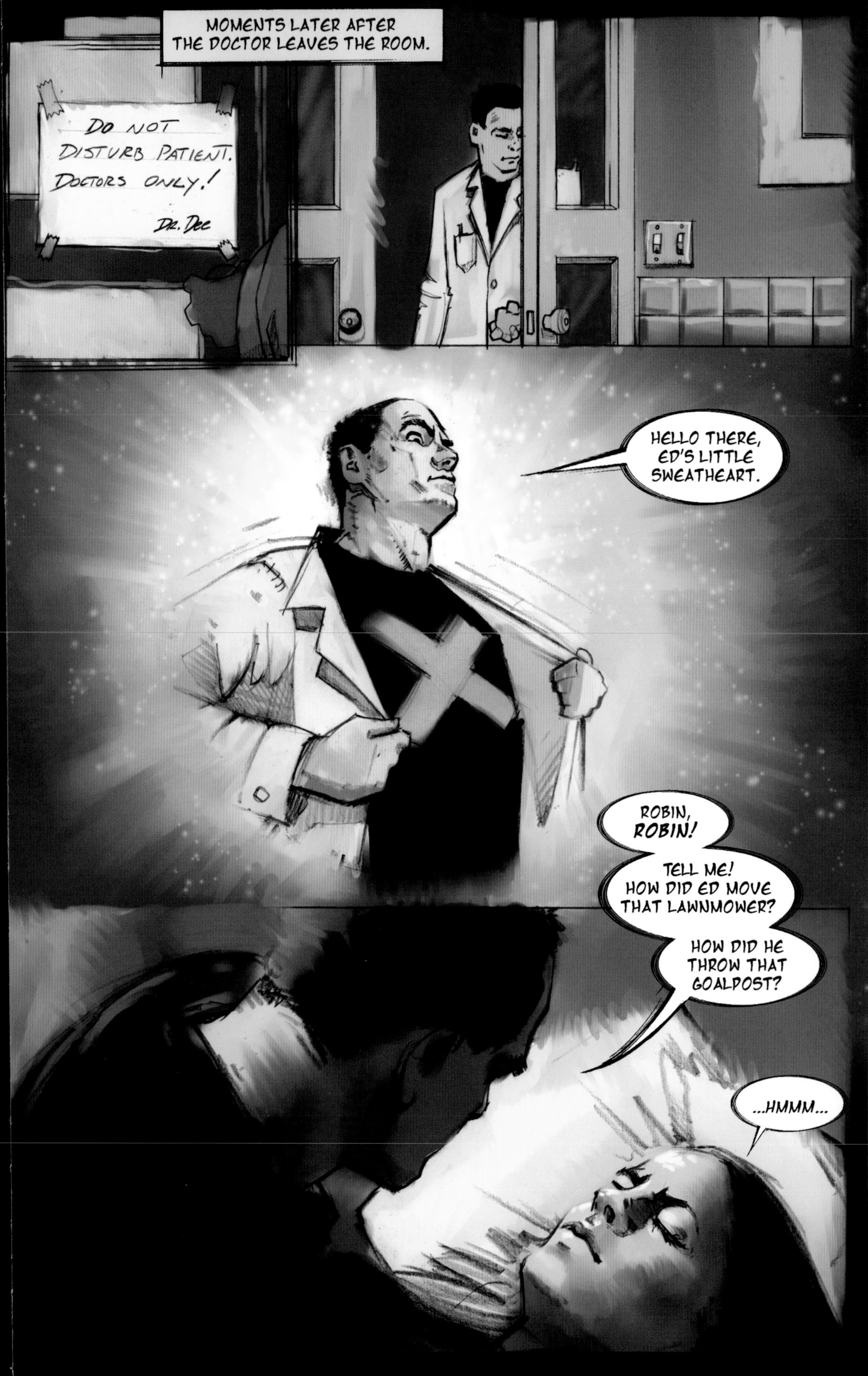
MOMENTS LATER AFTER
THE DOCTOR LEAVES THE ROOM.
DO NOT
DISTURB PATIENT.
DOCTORS ONLY!
DR. DEE
HELLO THERE,
ED'S LITTLE
SWEATHEART.
ROBIN,
ROBIN!
TELL ME!
HOW DID ED MOVE
THAT LAWNMOWER?
HOW DID HE
THROW THAT
GOALPOST?
...HMMM...

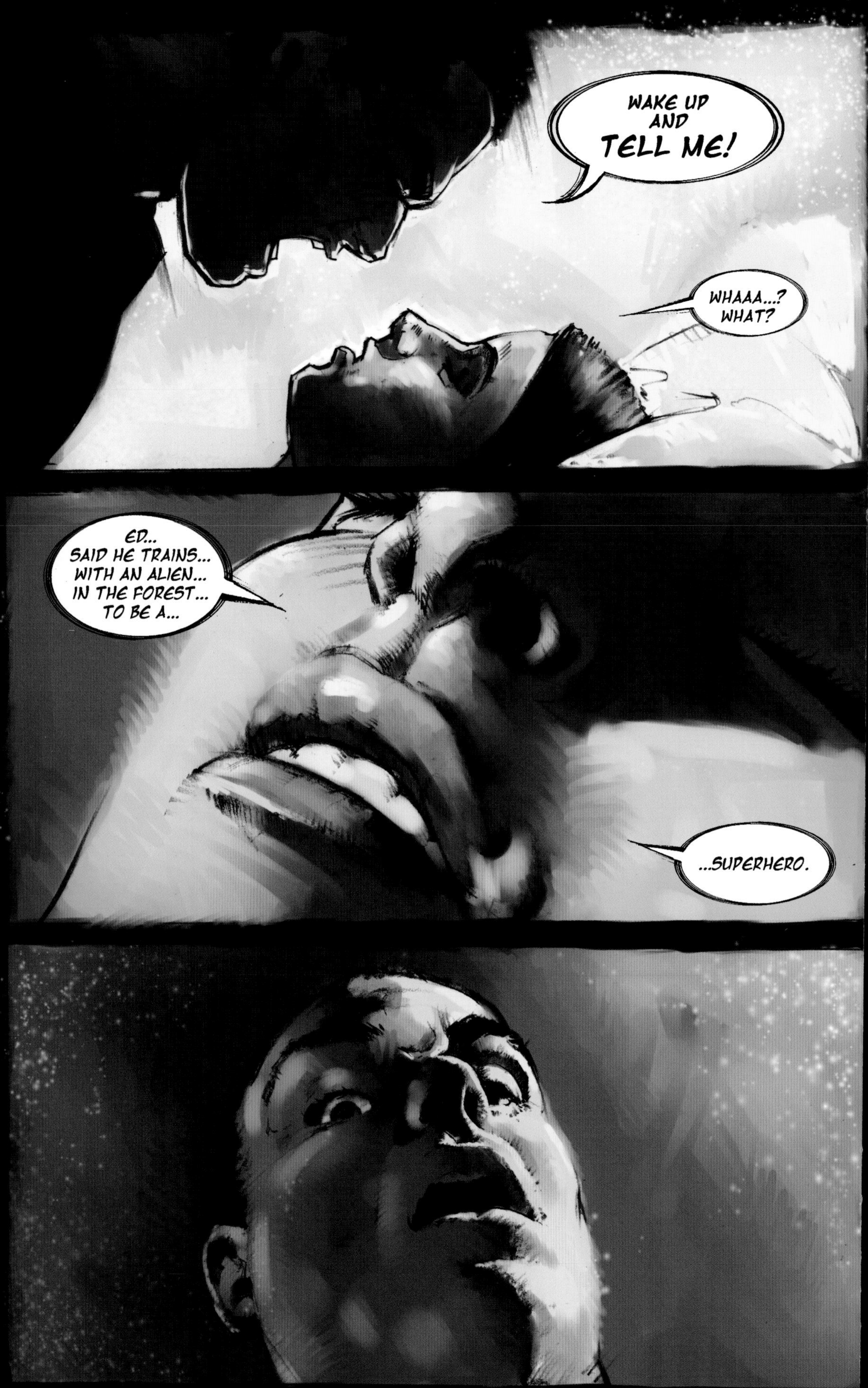
WAKE UP AND TELL ME!
WHAAA...? WHAT?
ED... SAID HE TRAINS... WITH AN ALIEN... IN THE FOREST... TO BE A...
...SUPERHERO.

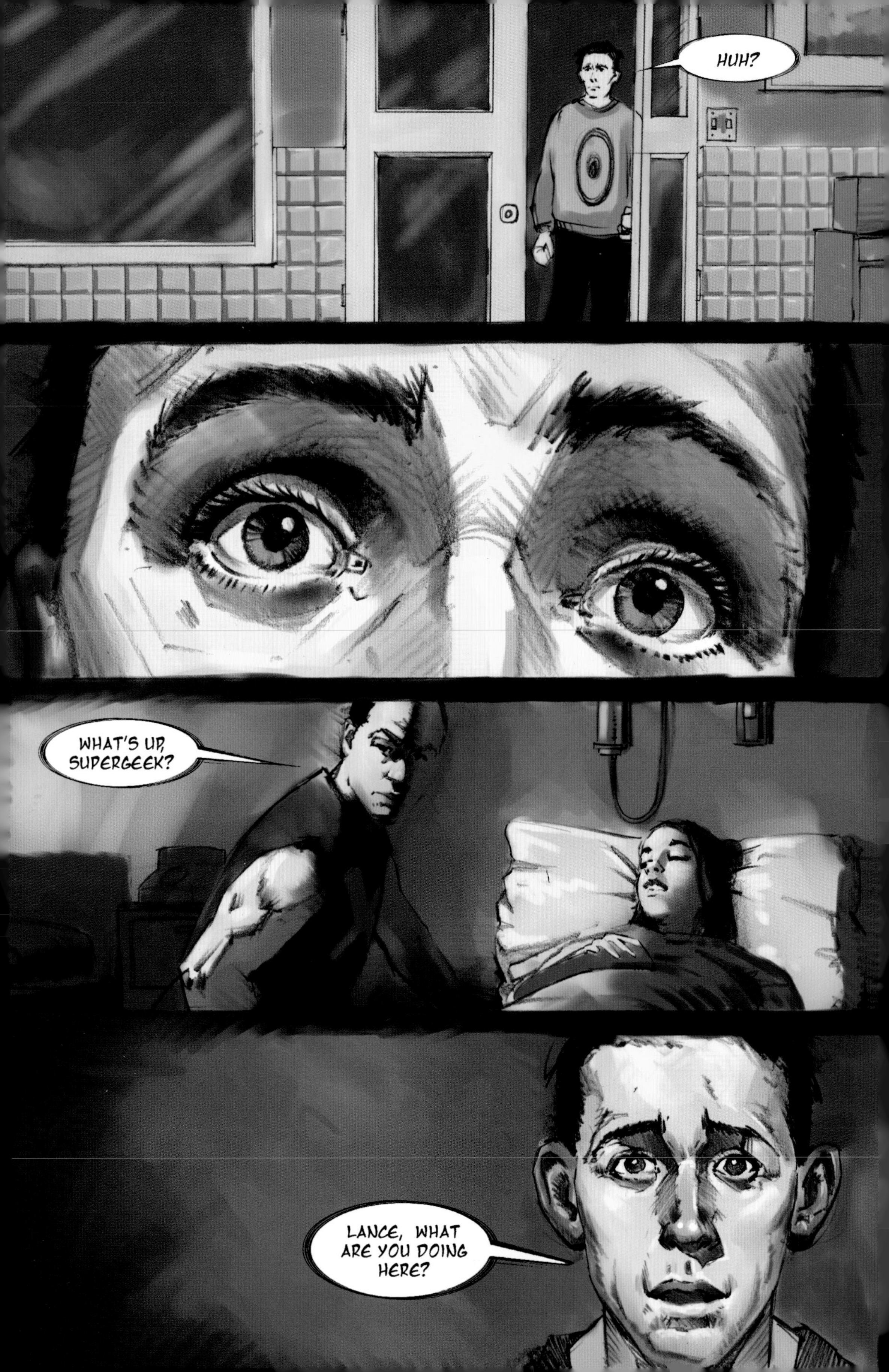
HUH?
WHAT'S UP, SUPERGEEK?
LANCE, WHAT ARE YOU DOING HERE?

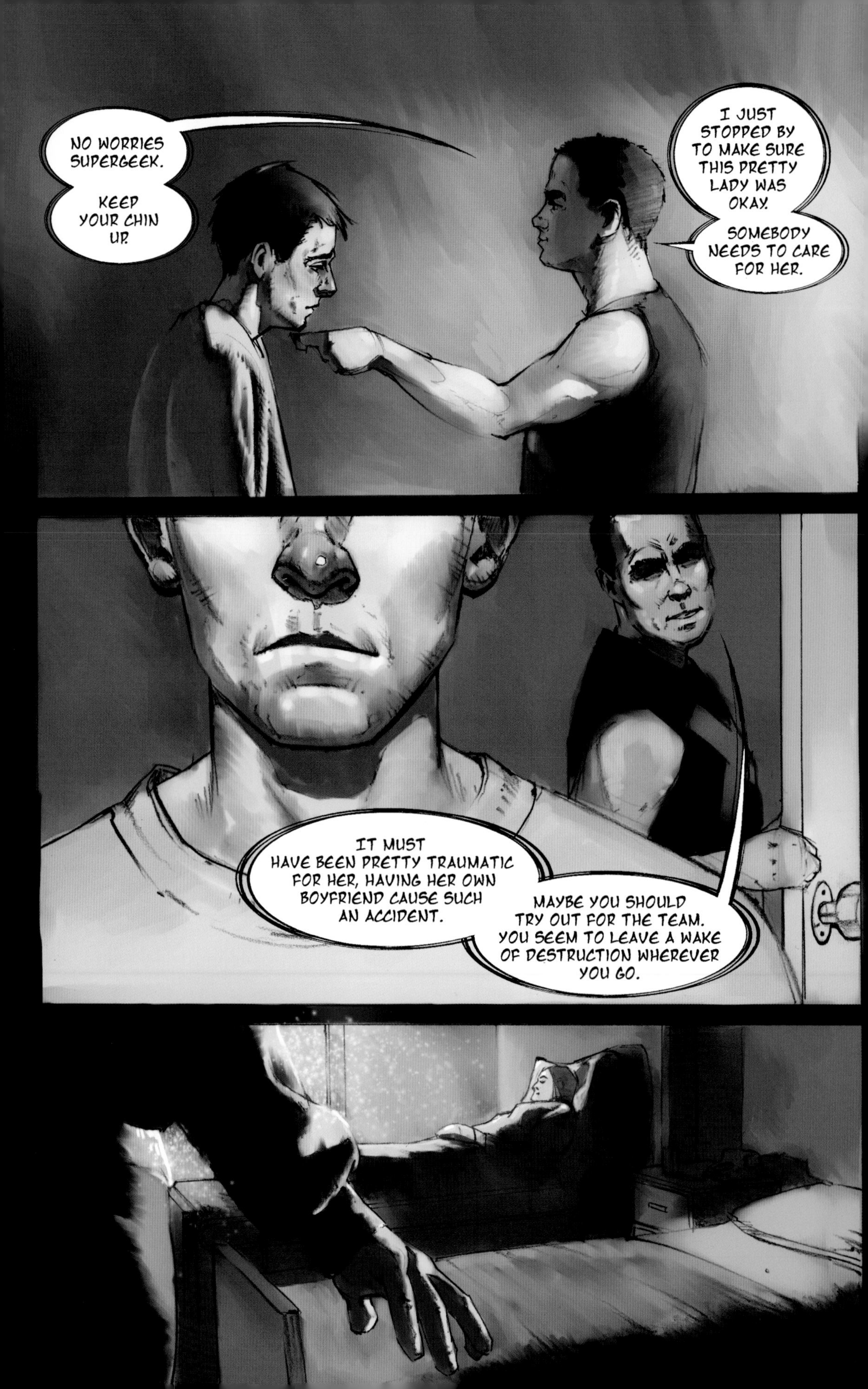
I JUST STOPPED BY TO MAKE SURE THIS PRETTY LADY WAS OKAY.
SOMEBODY NEEDS TO CARE FOR HER.
NO WORRIES SUPERGEEK.
KEEP YOUR CHIN UP.
IT MUST HAVE BEEN PRETTY TRAUMATIC FOR HER, HAVING HER OWN BOYFRIEND CAUSE SUCH AN ACCIDENT.
MAYBE YOU SHOULD TRY OUT FOR THE TEAM. YOU SEEM TO LEAVE A WAKE OF DESTRUCTION WHEREVER YOU GO.

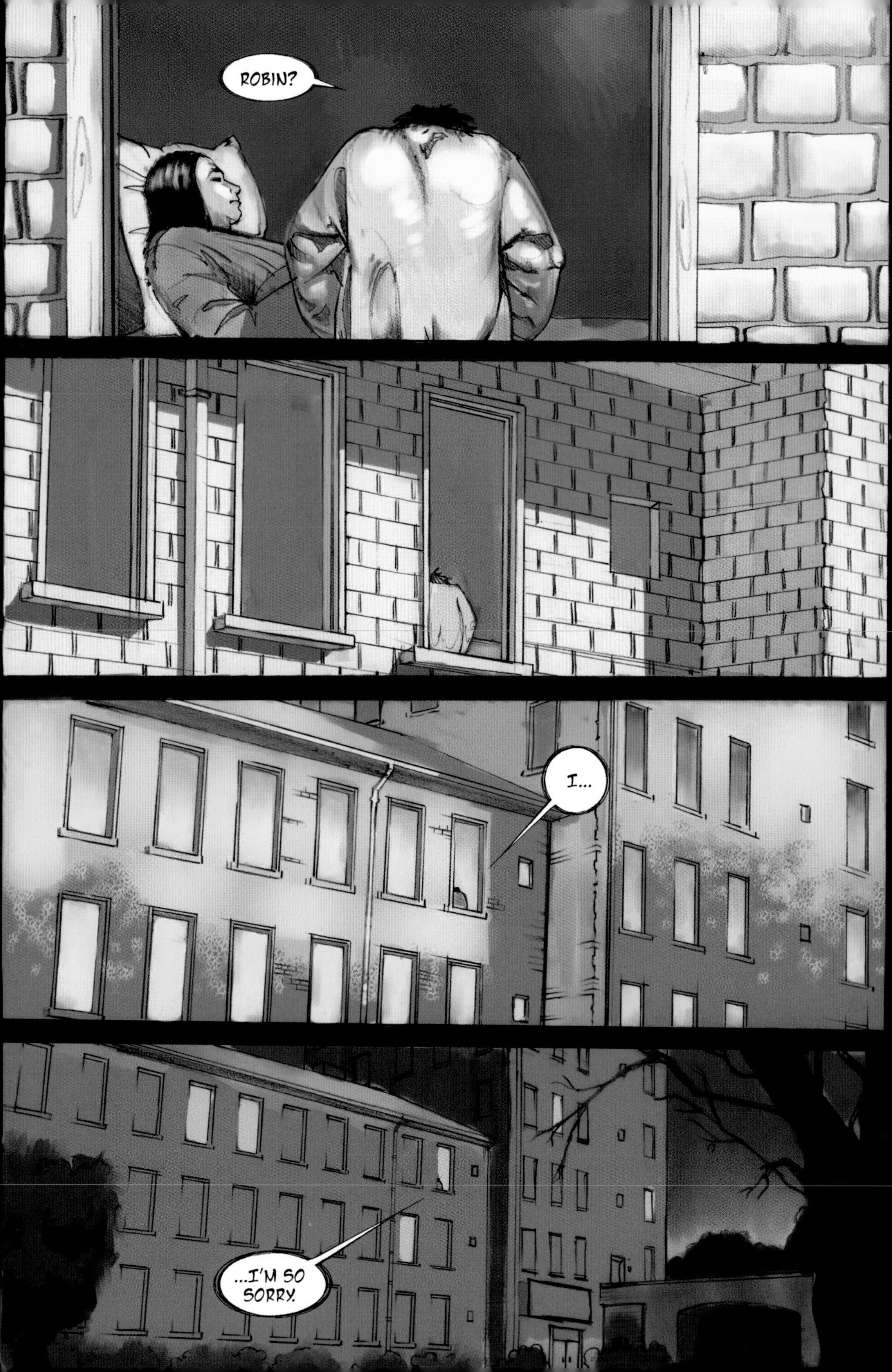
ROBIN?
I...
...I'M SO SORRY.

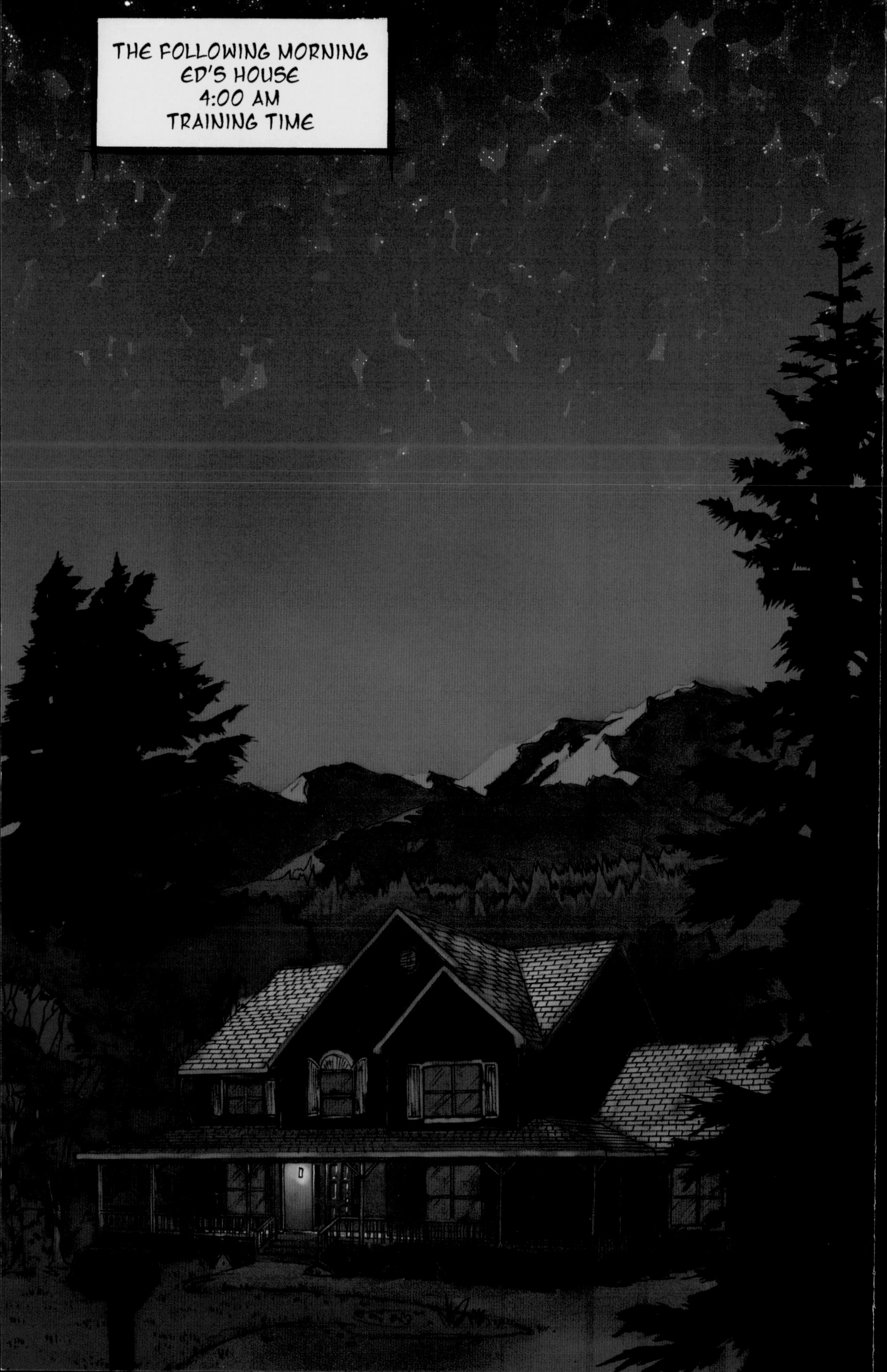
THE FOLLOWING MORNING
ED'S HOUSE
4:00 AM
TRAINING TIME

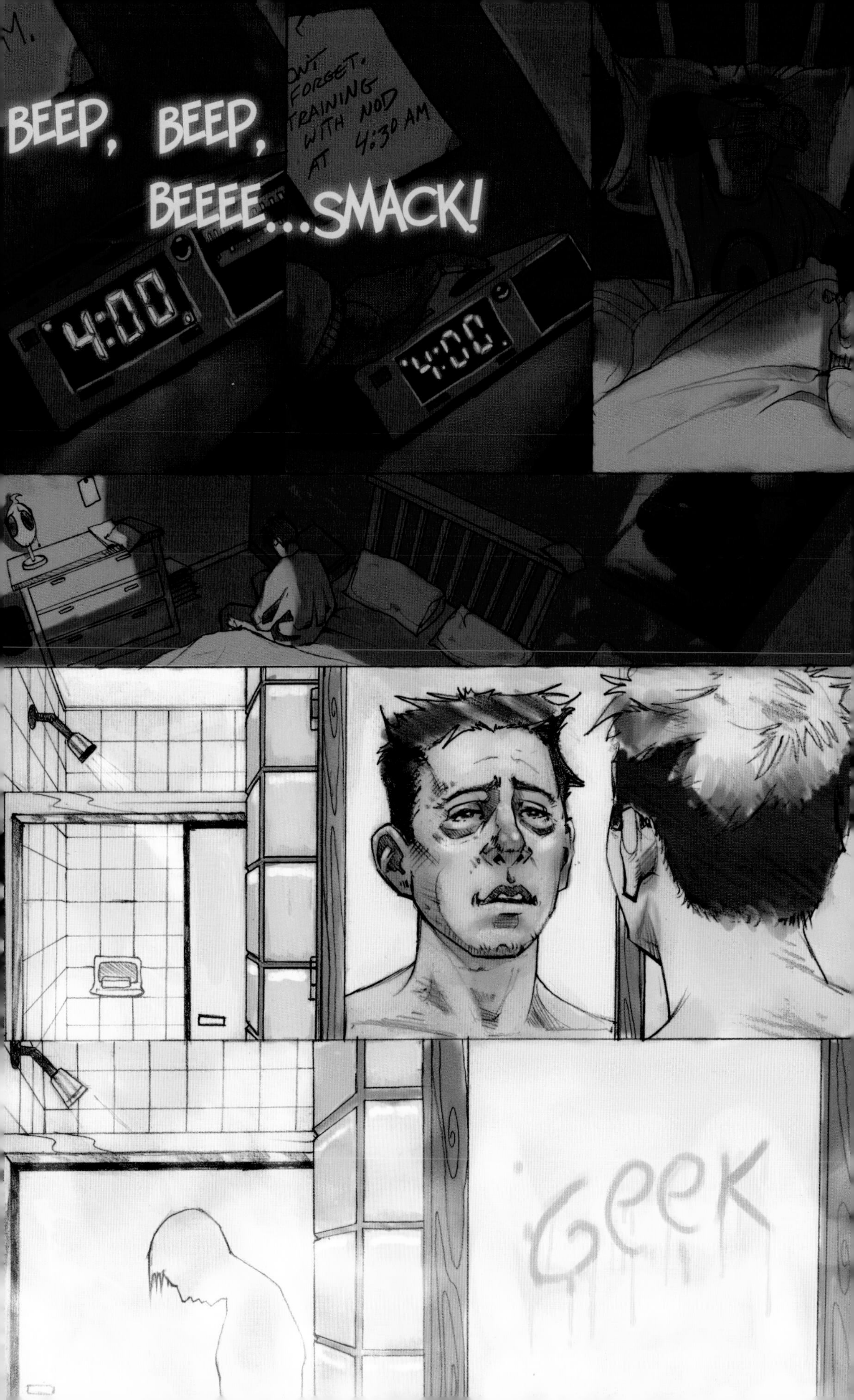

BEEP, BEEP,
BEEEE...SMACK!
DON'T FORGET. TRAINING WITH NOD AT 4:30 AM
4:00
4:00
GEEK

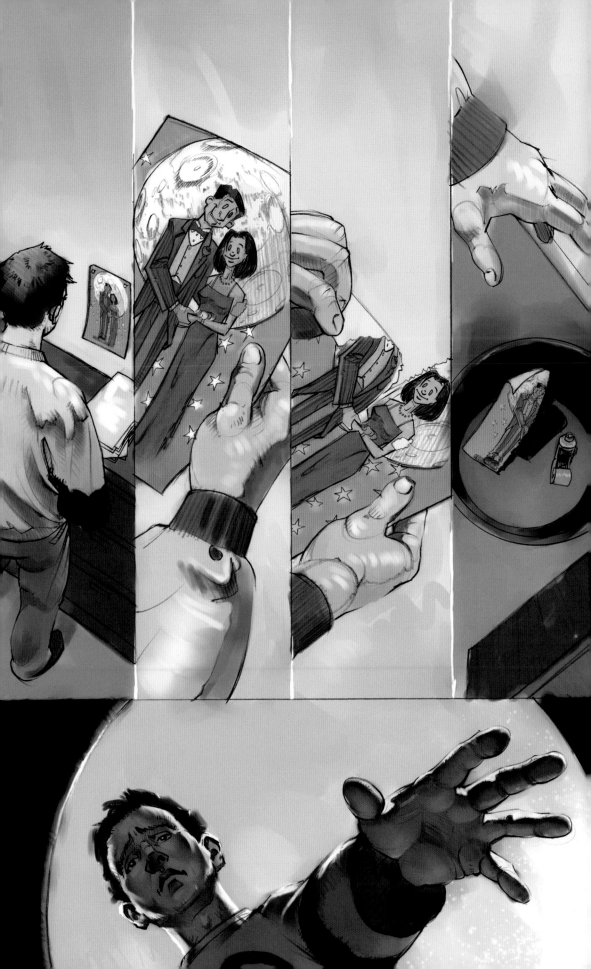

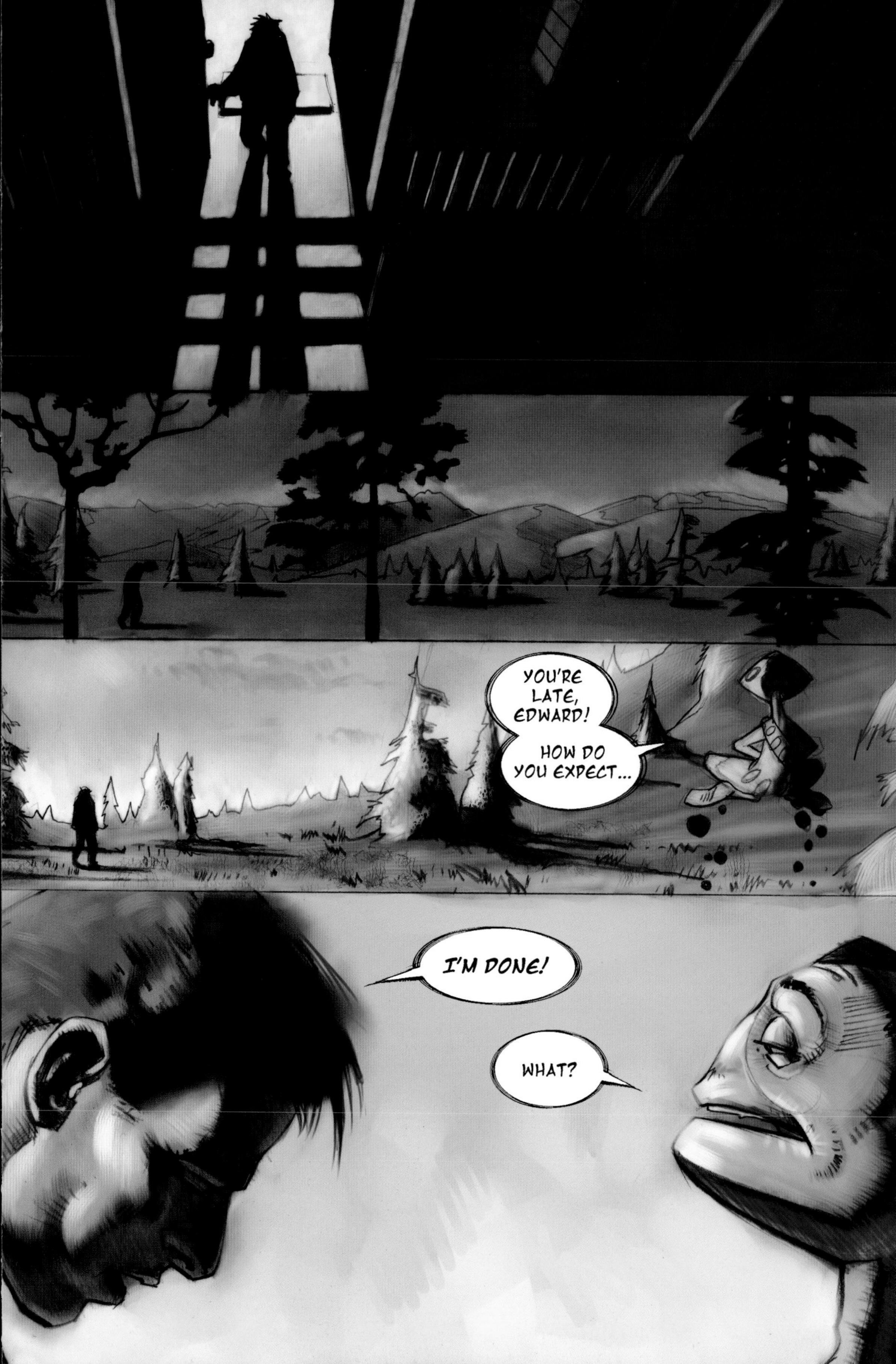
YOU'RE LATE, EDWARD!
HOW DO YOU EXPECT...
I'M DONE!
WHAT?

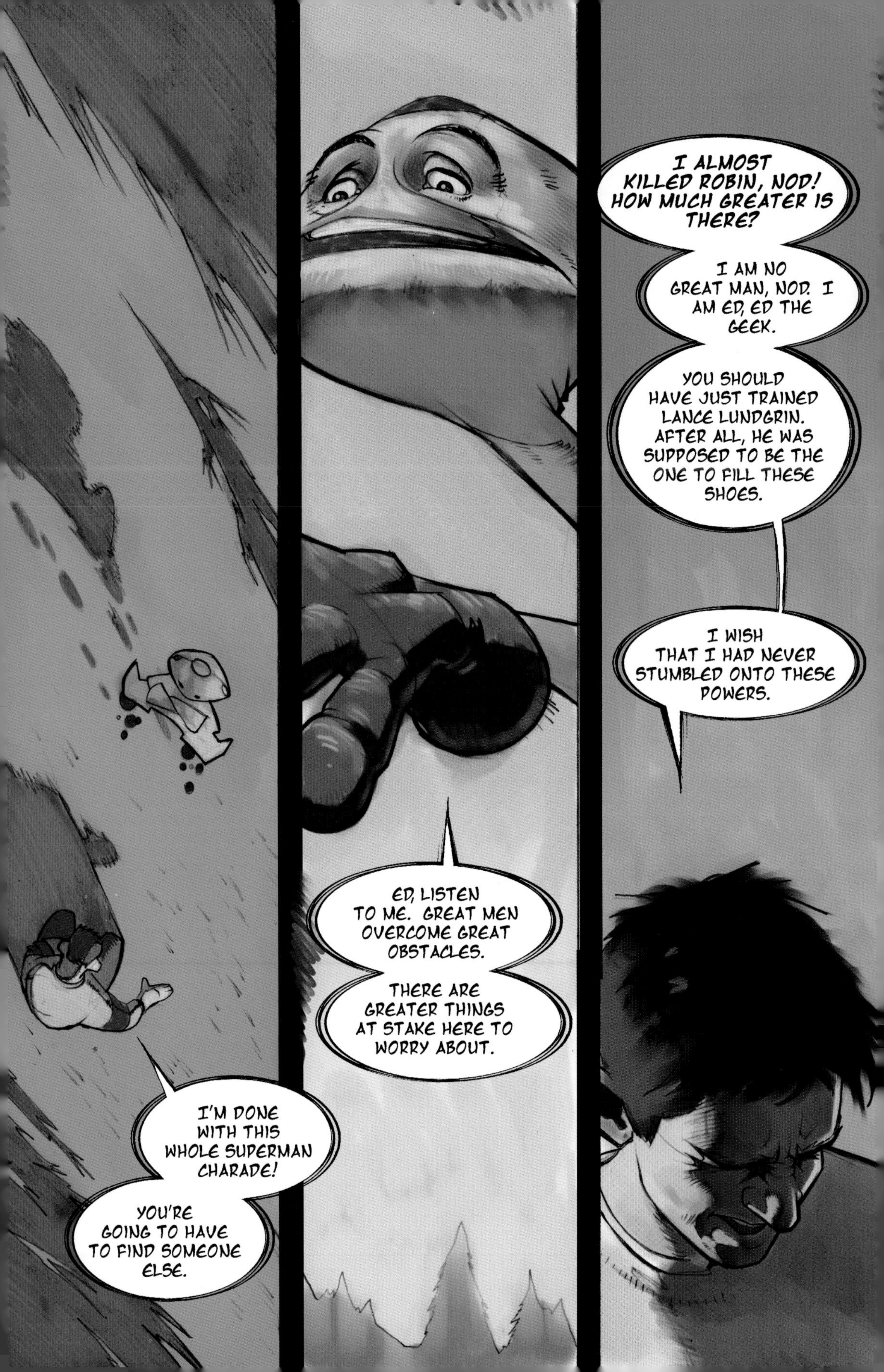
I'M DONE WITH THIS WHOLE SUPERMAN CHARADE!
YOU'RE GOING TO HAVE TO FIND SOMEONE ELSE.
ED, LISTEN TO ME. GREAT MEN OVERCOME GREAT OBSTACLES.
THERE ARE GREATER THINGS AT STAKE HERE TO WORRY ABOUT.
I ALMOST KILLED ROBIN, NOD! HOW MUCH GREATER IS THERE?
I AM NO GREAT MAN, NOD. I AM ED, ED THE GEEK.
YOU SHOULD HAVE JUST TRAINED LANCE LUNDGRIN. AFTER ALL, HE WAS SUPPOSED TO BE THE ONE TO FILL THESE SHOES.
I WISH THAT I HAD NEVER STUMBLED ONTO THESE POWERS.

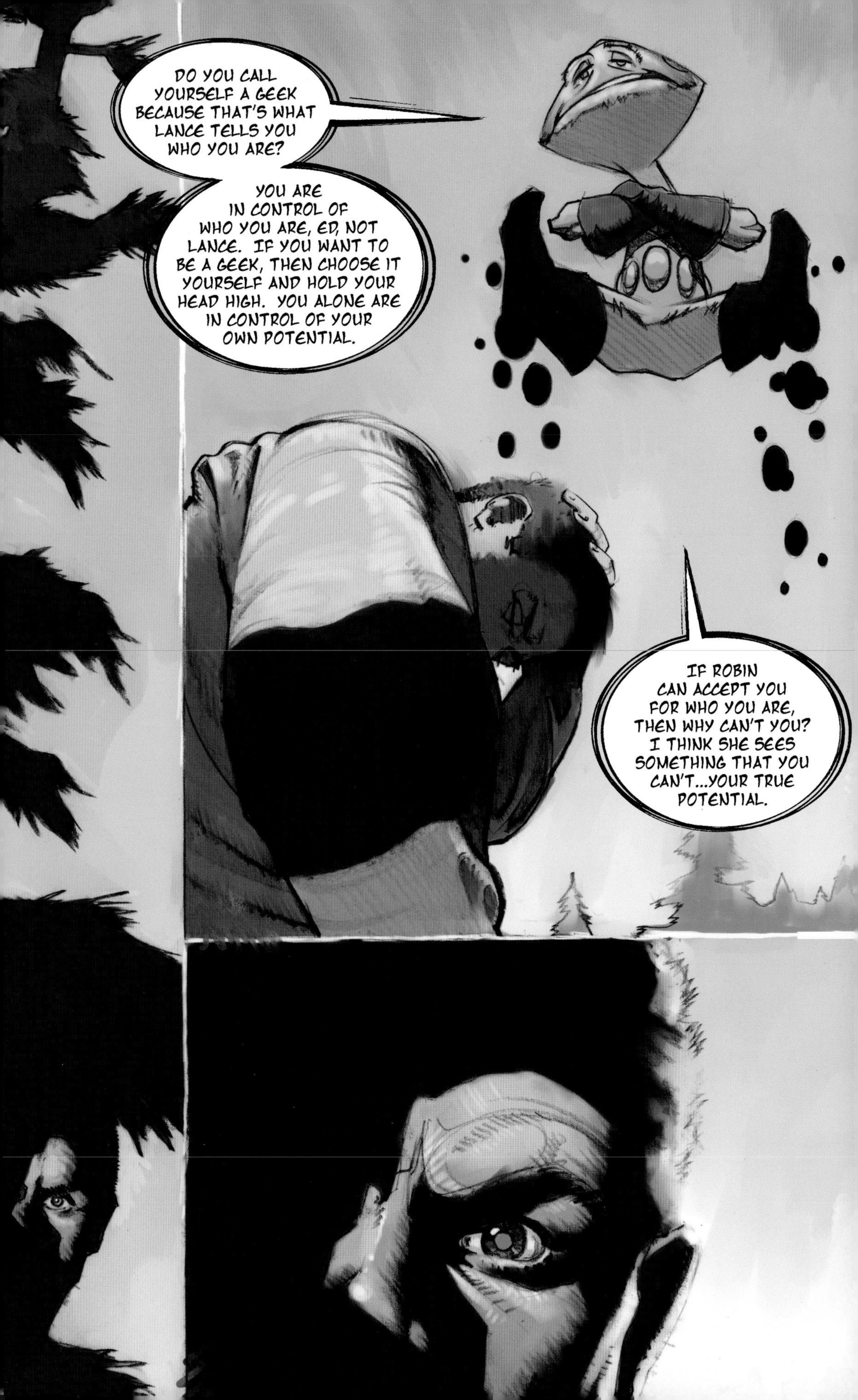
DO YOU CALL YOURSELF A GEEK BECAUSE THAT'S WHAT LANCE TELLS YOU WHO YOU ARE?
YOU ARE IN CONTROL OF WHO YOU ARE, ED, NOT LANCE. IF YOU WANT TO BE A GEEK, THEN CHOOSE IT YOURSELF AND HOLD YOUR HEAD HIGH. YOU ALONE ARE IN CONTROL OF YOUR OWN POTENTIAL.
IF ROBIN CAN ACCEPT YOU FOR WHO YOU ARE, THEN WHY CAN'T YOU? I THINK SHE SEES SOMETHING THAT YOU CAN'T...YOUR TRUE POTENTIAL.

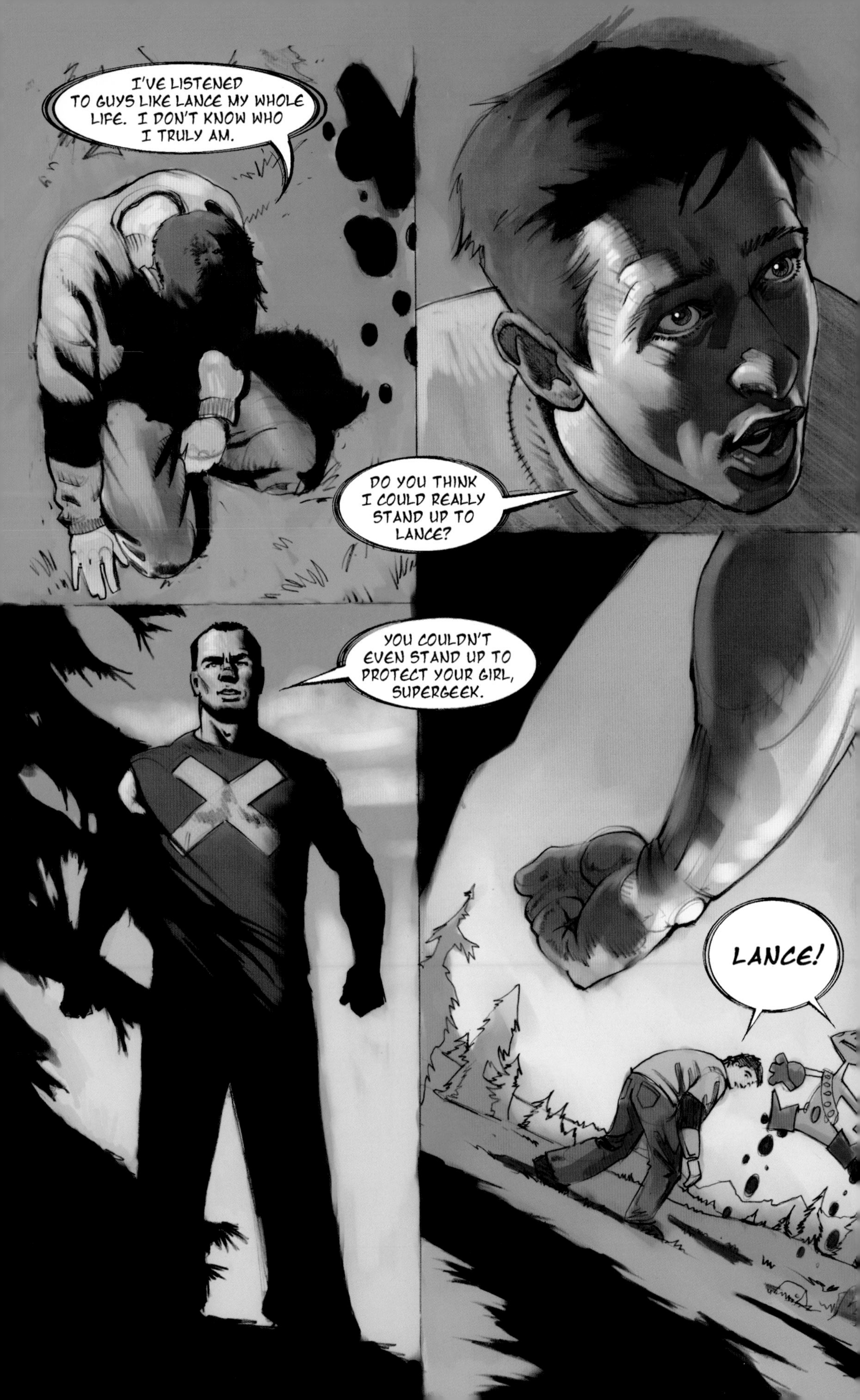
I'VE LISTENED TO GUYS LIKE LANCE MY WHOLE LIFE. I DON'T KNOW WHO I TRULY AM.
DO YOU THINK I COULD REALLY STAND UP TO LANCE?
YOU COULDN'T EVEN STAND UP TO PROTECT YOUR GIRL, SUPERGEEK.
LANCE!

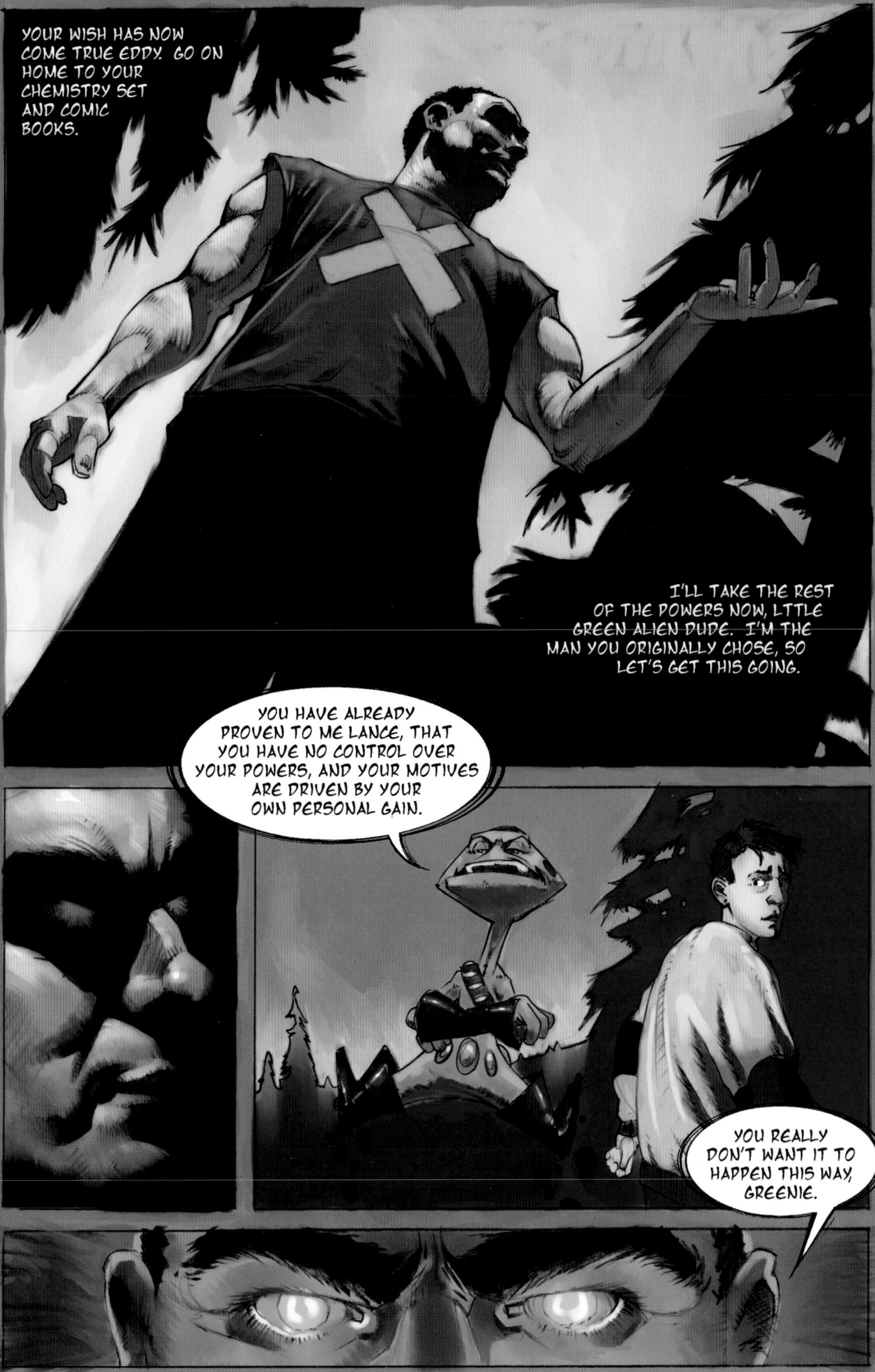
YOUR WISH HAS NOW COME TRUE EDDY. GO ON HOME TO YOUR CHEMISTRY SET AND COMIC BOOKS.
I'LL TAKE THE REST OF THE POWERS NOW, LTTLE GREEN ALIEN DUDE. I'M THE MAN YOU ORIGINALLY CHOSE, SO LET'S GET THIS GOING.
YOU HAVE ALREADY PROVEN TO ME LANCE, THAT YOU HAVE NO CONTROL OVER YOUR POWERS, AND YOUR MOTIVES ARE DRIVEN BY YOUR OWN PERSONAL GAIN.
YOU REALLY DON'T WANT IT TO HAPPEN THIS WAY, GREENIE.

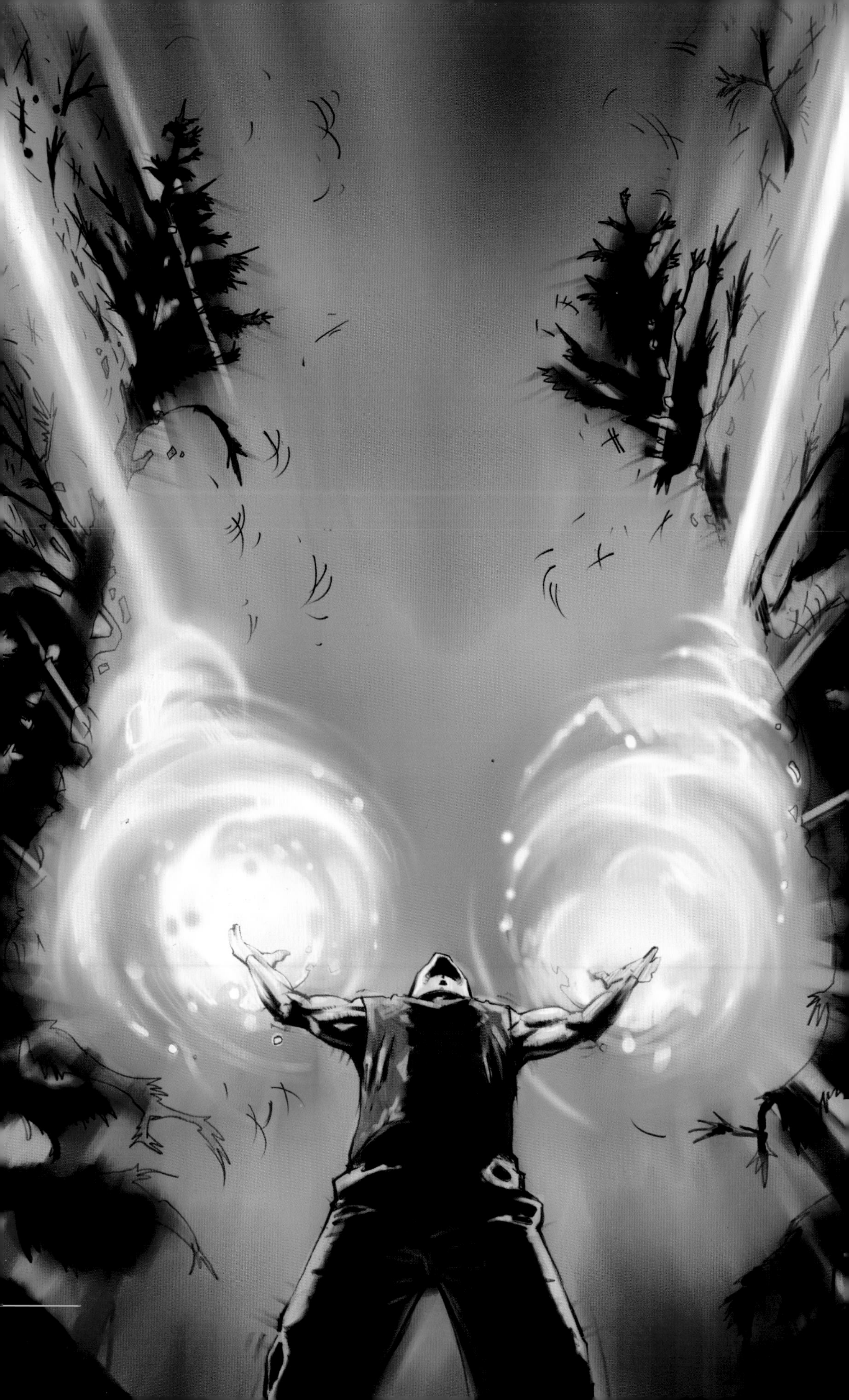

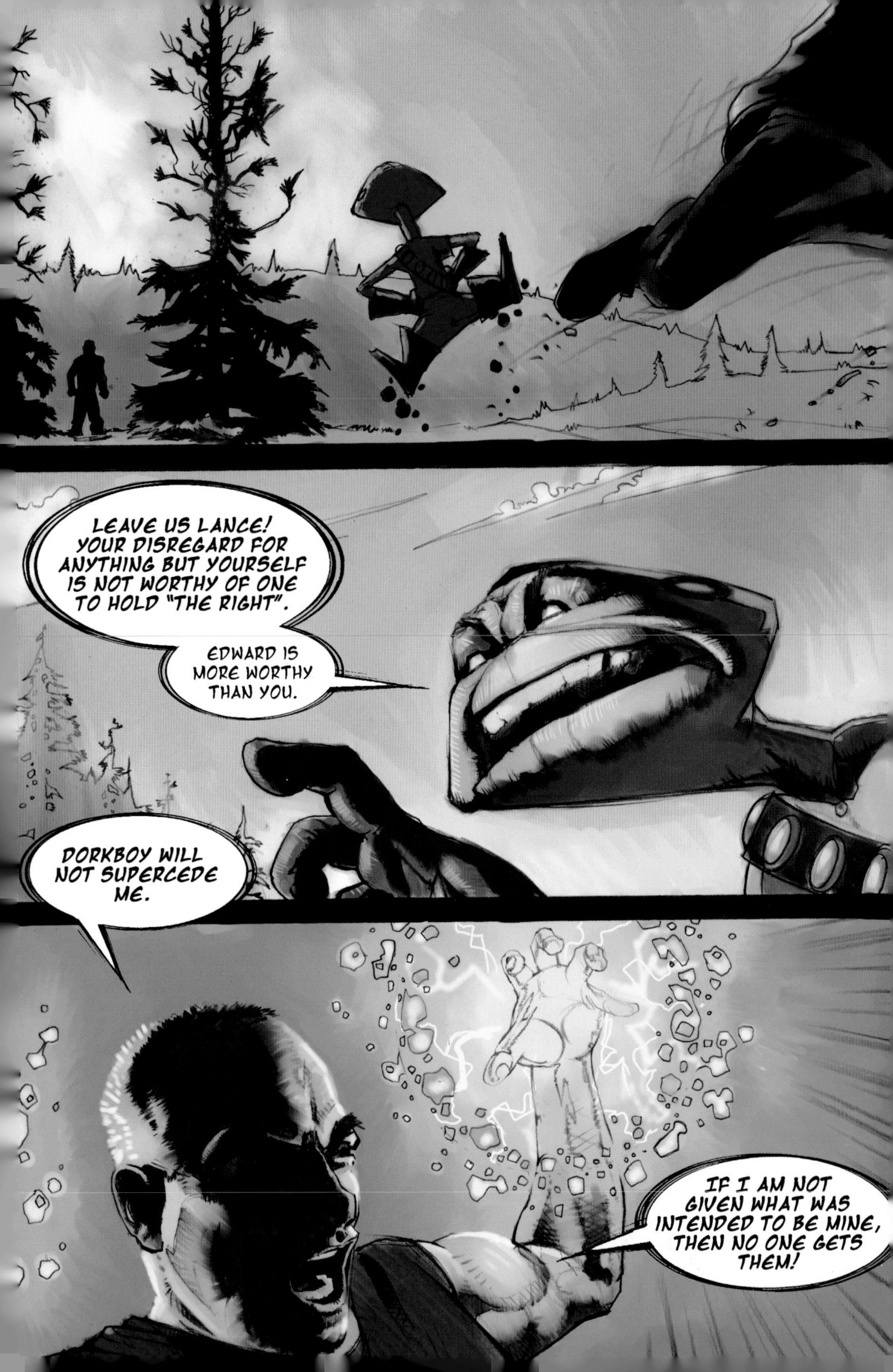

LEAVE US LANCE! YOUR DISREGARD FOR ANYTHING BUT YOURSELF IS NOT WORTHY OF ONE TO HOLD "THE RIGHT".
EDWARD IS MORE WORTHY THAN YOU.
DORKBOY WILL NOT SUPERCEDE ME.
IF I AM NOT GIVEN WHAT WAS INTENDED TO BE MINE, THEN NO ONE GETS THEM!

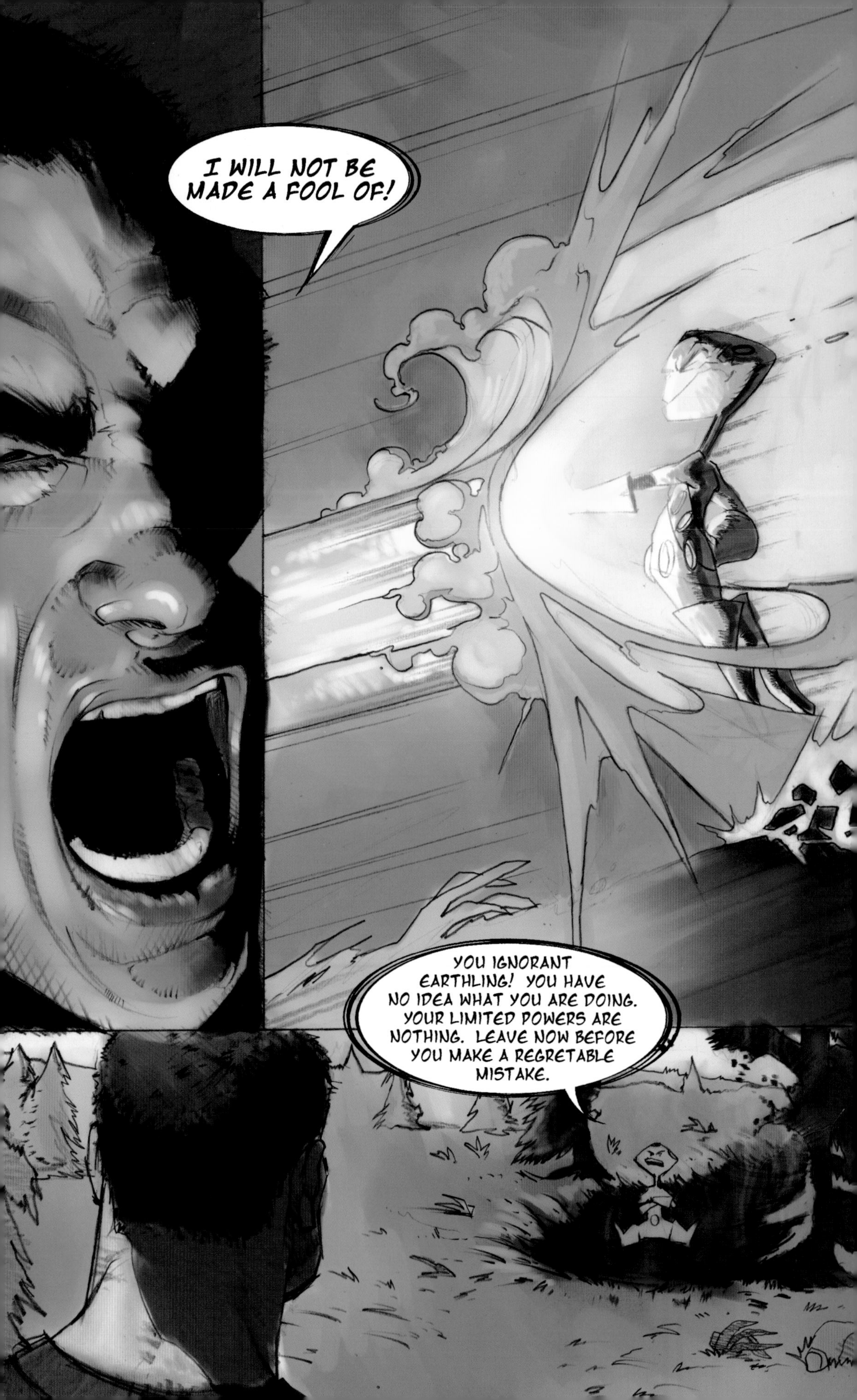
I WILL NOT BE MADE A FOOL OF!
YOU IGNORANT EARTHLING! YOU HAVE NO IDEA WHAT YOU ARE DOING. YOUR LIMITED POWERS ARE NOTHING. LEAVE NOW BEFORE YOU MAKE A REGRETABLE MISTAKE.

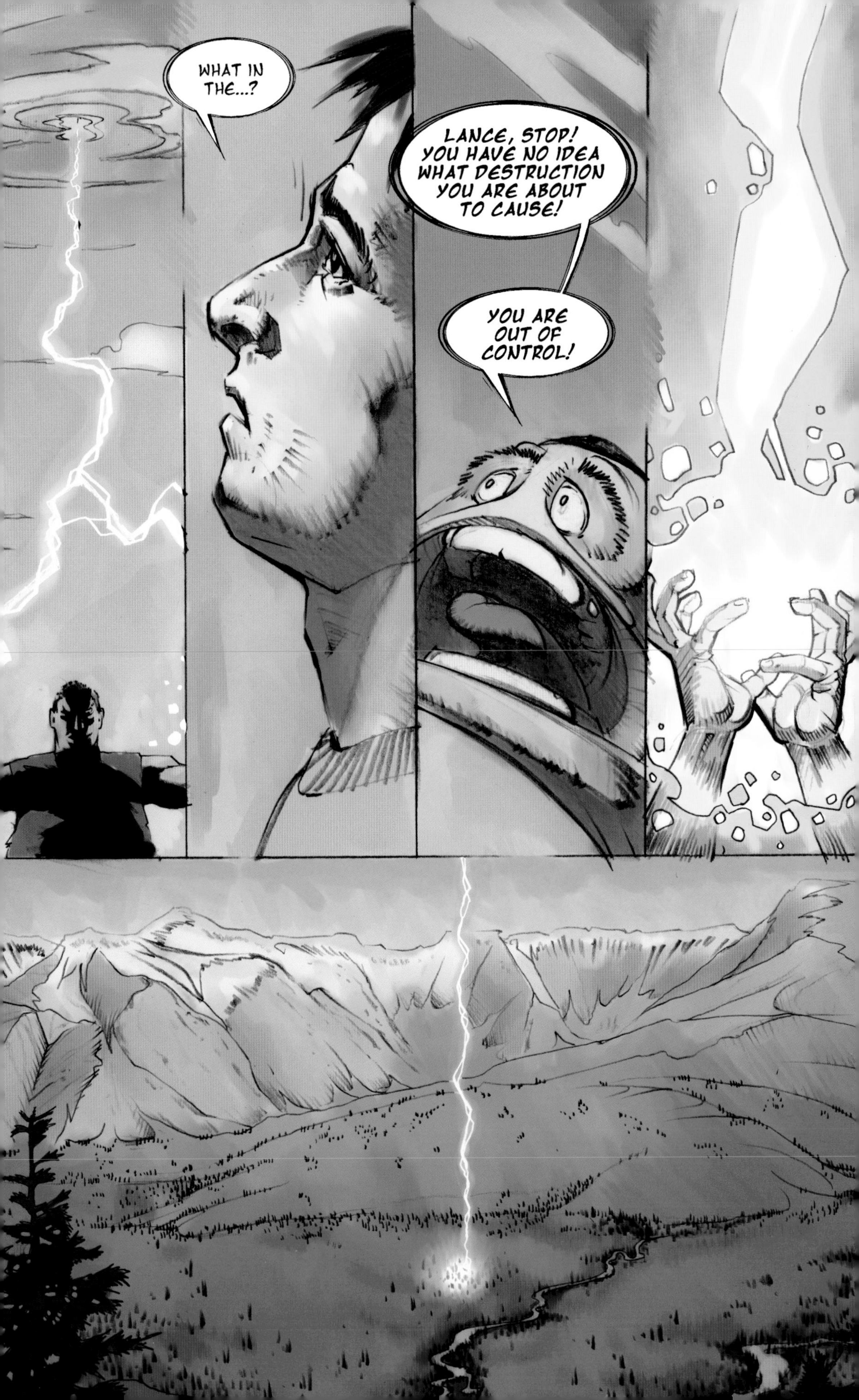
WHAT IN THE...?
LANCE, STOP! YOU HAVE NO IDEA WHAT DESTRUCTION YOU ARE ABOUT TO CAUSE!
YOU ARE OUT OF CONTROL!

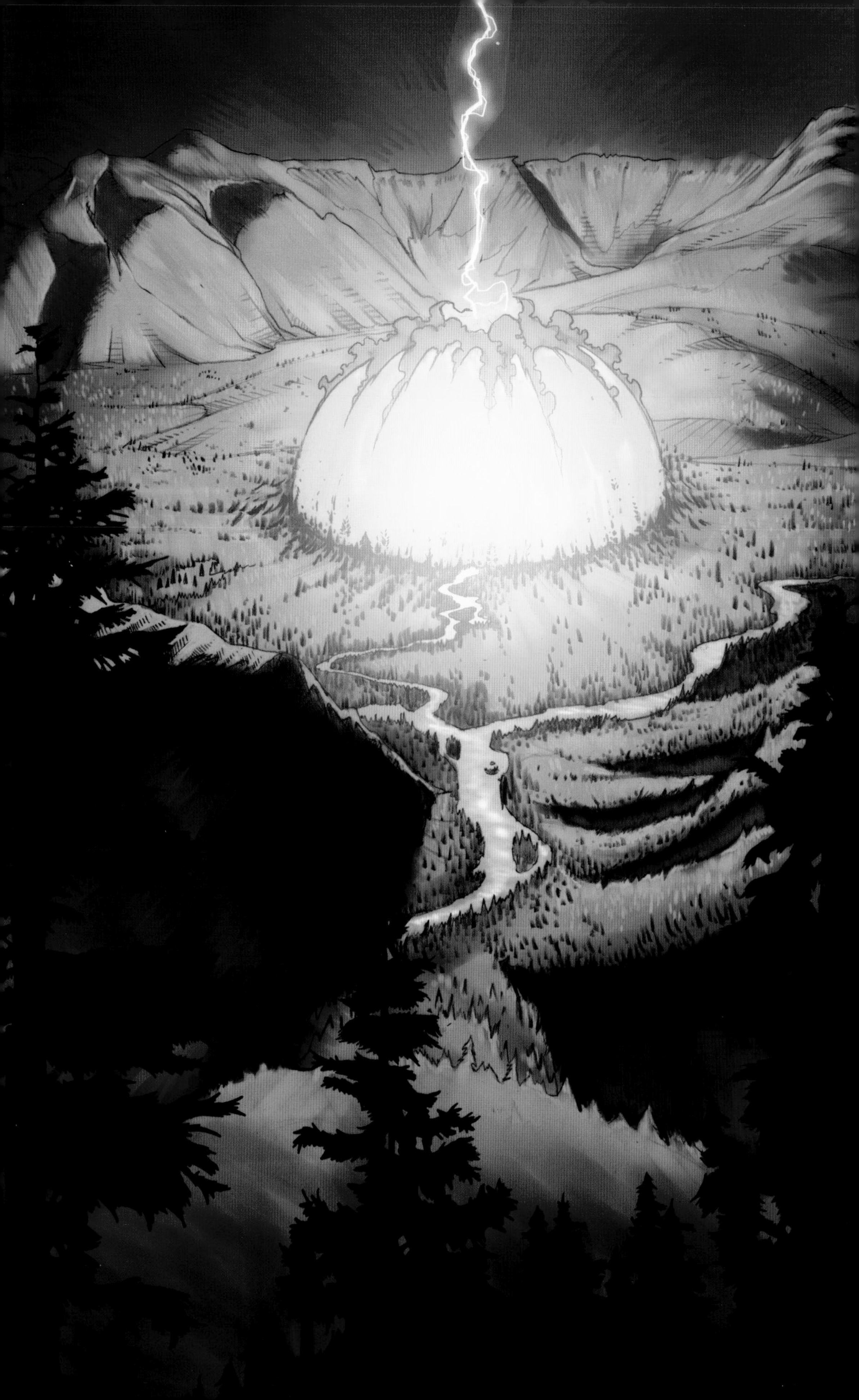

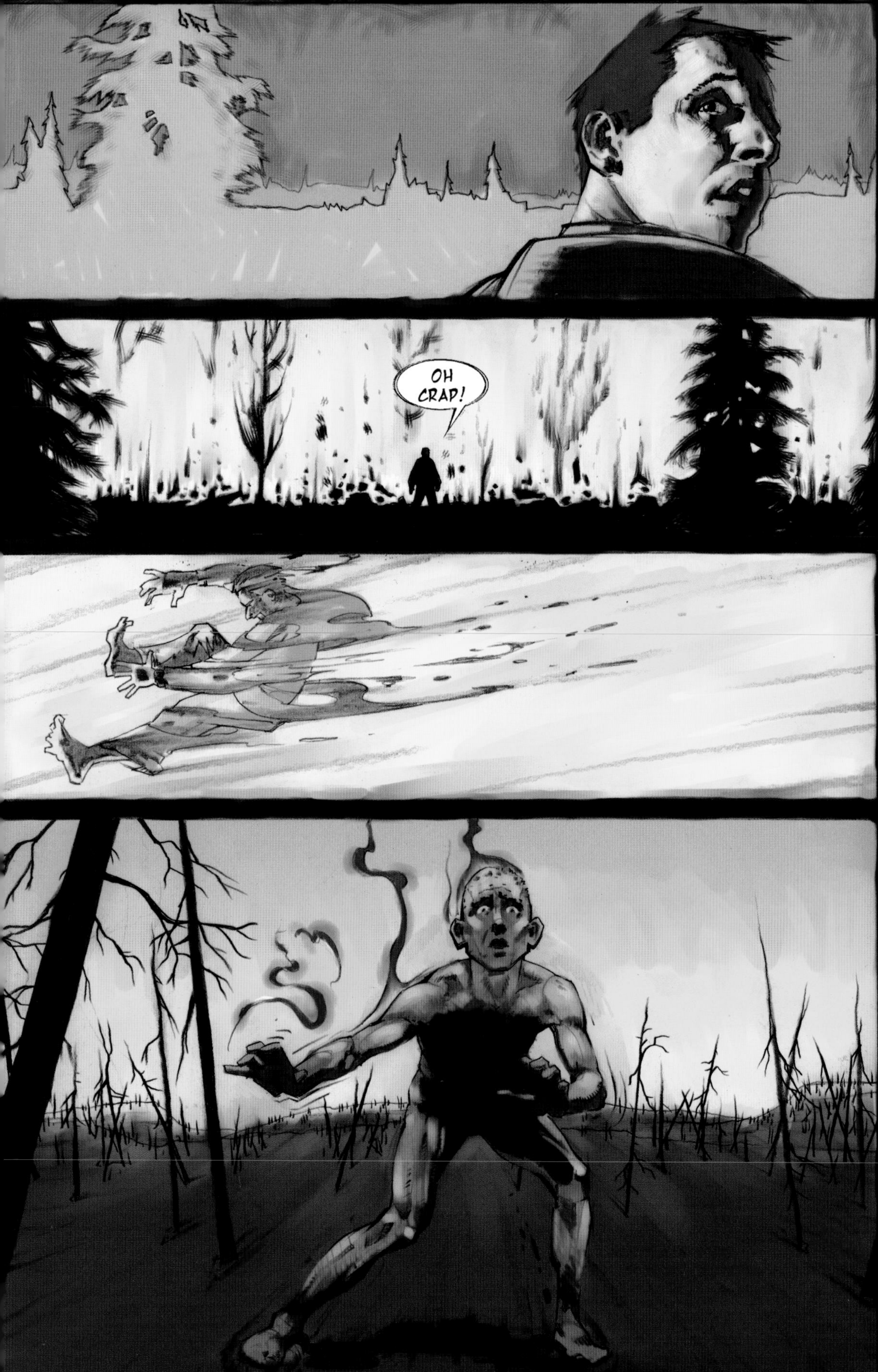
OH CRAP!

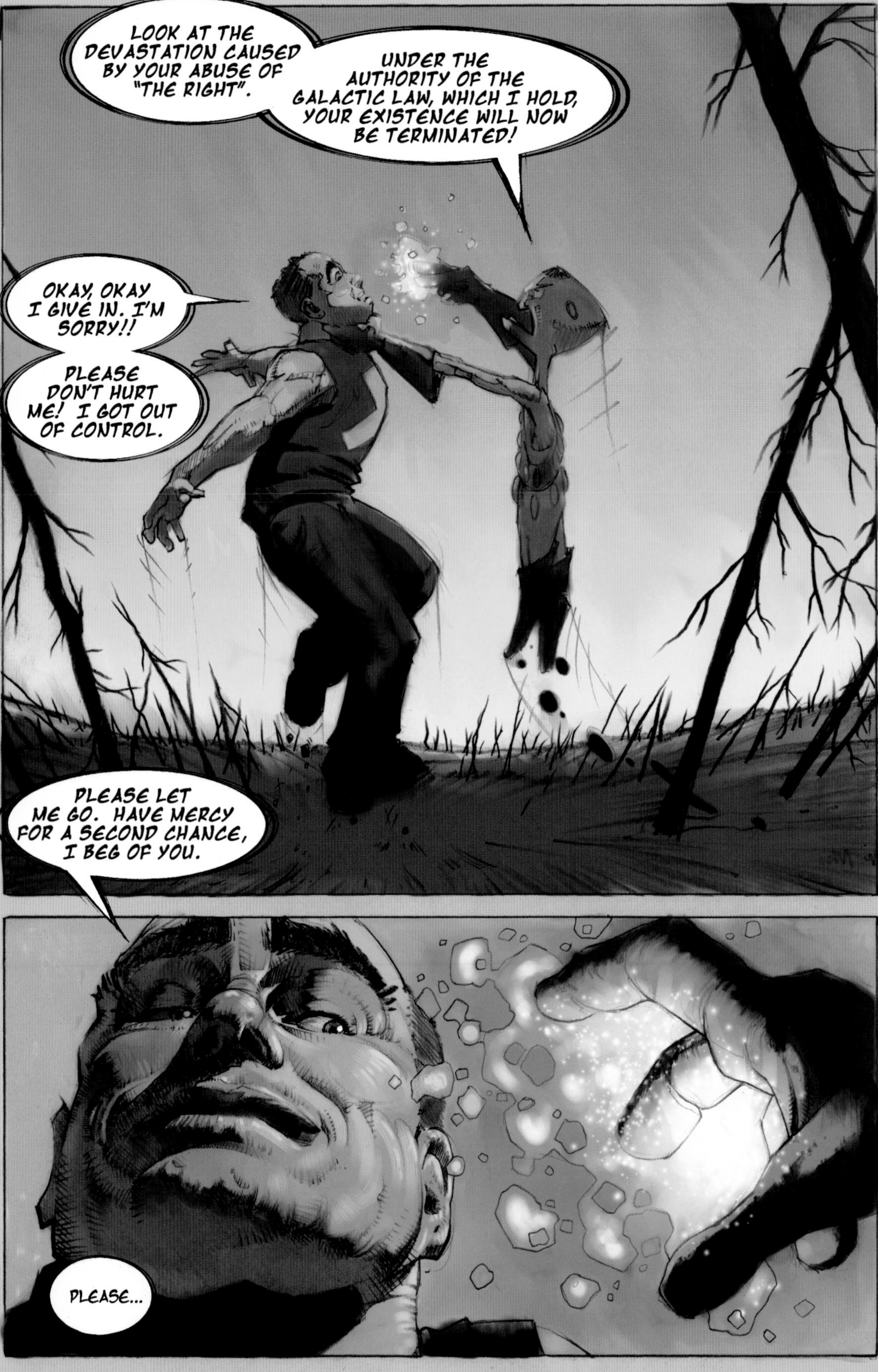
LOOK AT THE DEVASTATION CAUSED BY YOUR ABUSE OF "THE RIGHT".
UNDER THE AUTHORITY OF THE GALACTIC LAW, WHICH I HOLD, YOUR EXISTENCE WILL NOW BE TERMINATED!
OKAY, OKAY I GIVE IN. I'M SORRY!!
PLEASE DON'T HURT ME! I GOT OUT OF CONTROL.
PLEASE LET ME GO. HAVE MERCY FOR A SECOND CHANCE, I BEG OF YOU.
PLEASE...

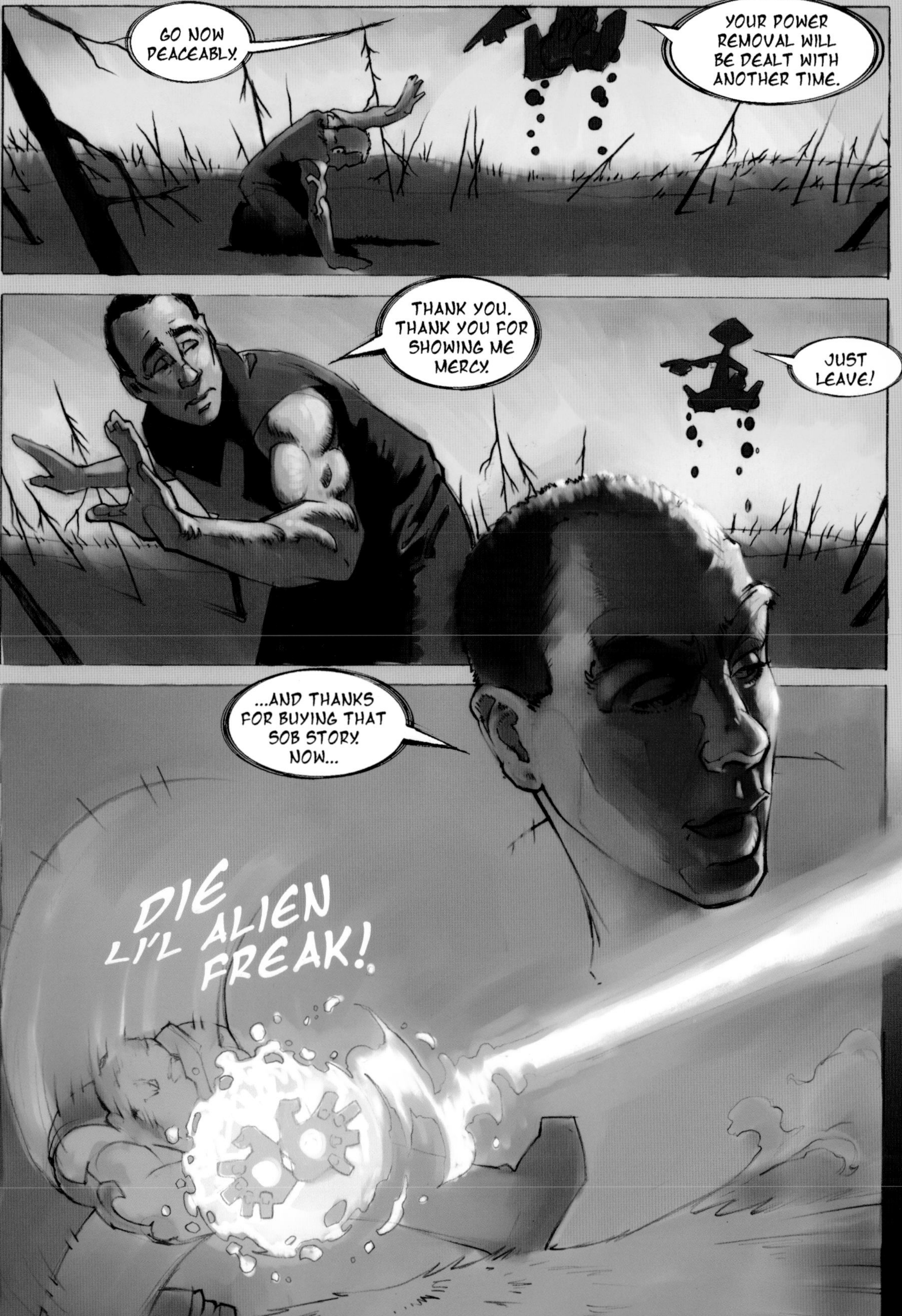
GO NOW PEACEABLY.
YOUR POWER REMOVAL WILL BE DEALT WITH ANOTHER TIME.
THANK YOU. THANK YOU FOR SHOWING ME MERCY.
JUST LEAVE!
...AND THANKS FOR BUYING THAT SOB STORY. NOW...
DIE LI'L ALIEN FREAK!

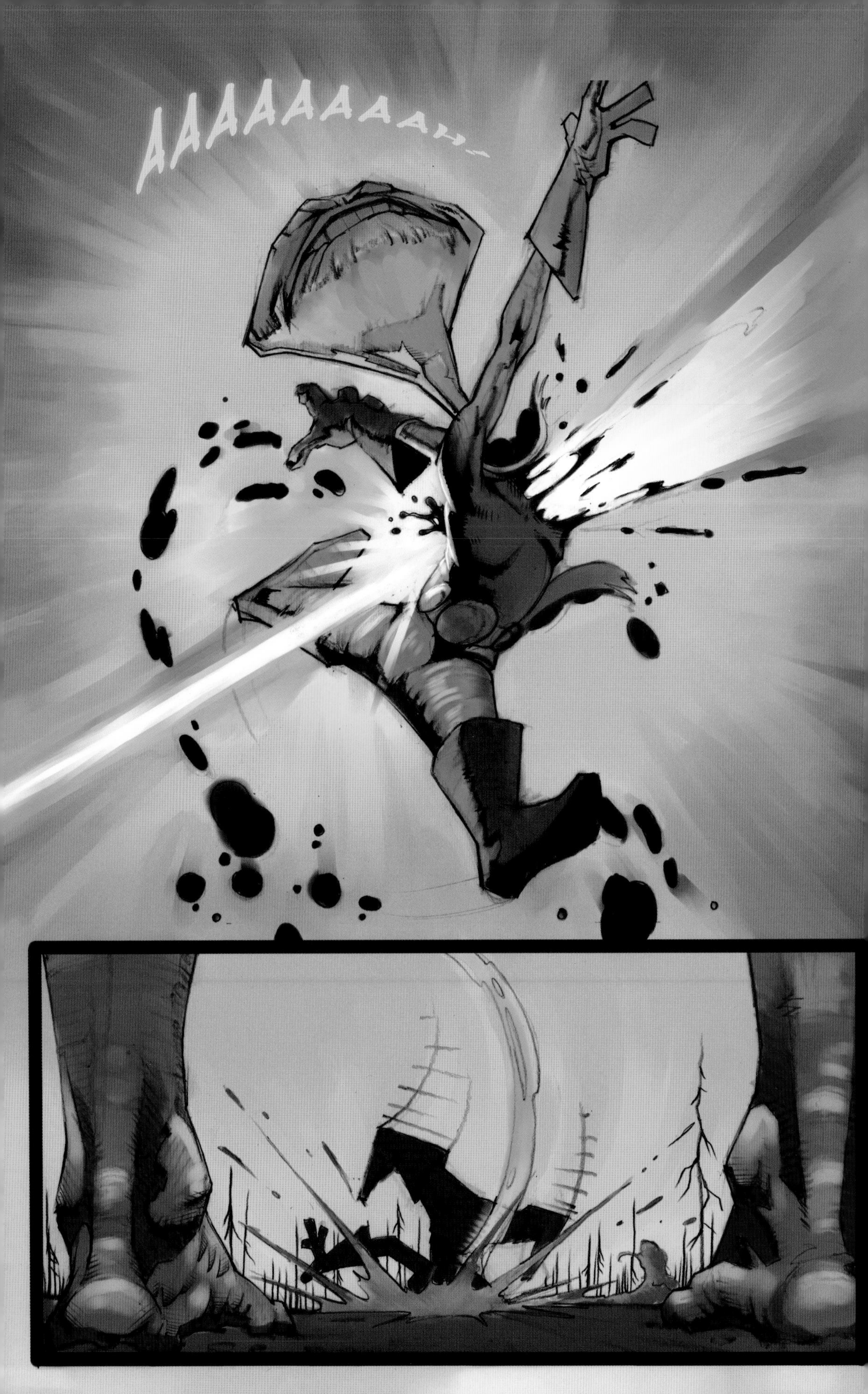
AAAAAAAAH–

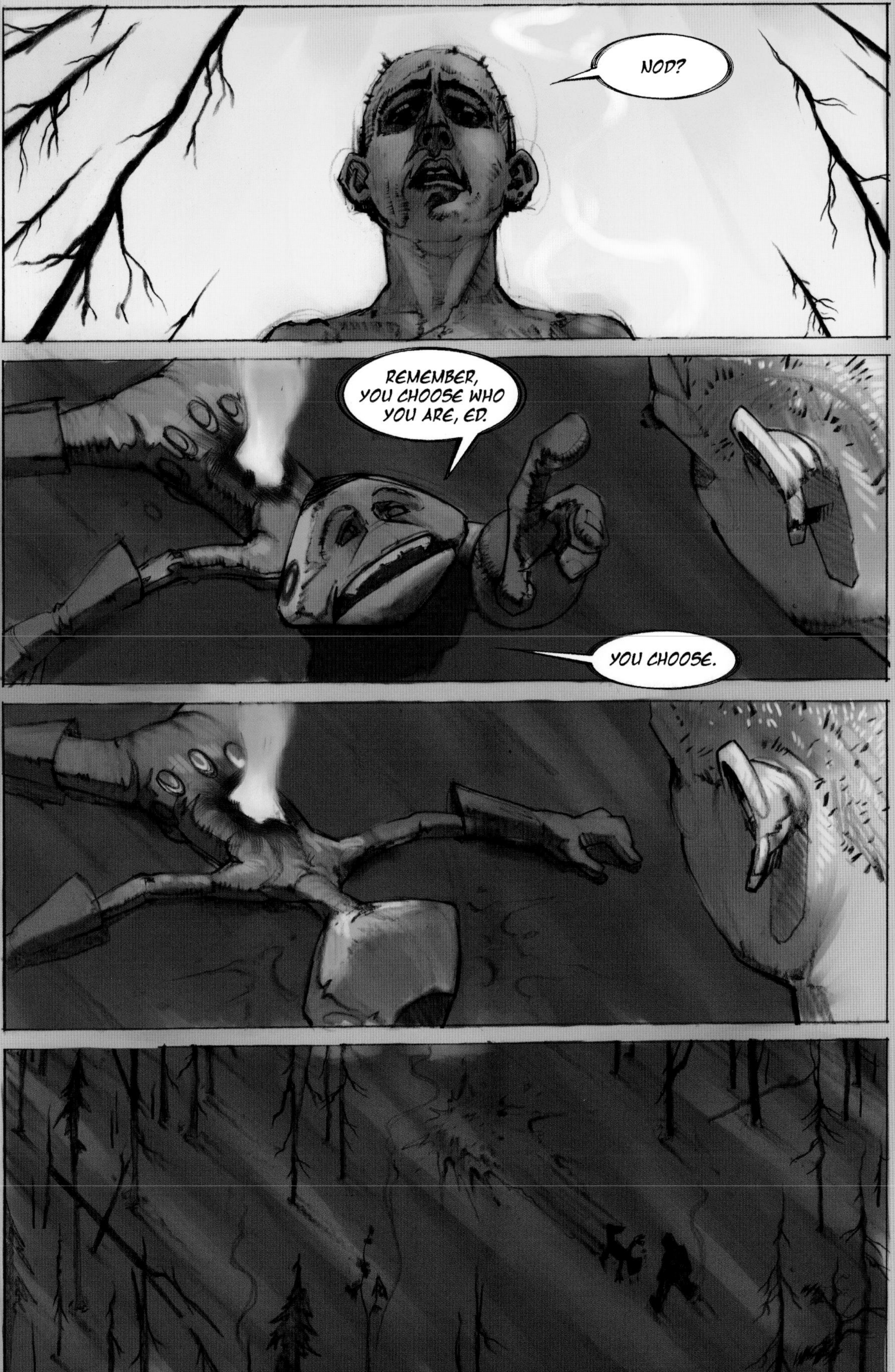
NOD?
REMEMBER, YOU CHOOSE WHO YOU ARE, ED.
YOU CHOOSE.

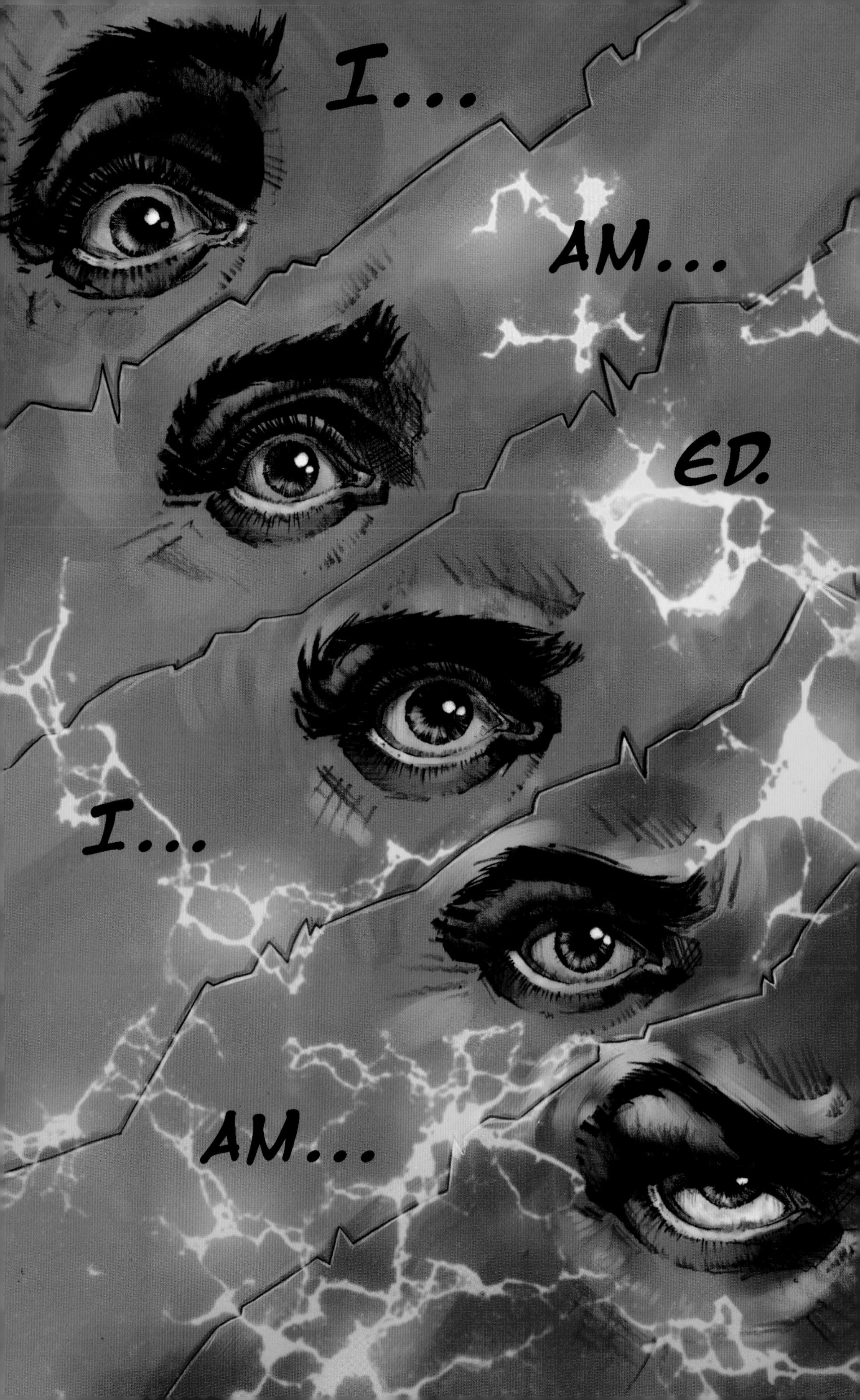
I...
AM...
ED.
I...
AM...

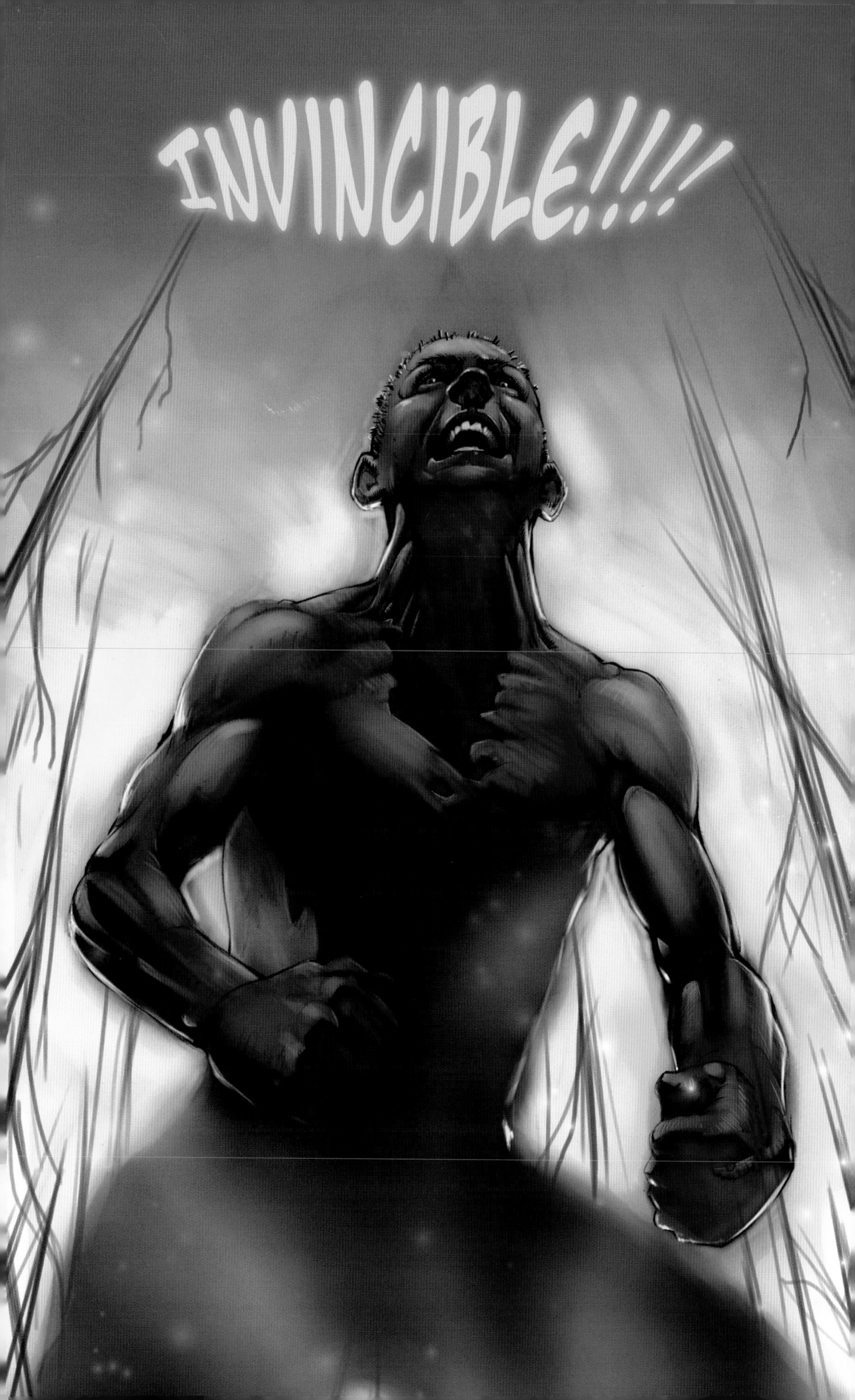
INVINCIBLE!!!!

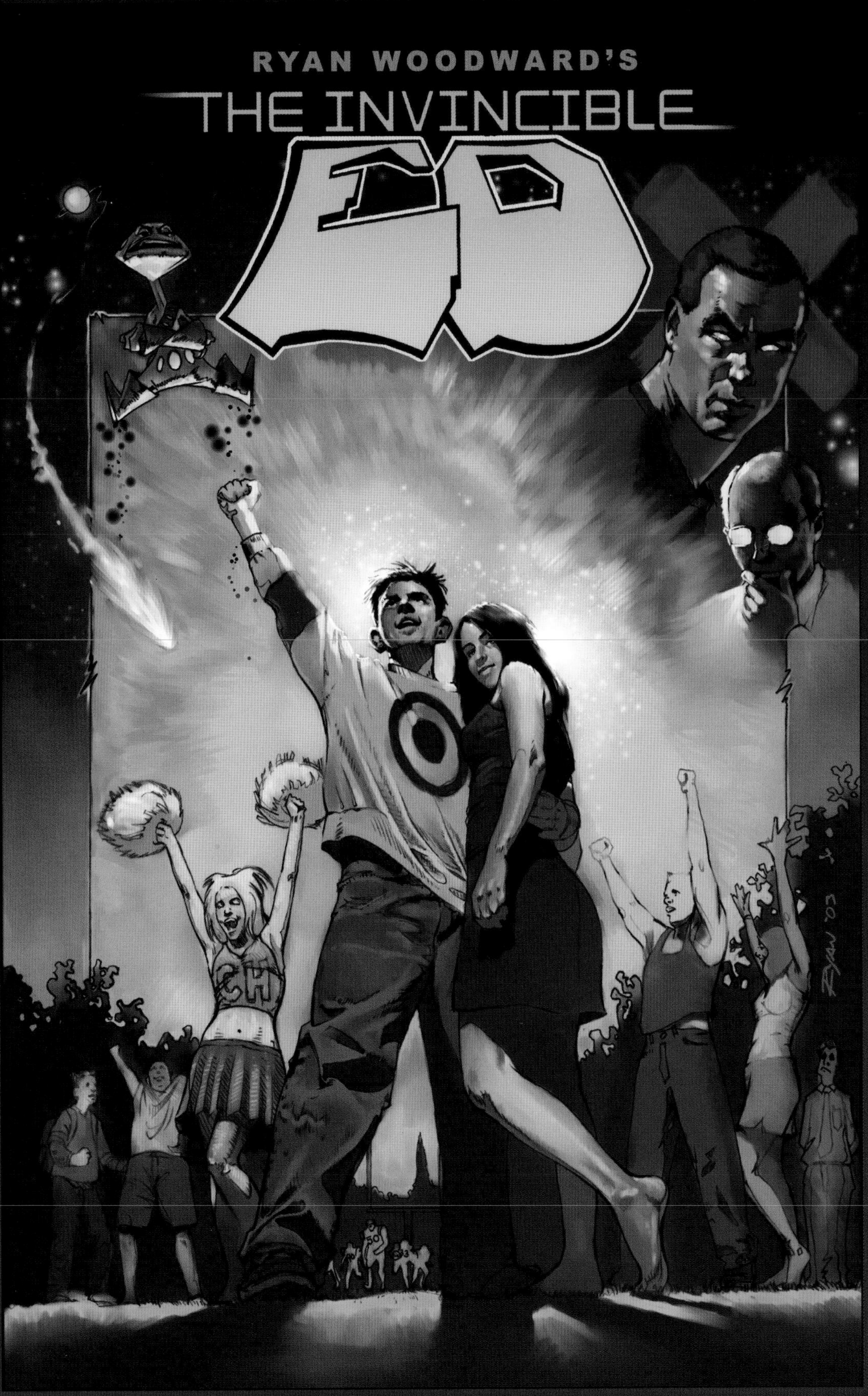
RYAN WOODWARD'S
THE INVINCIBLE
ED
CH
RYAN '03

written
RYAN WOODWARD

pencils
MIKE O'HARE

colors
RYAN WOODWARD

comic fonts
NATE PIEKOS

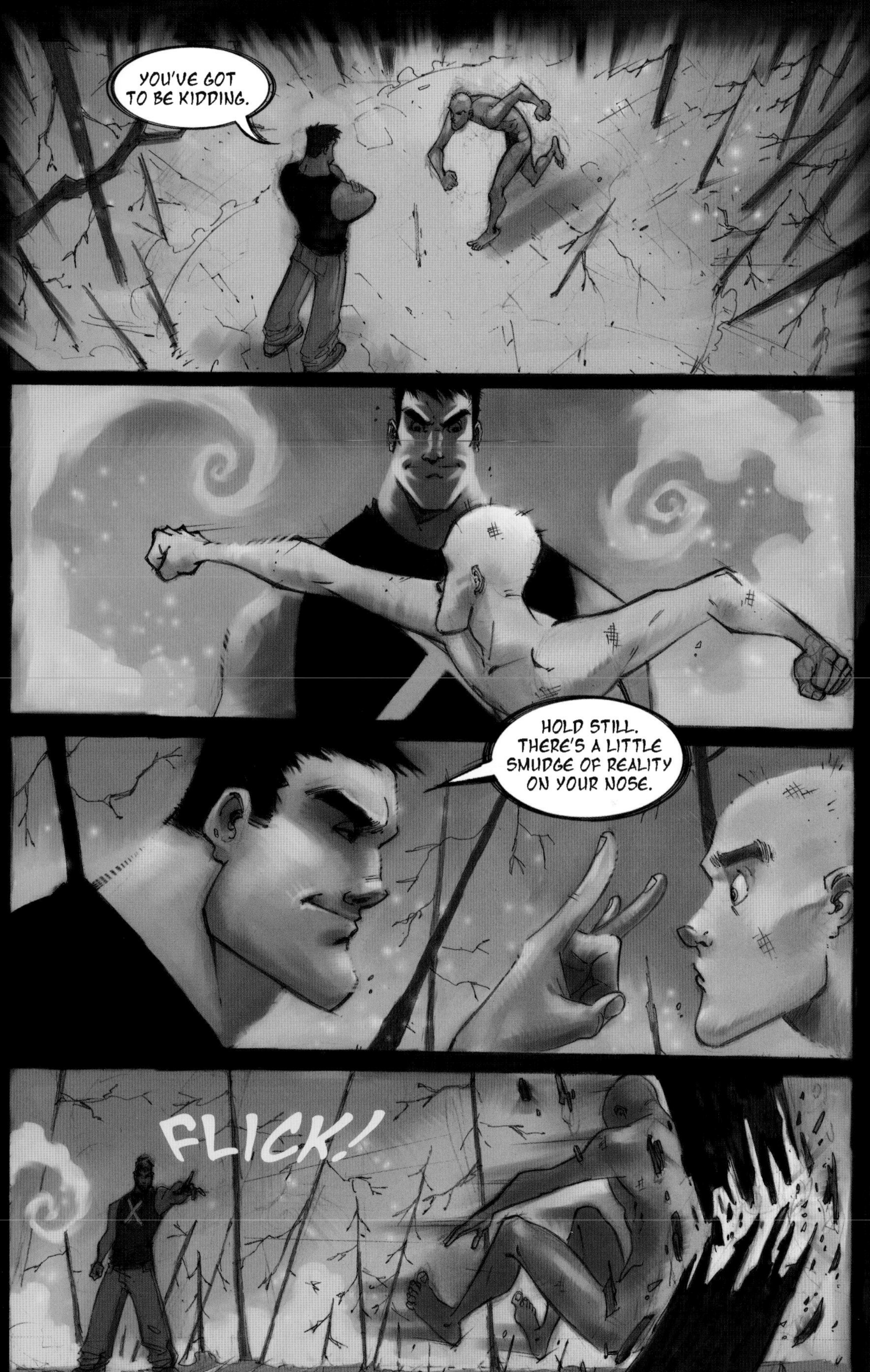
YOU'VE GOT TO BE KIDDING.
HOLD STILL. THERE'S A LITTLE SMUDGE OF REALITY ON YOUR NOSE.
FLICK!

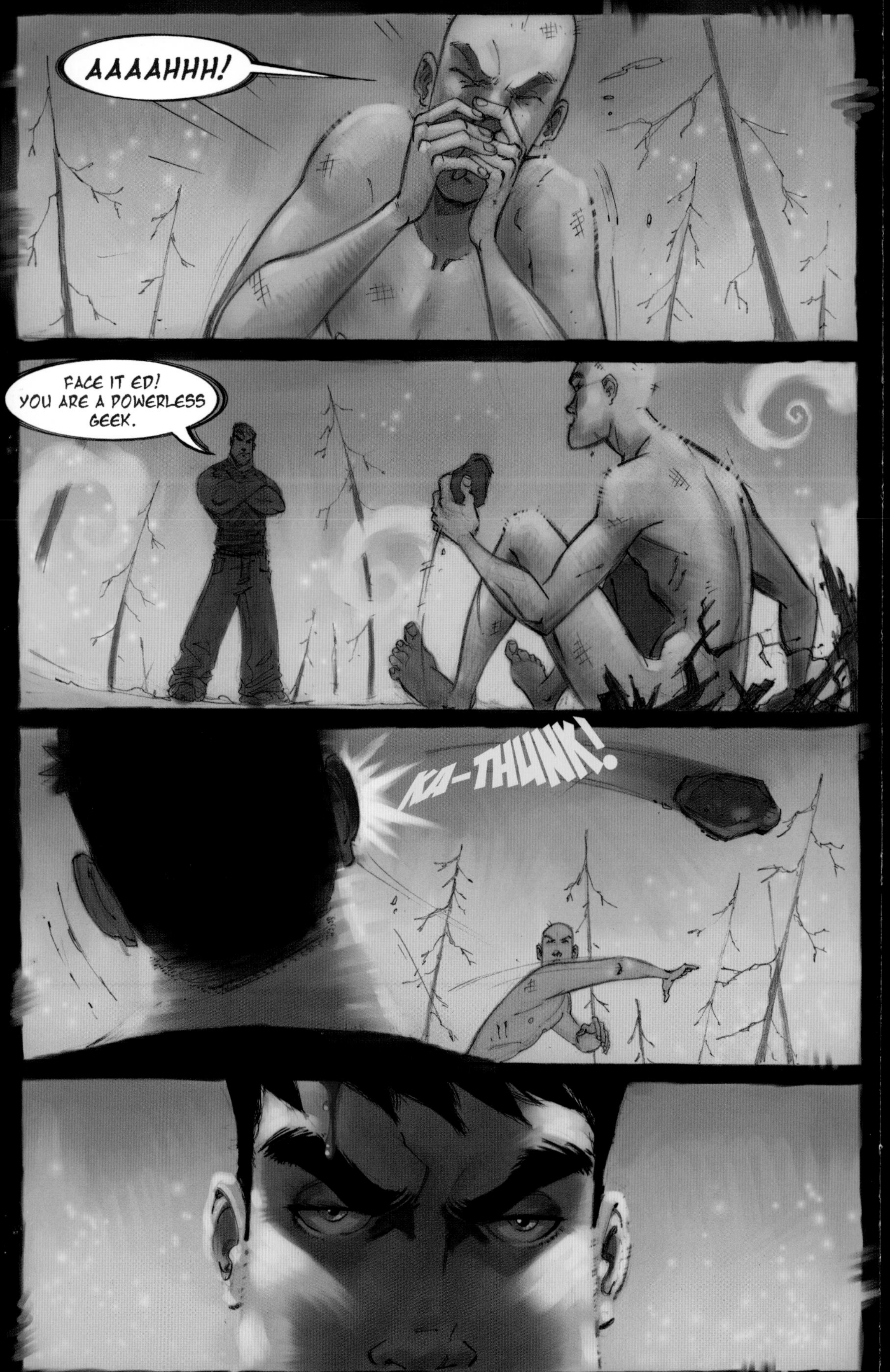
AAAAHHH!
FACE IT ED! YOU ARE A POWERLESS GEEK.
KA-THUNK!

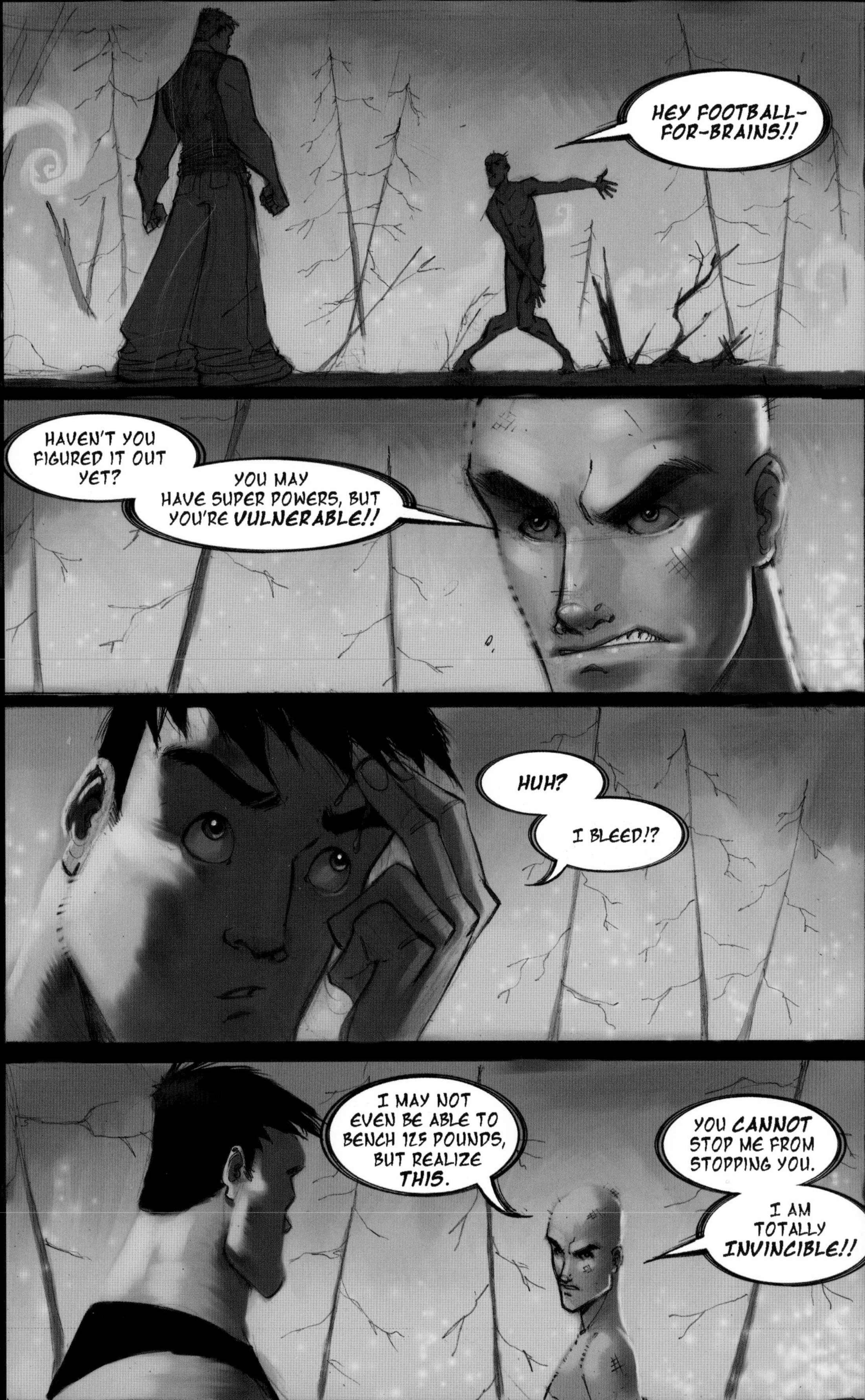
HEY FOOTBALL-FOR-BRAINS!!
HAVEN'T YOU FIGURED IT OUT YET?
YOU MAY HAVE SUPER POWERS, BUT YOU'RE **VULNERABLE!!**
HUH?
I BLEED!?
I MAY NOT EVEN BE ABLE TO BENCH 125 POUNDS, BUT REALIZE **THIS.**
YOU **CANNOT** STOP ME FROM STOPPING YOU.
I AM TOTALLY **INVINCIBLE!!**

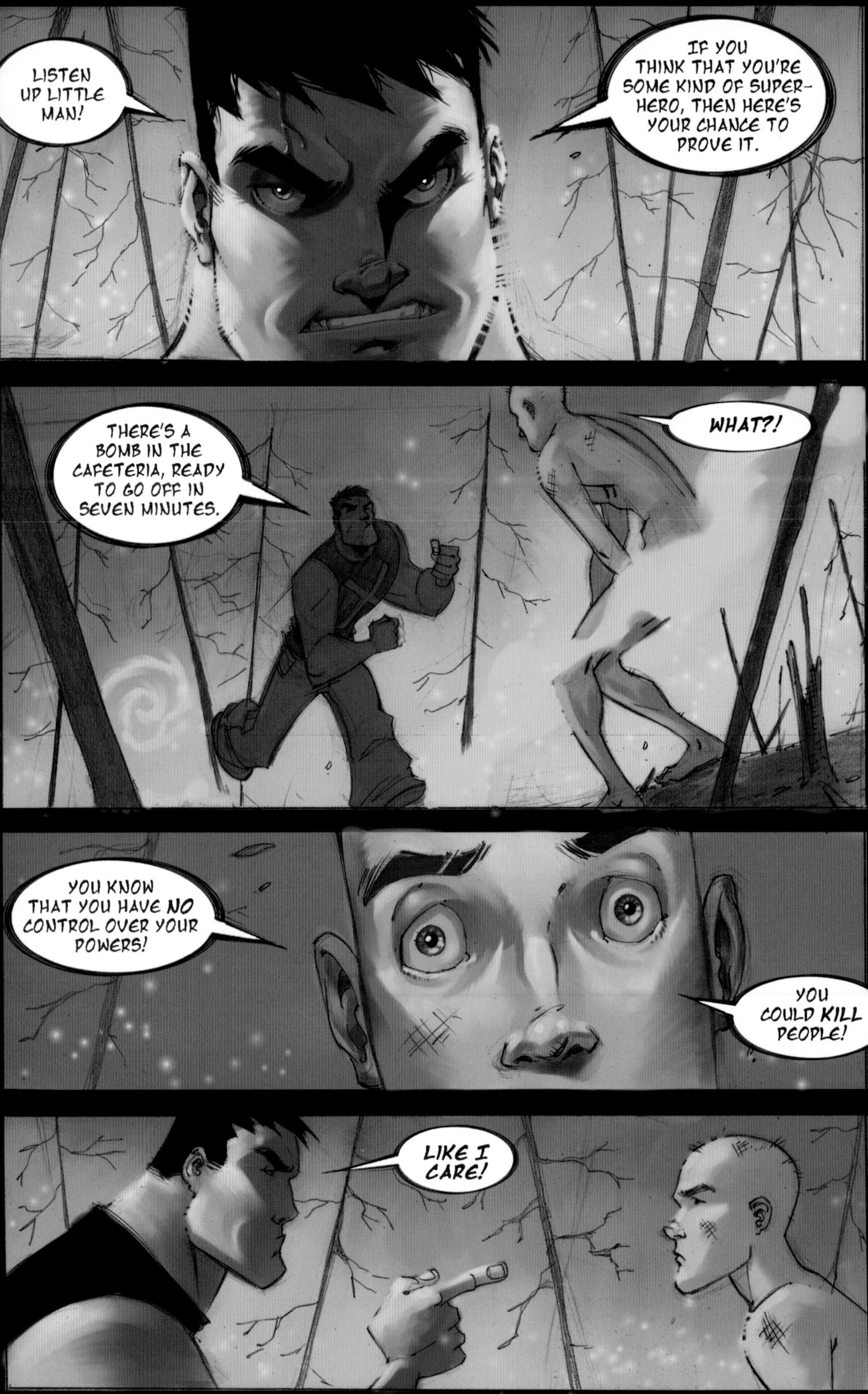
LISTEN UP LITTLE MAN!
IF YOU THINK THAT YOU'RE SOME KIND OF SUPER-HERO, THEN HERE'S YOUR CHANCE TO PROVE IT.
THERE'S A BOMB IN THE CAFETERIA, READY TO GO OFF IN SEVEN MINUTES.
WHAT?!
YOU KNOW THAT YOU HAVE NO CONTROL OVER YOUR POWERS!
YOU COULD KILL PEOPLE!
LIKE I CARE!

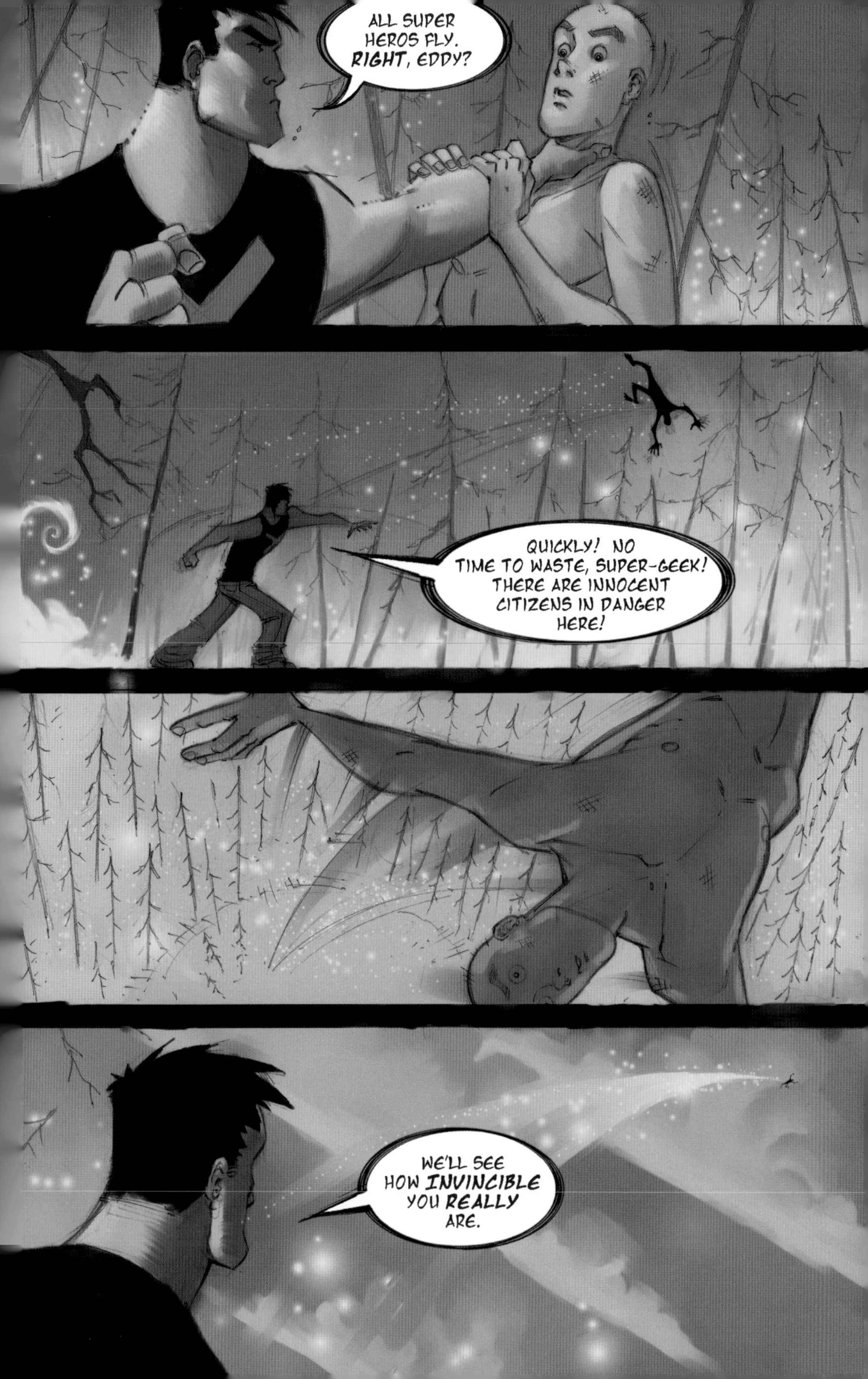
ALL SUPER HEROS FLY. RIGHT, EDDY?
QUICKLY! NO TIME TO WASTE, SUPER-GEEK! THERE ARE INNOCENT CITIZENS IN DANGER HERE!
WE'LL SEE HOW INVINCIBLE YOU REALLY ARE.

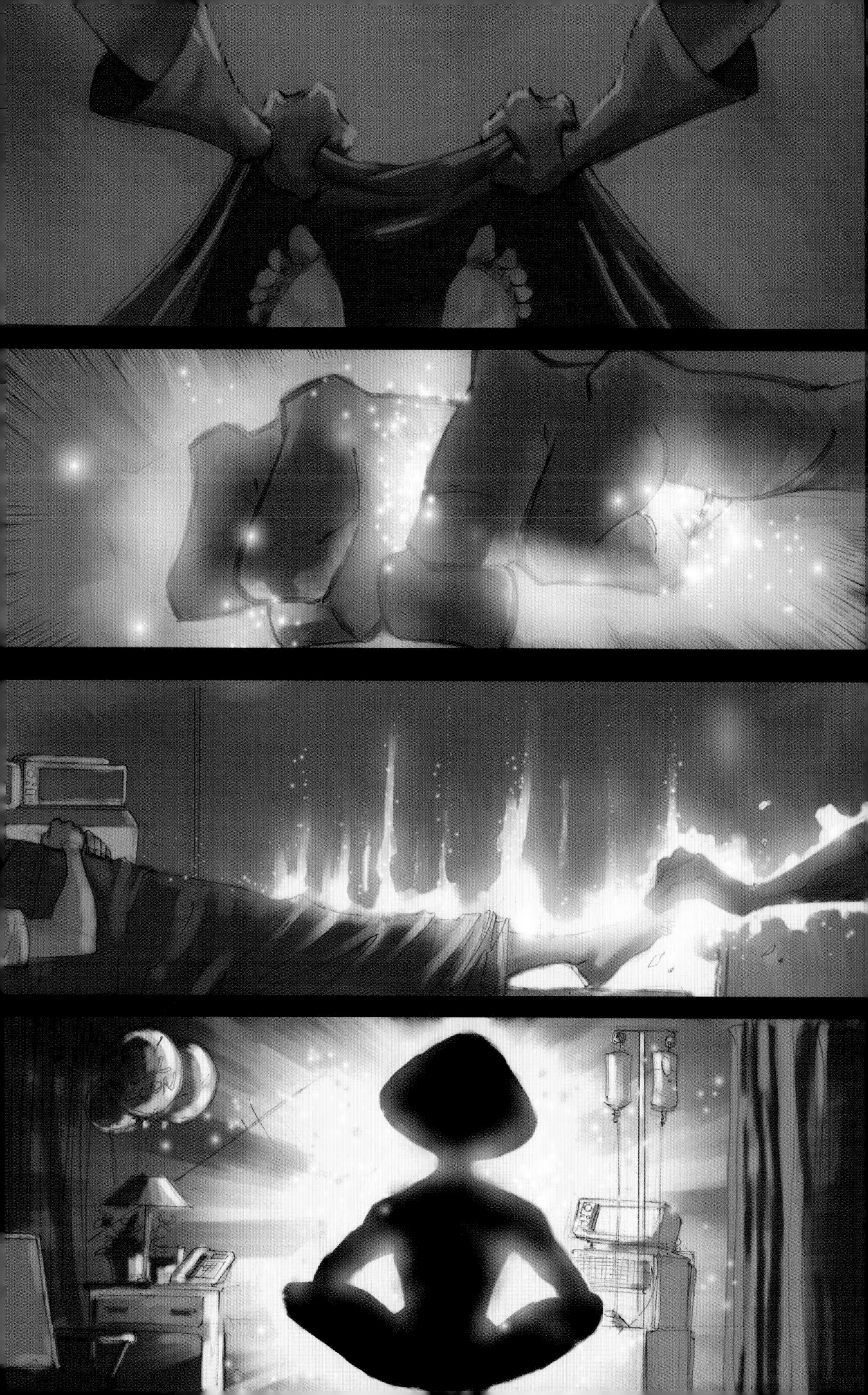

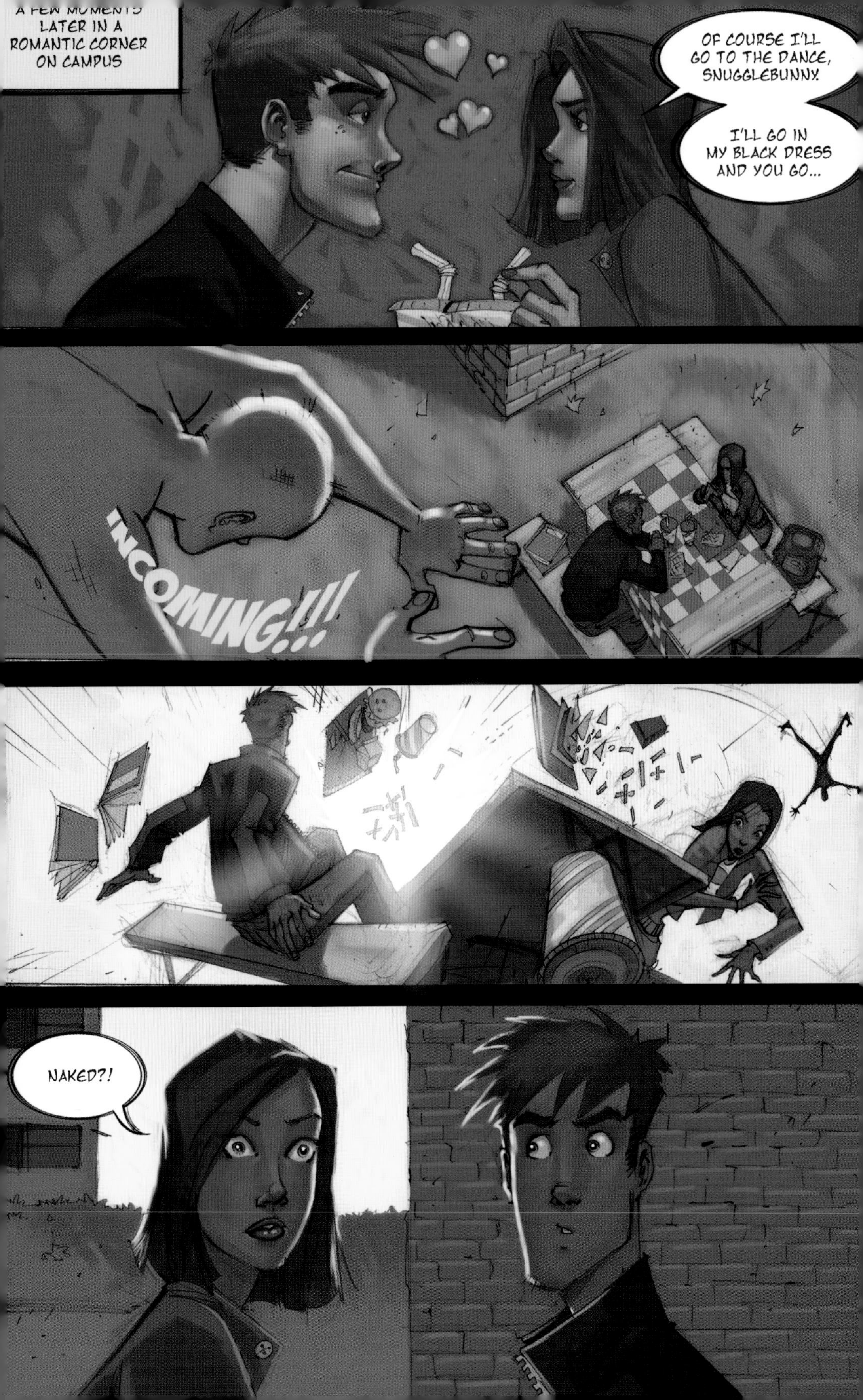
A FEW MOMENTS LATER IN A ROMANTIC CORNER ON CAMPUS
OF COURSE I'LL GO TO THE DANCE, SNUGGLEBUNNY.
I'LL GO IN MY BLACK DRESS AND YOU GO...
INCOMING!!!...
NAKED?!

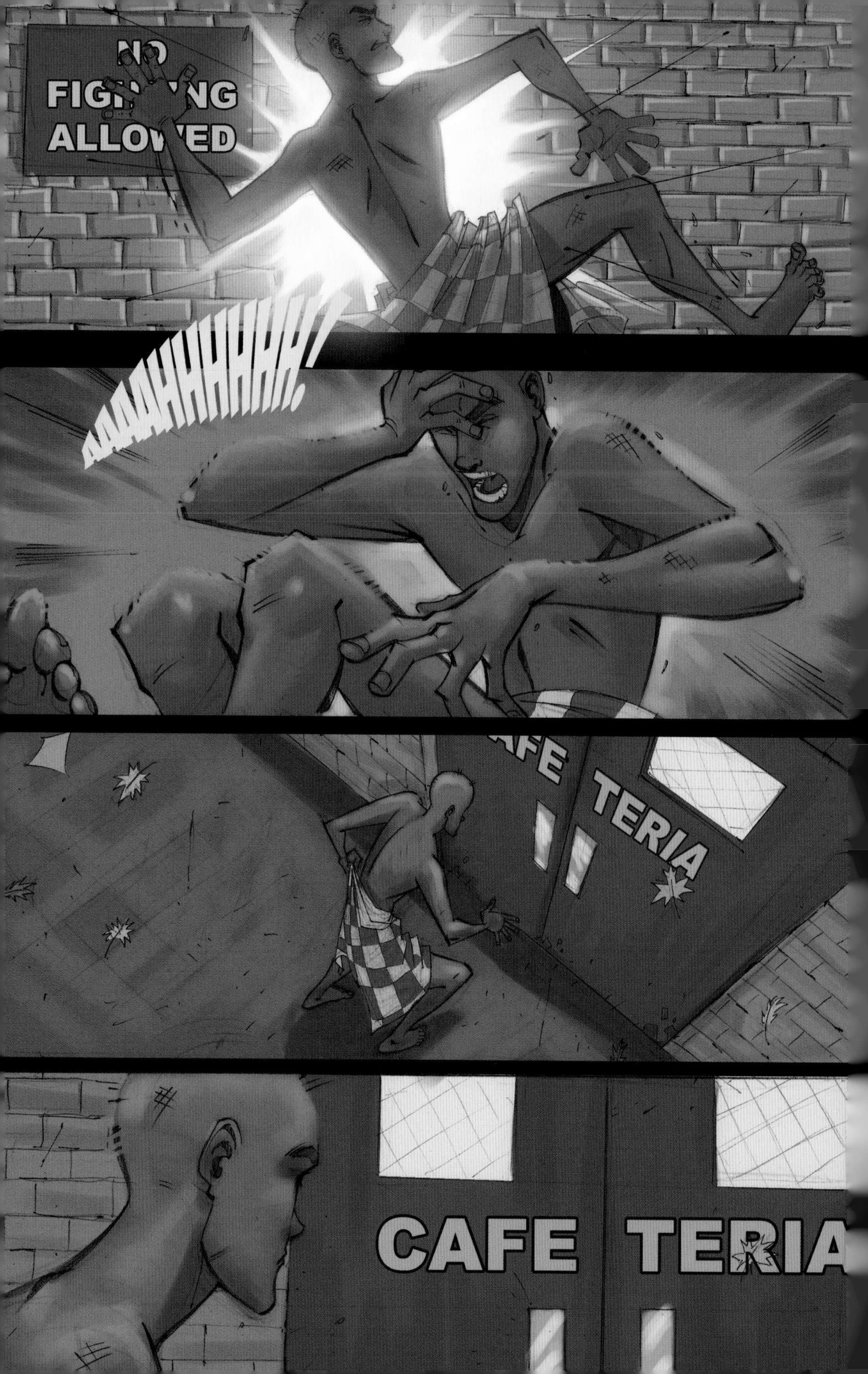

NO FIGHTING ALLOWED
AAAAHHHHHH!!
CAFE TERIA
CAFE TERIA

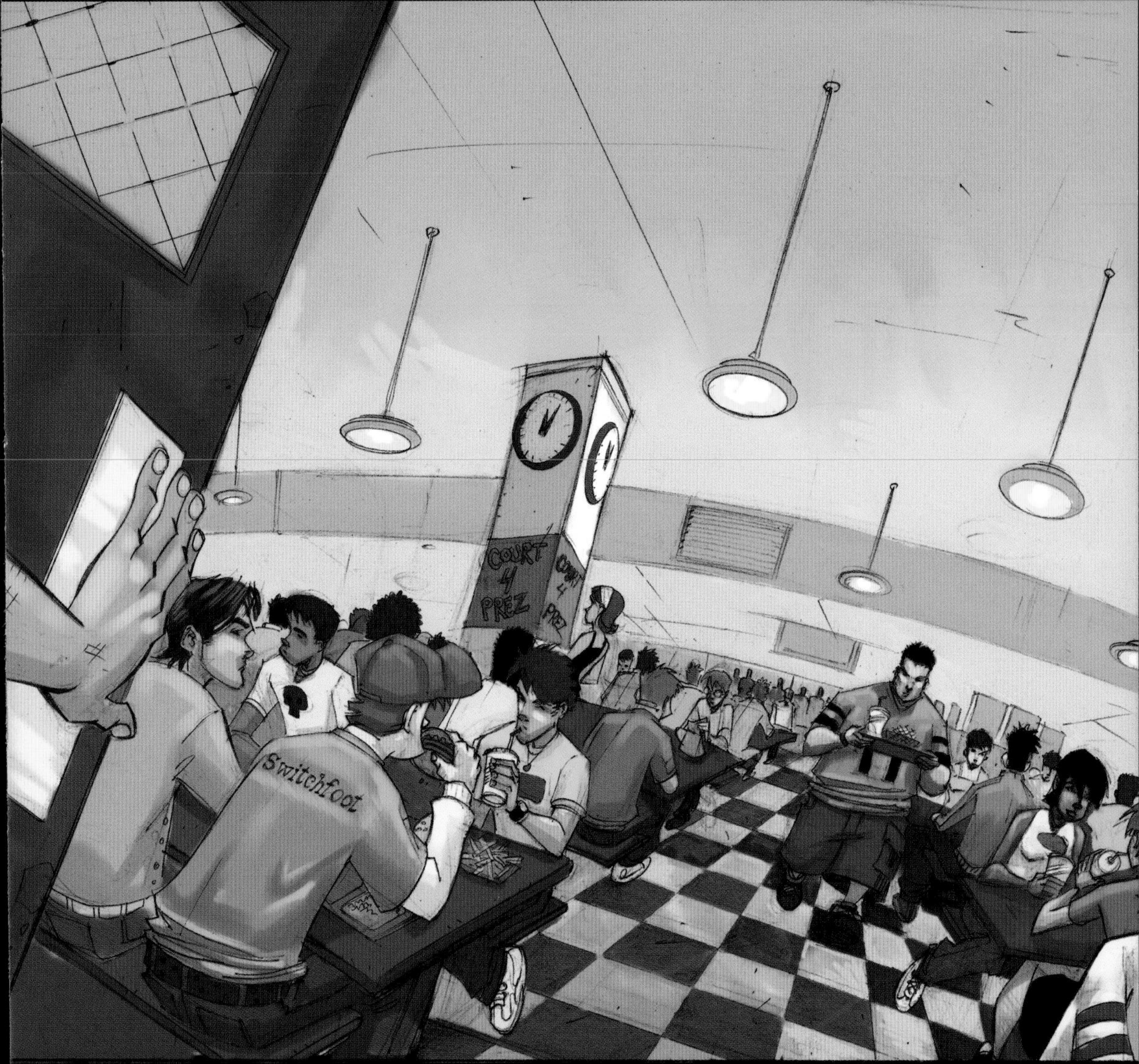
COURT 4 PREZ
Switchfoot

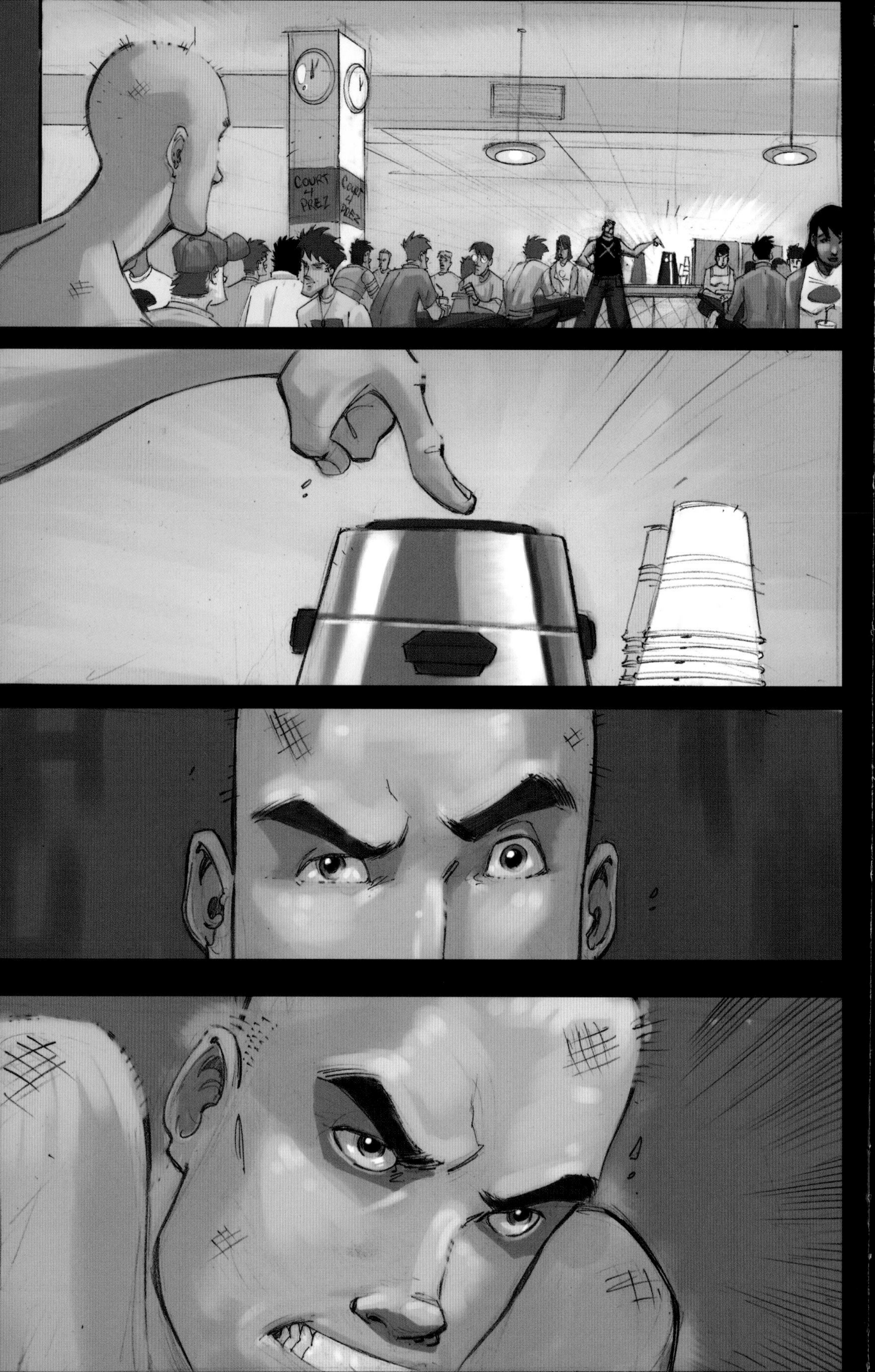
COURT 4 PREZ
COURT 4 PREZ

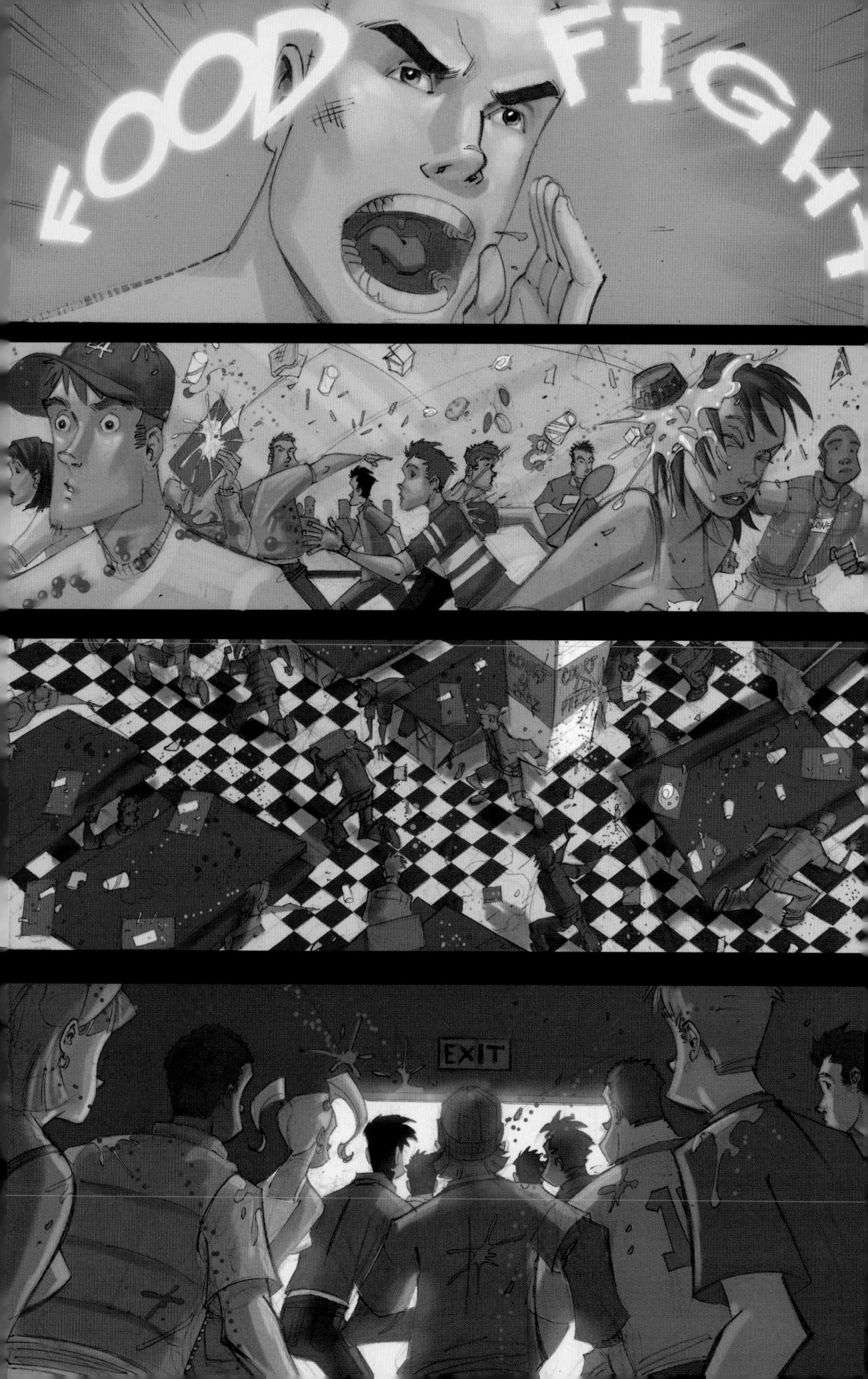
FOOD FIGHT
EXIT

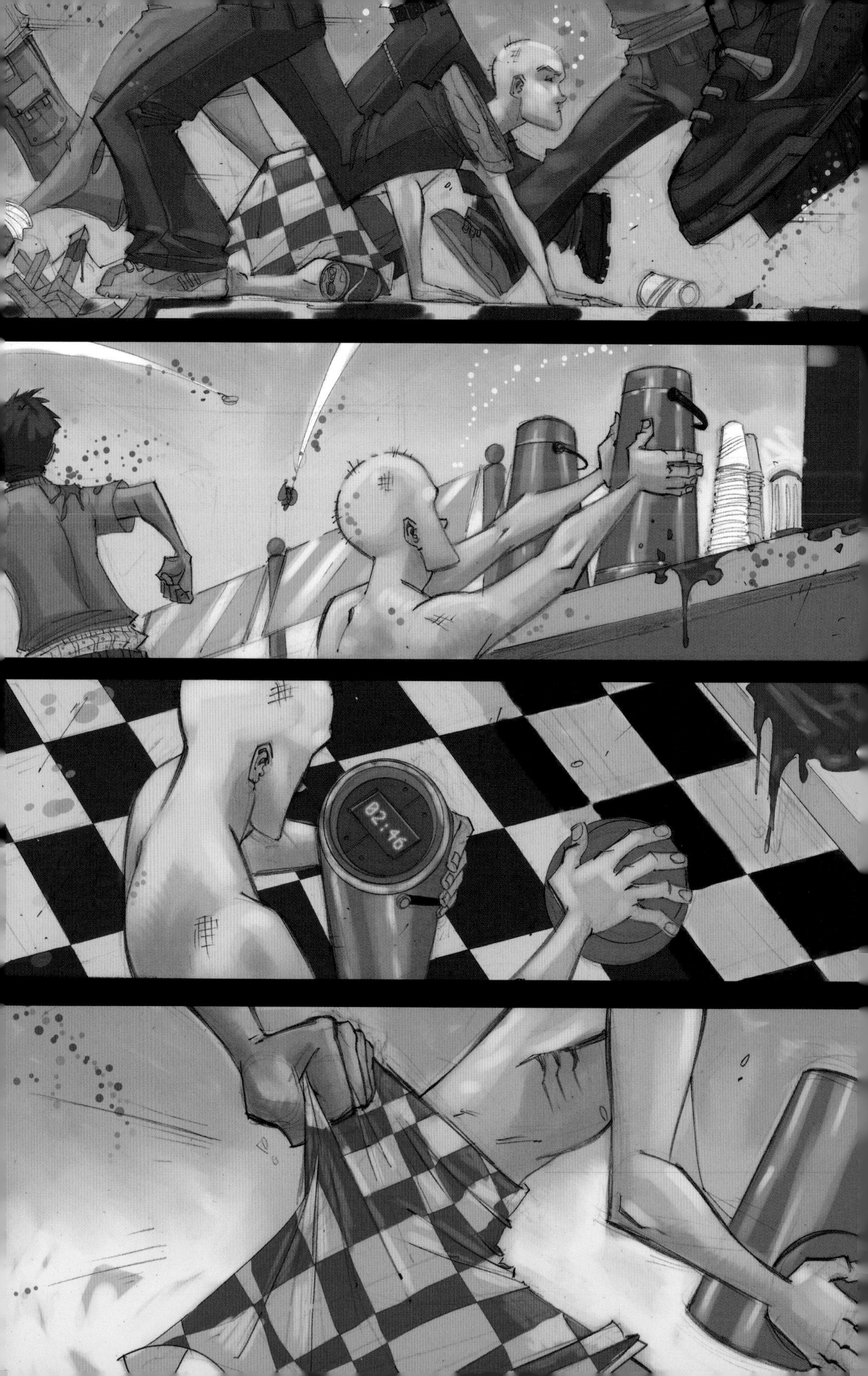
02:46

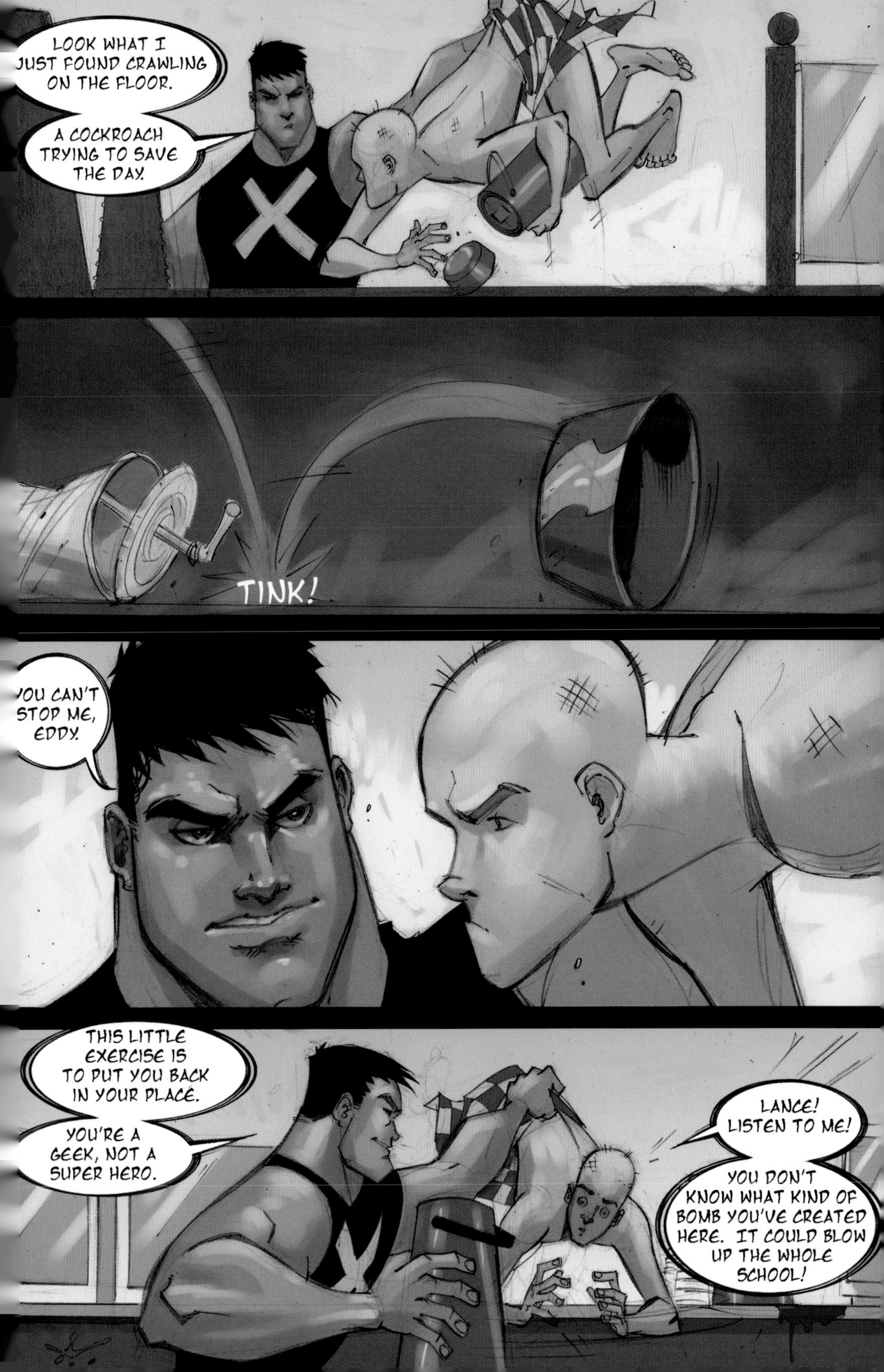

LOOK WHAT I JUST FOUND CRAWLING ON THE FLOOR.
A COCKROACH TRYING TO SAVE THE DAY.
TINK!
YOU CAN'T STOP ME, EDDY.
THIS LITTLE EXERCISE IS TO PUT YOU BACK IN YOUR PLACE.
YOU'RE A GEEK, NOT A SUPER HERO.
LANCE! LISTEN TO ME!
YOU DON'T KNOW WHAT KIND OF BOMB YOU'VE CREATED HERE. IT COULD BLOW UP THE WHOLE SCHOOL!

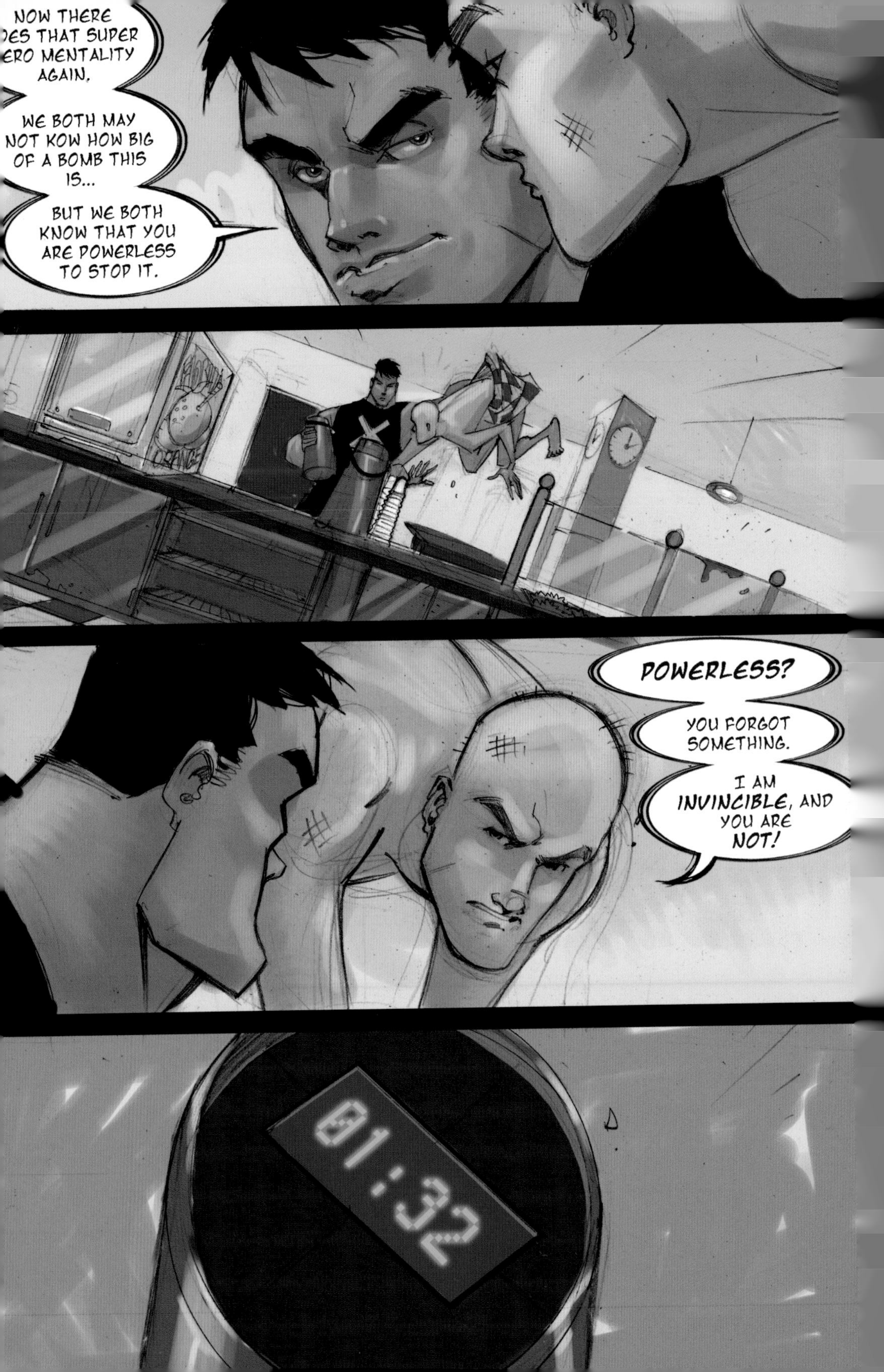
NOW THERE
ƆES THAT SUPER
ERO MENTALITY
AGAIN.
WE BOTH MAY
NOT KOW HOW BIG
OF A BOMB THIS
IS...
BUT WE BOTH
KNOW THAT YOU
ARE POWERLESS
TO STOP IT.
ORANGE
POWERLESS?
YOU FORGOT
SOMETHING.
I AM
INVINCIBLE, AND
YOU ARE
NOT!
01:32

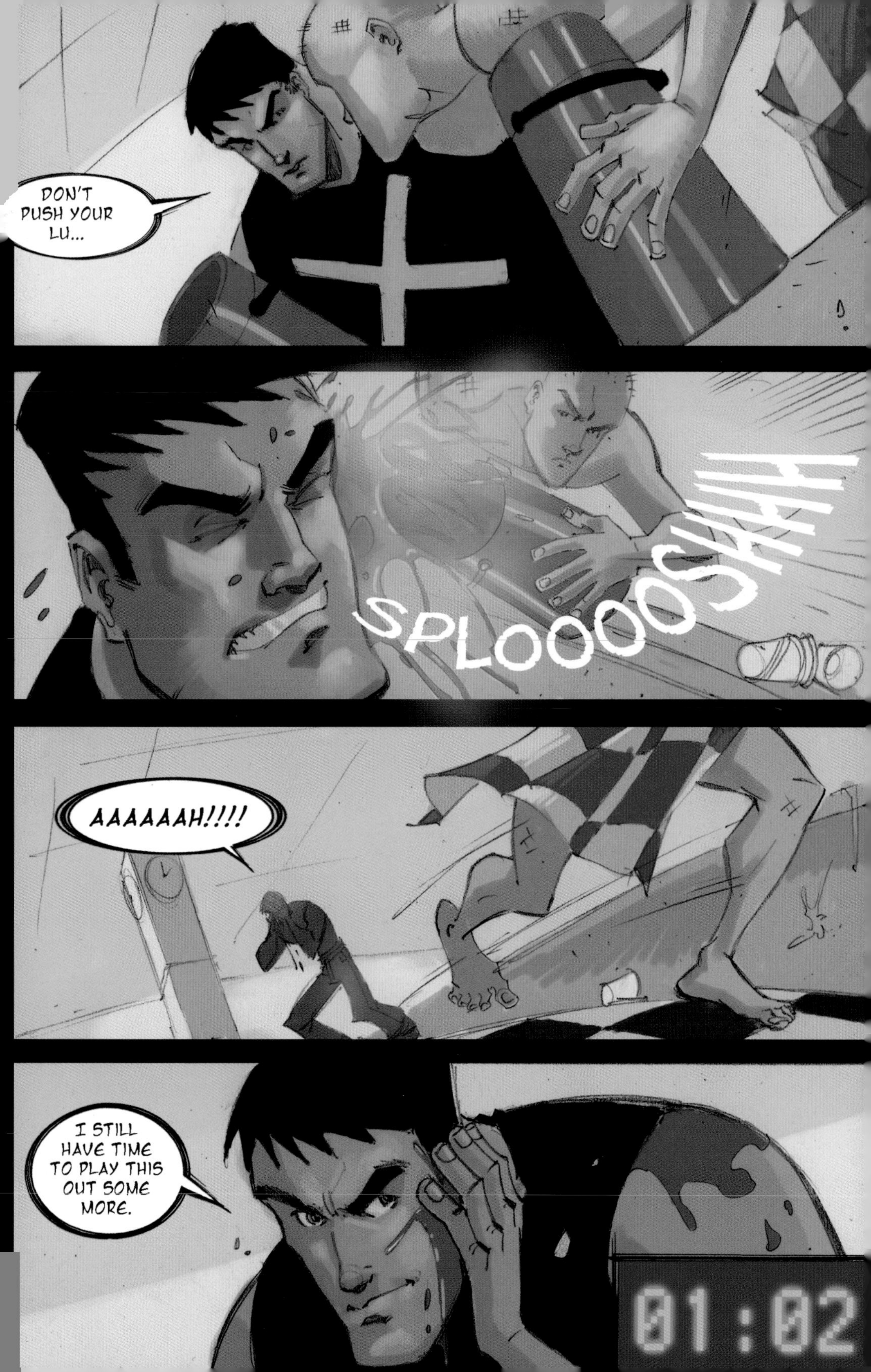
DON'T PUSH YOUR LU...
SPLOOOOSHHH
AAAAAAH!!!!
I STILL HAVE TIME TO PLAY THIS OUT SOME MORE.
01:02

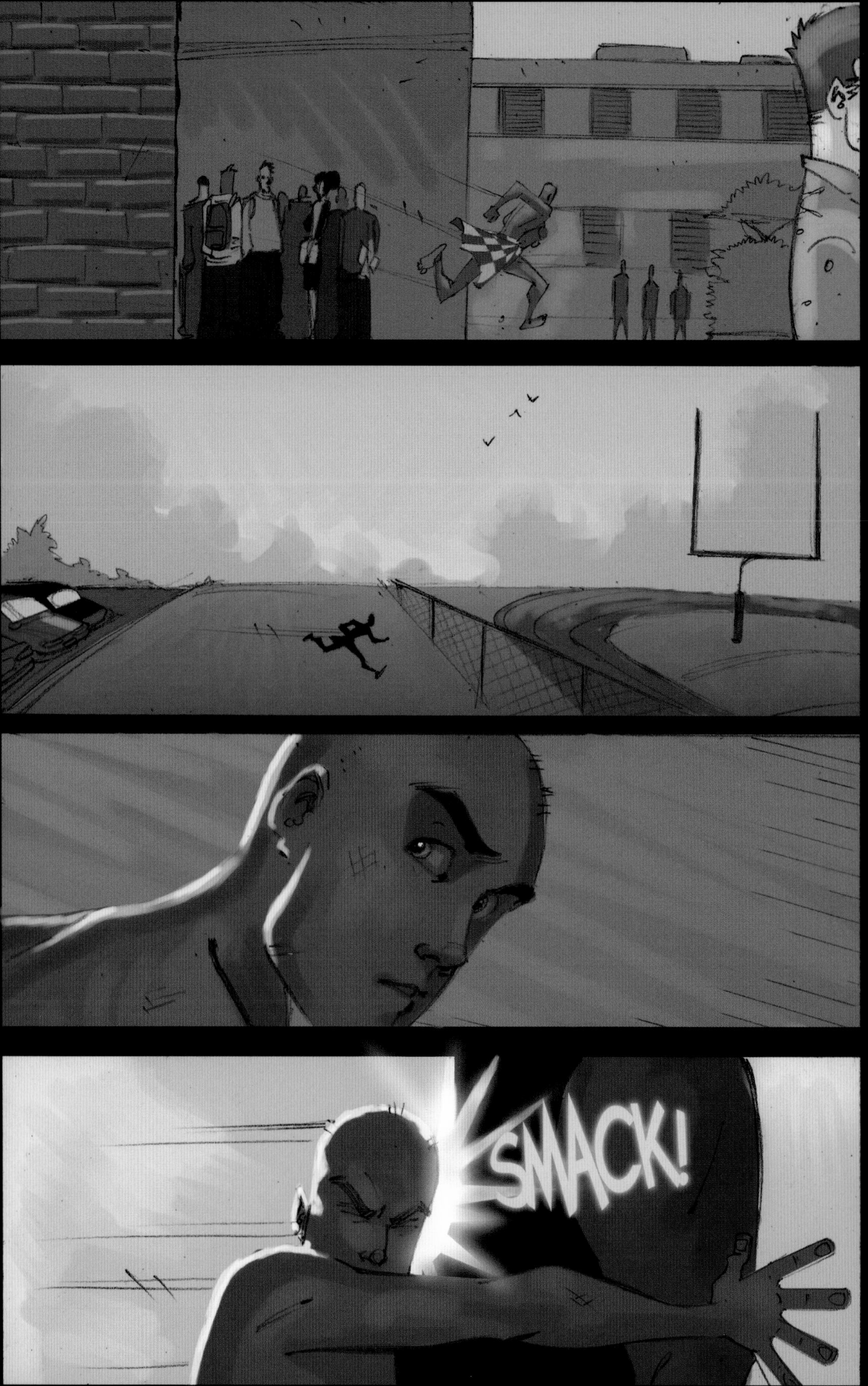
SMACK!

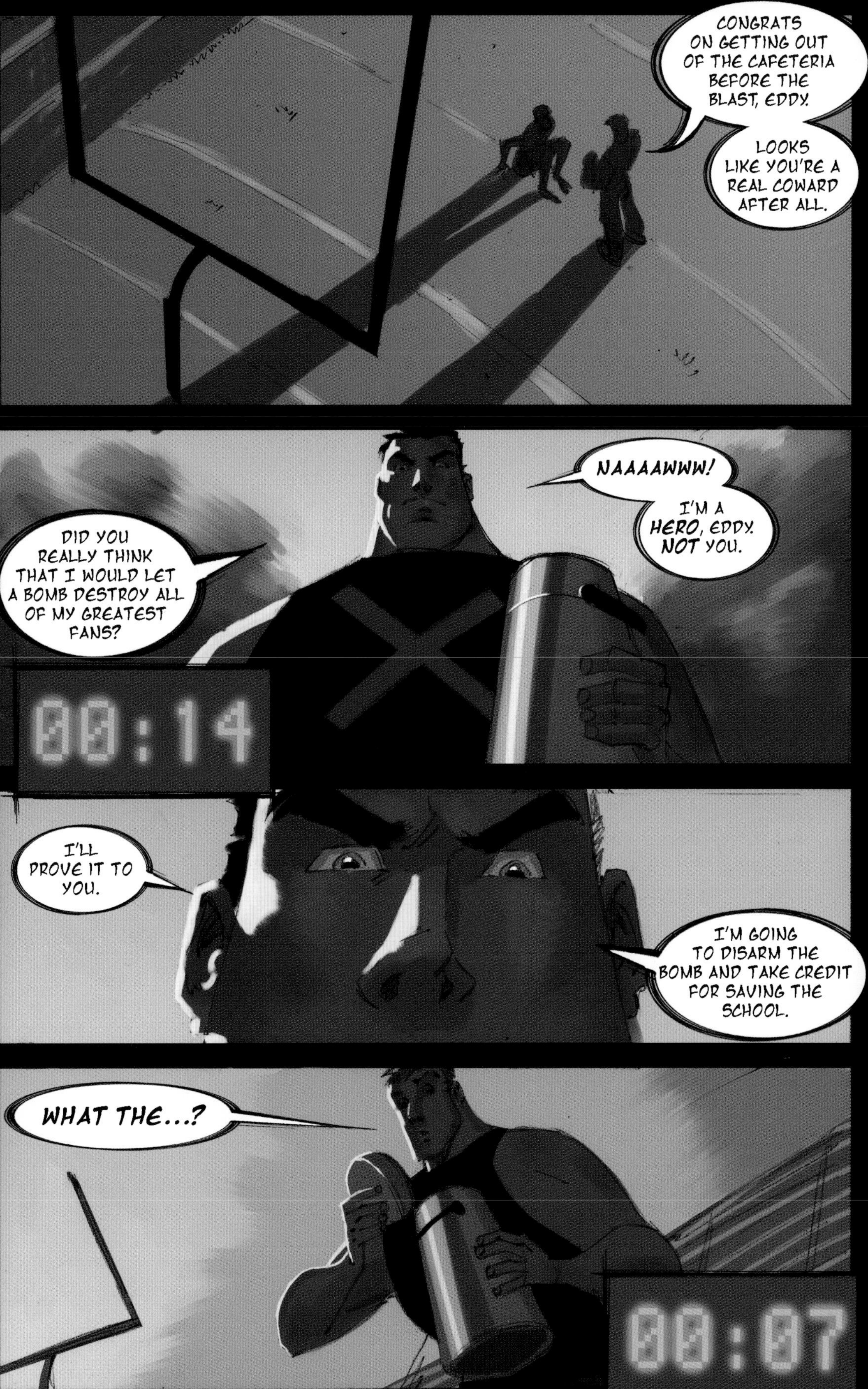

CONGRATS ON GETTING OUT OF THE CAFETERIA BEFORE THE BLAST, EDDY.
LOOKS LIKE YOU'RE A REAL COWARD AFTER ALL.
NAAAAWWW!
I'M A HERO, EDDY. NOT YOU.
DID YOU REALLY THINK THAT I WOULD LET A BOMB DESTROY ALL OF MY GREATEST FANS?
00:14
I'LL PROVE IT TO YOU.
I'M GOING TO DISARM THE BOMB AND TAKE CREDIT FOR SAVING THE SCHOOL.
WHAT THE...?
00:07

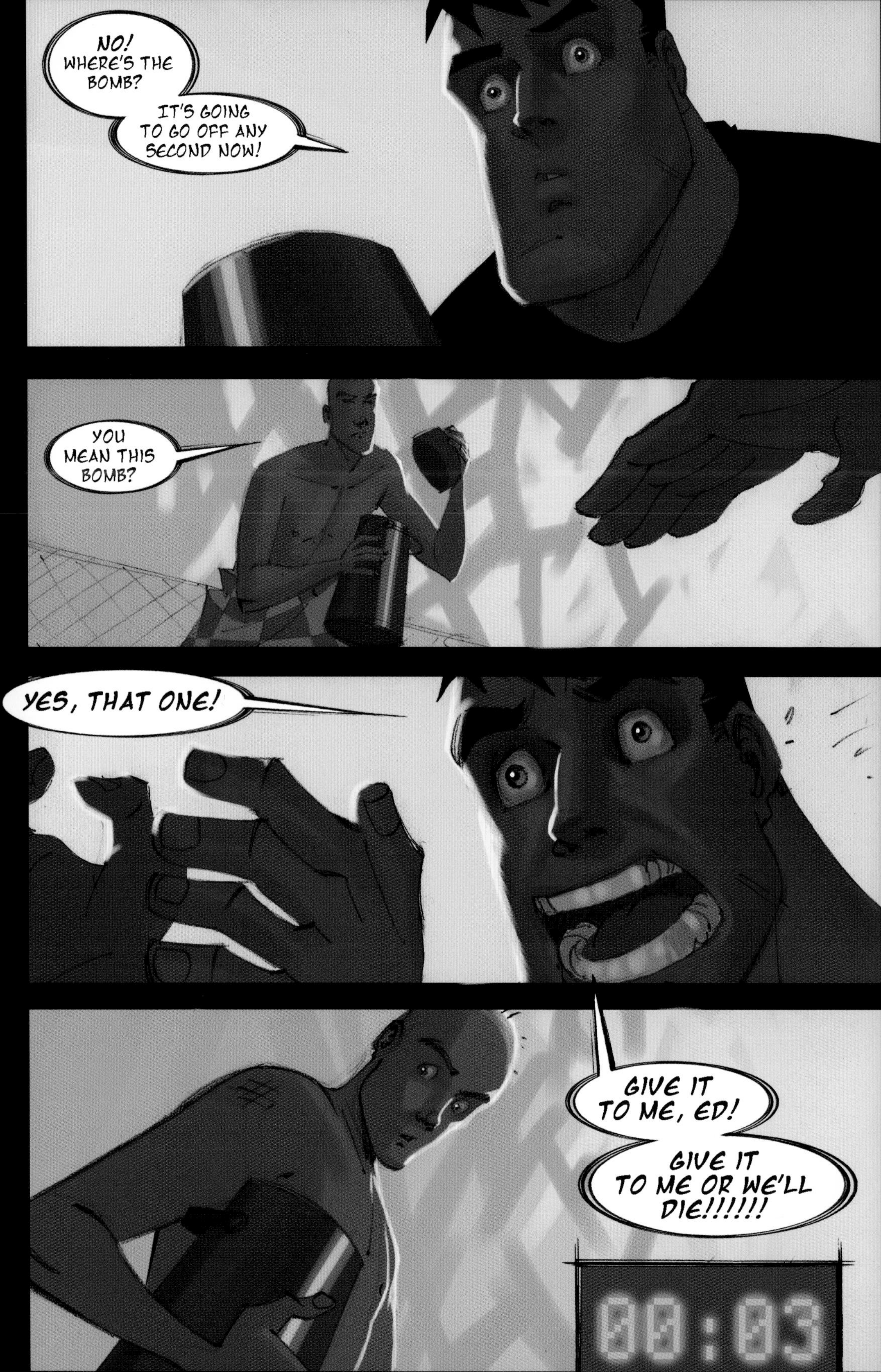
NO! WHERE'S THE BOMB?
IT'S GOING TO GO OFF ANY SECOND NOW!
YOU MEAN THIS BOMB?
YES, THAT ONE!
GIVE IT TO ME, ED!
GIVE IT TO ME OR WE'LL DIE!!!!!!
00:03

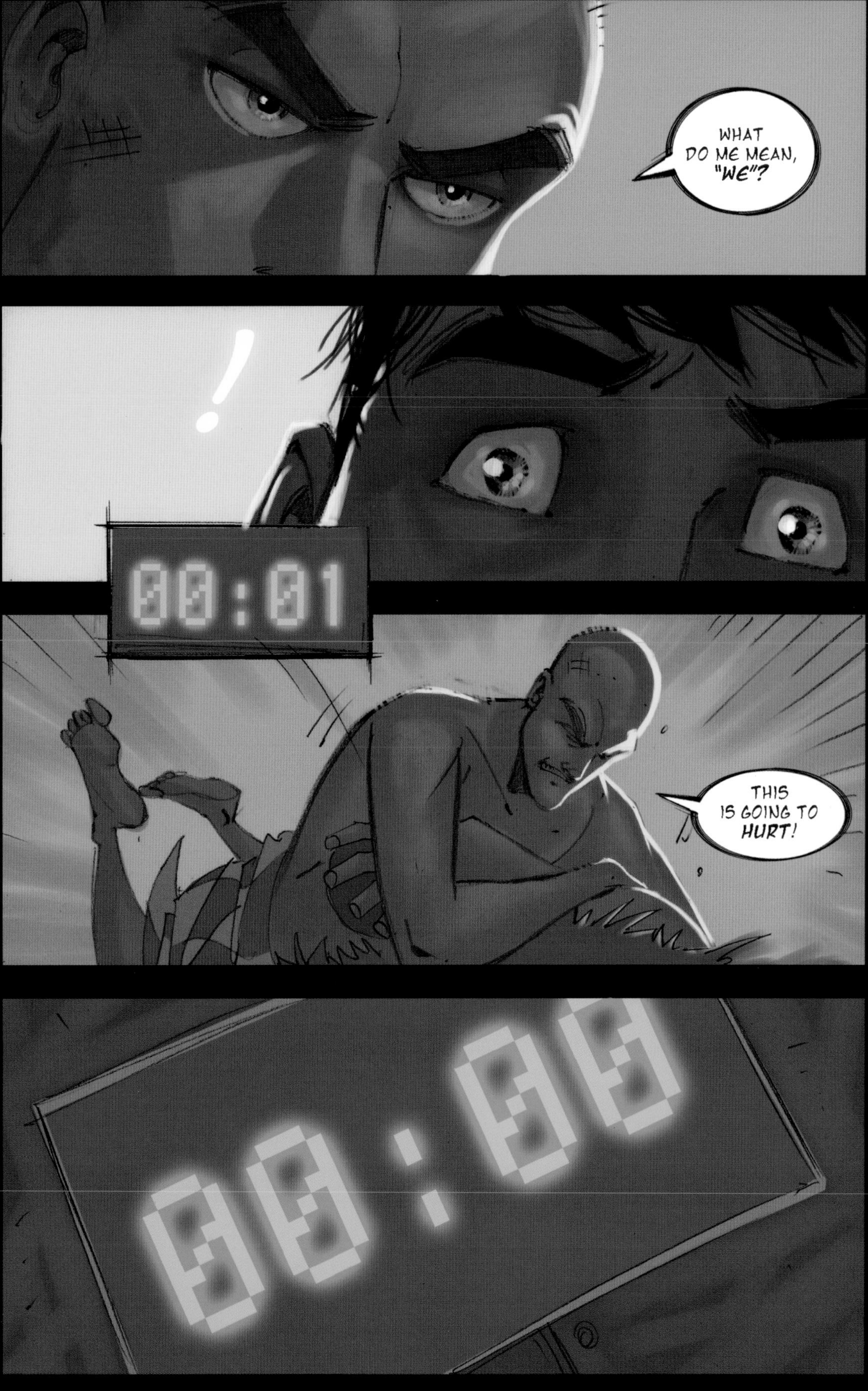
WHAT DO ME MEAN, "WE"?
!
00:01
THIS IS GOING TO HURT!
00:00

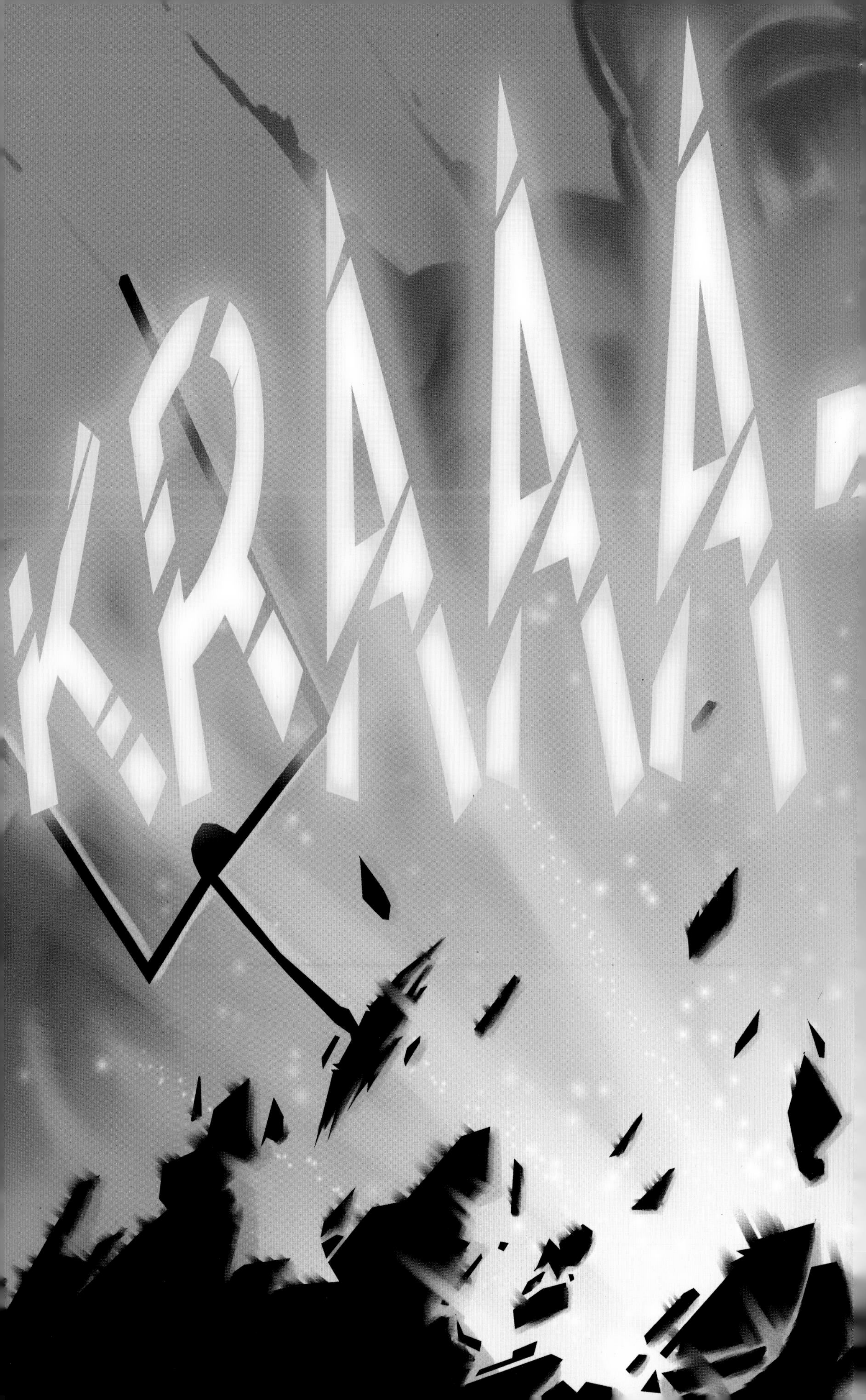
KRAAA

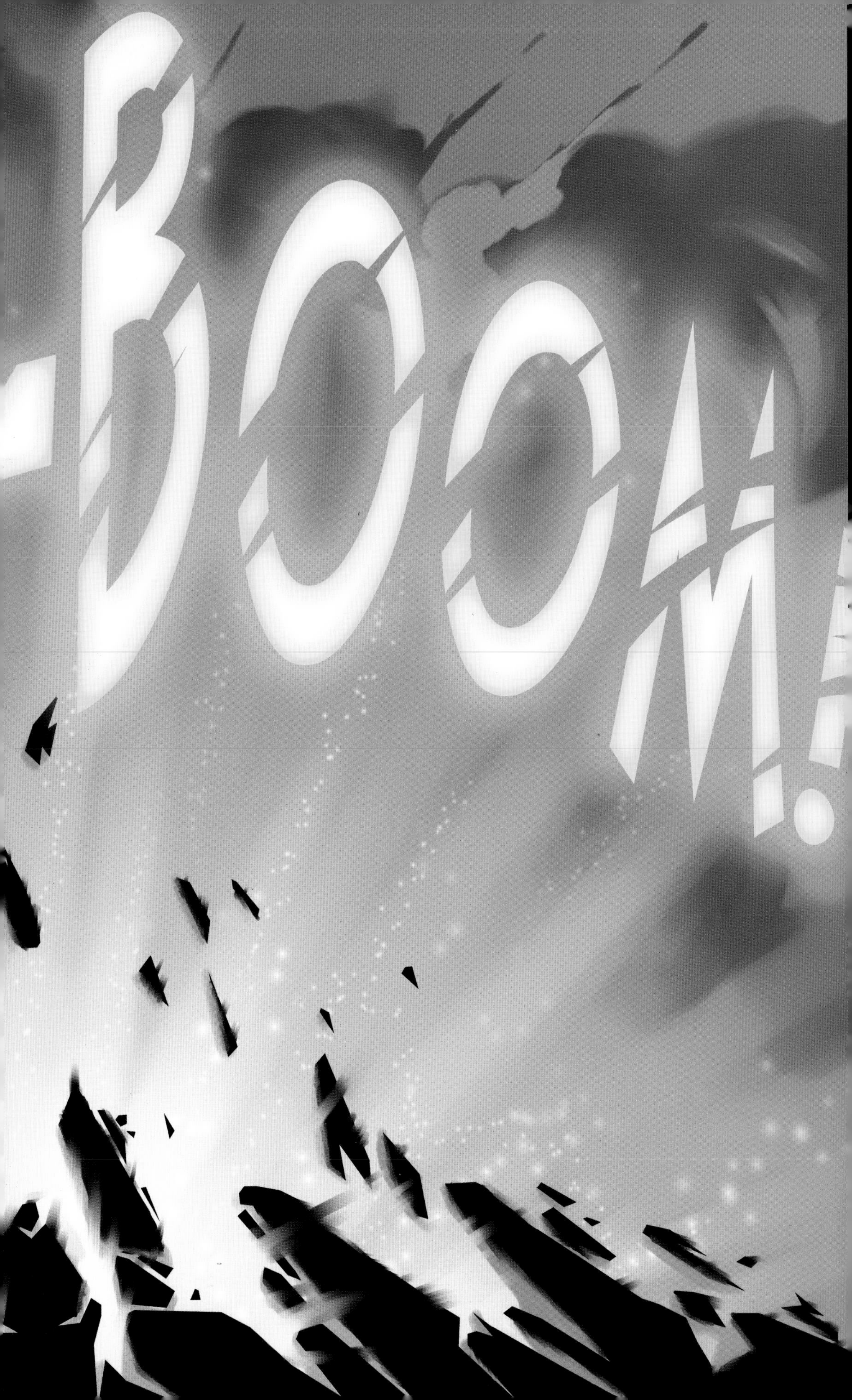
BOOM!

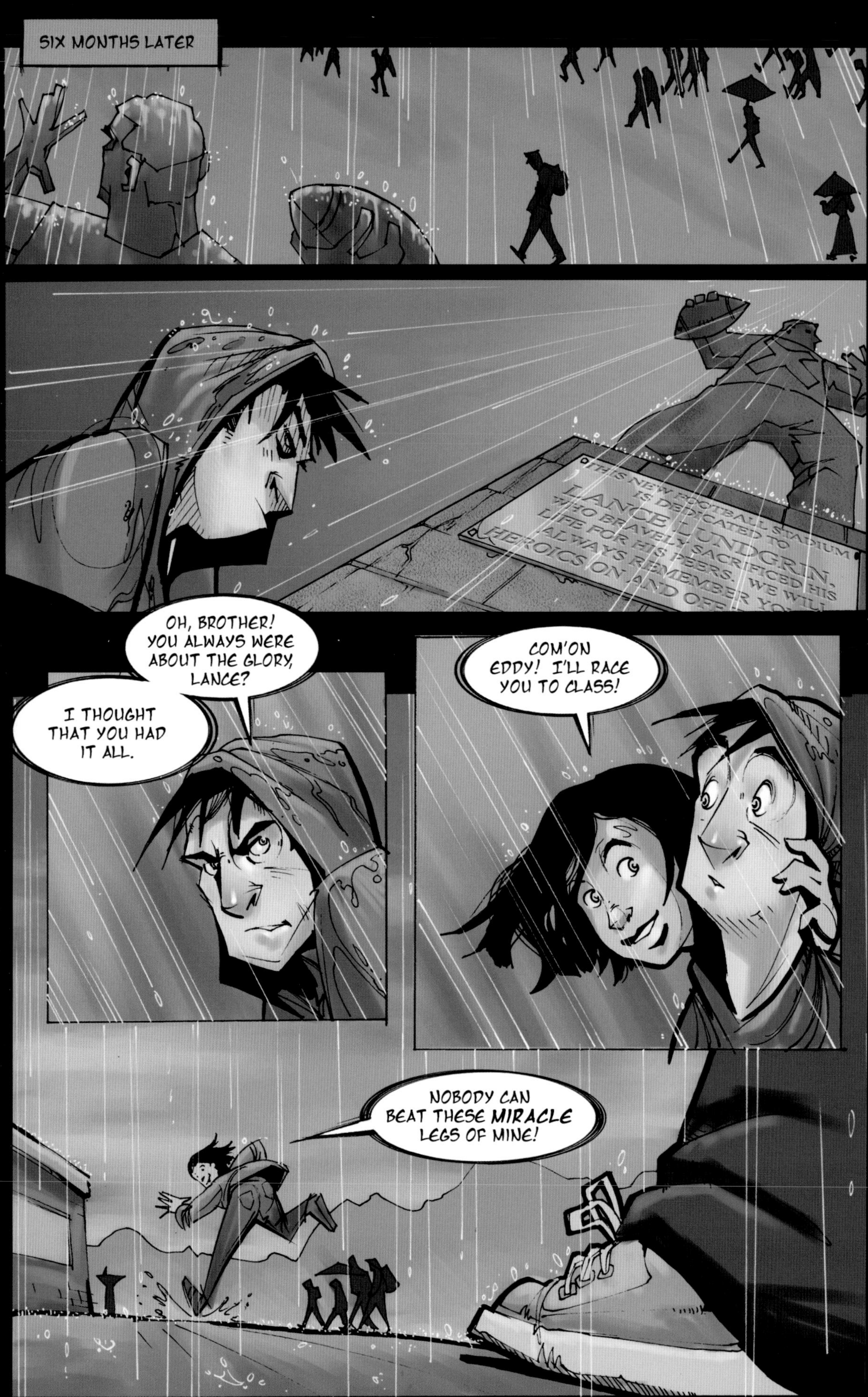
SIX MONTHS LATER
THIS NEW FOOTBALL STADIUM
IS DEDICATED TO
LANCE LUNDGRIN,
WHO BRAVELY SACRIFICED HIS
LIFE FOR HIS PEERS. WE WILL
ALWAYS REMEMBER YOU
HEROICS ON AND OFF
OH, BROTHER! YOU ALWAYS WERE ABOUT THE GLORY, LANCE?
I THOUGHT THAT YOU HAD IT ALL.
COM'ON EDDY! I'LL RACE YOU TO CLASS!
NOBODY CAN BEAT THESE MIRACLE LEGS OF MINE!

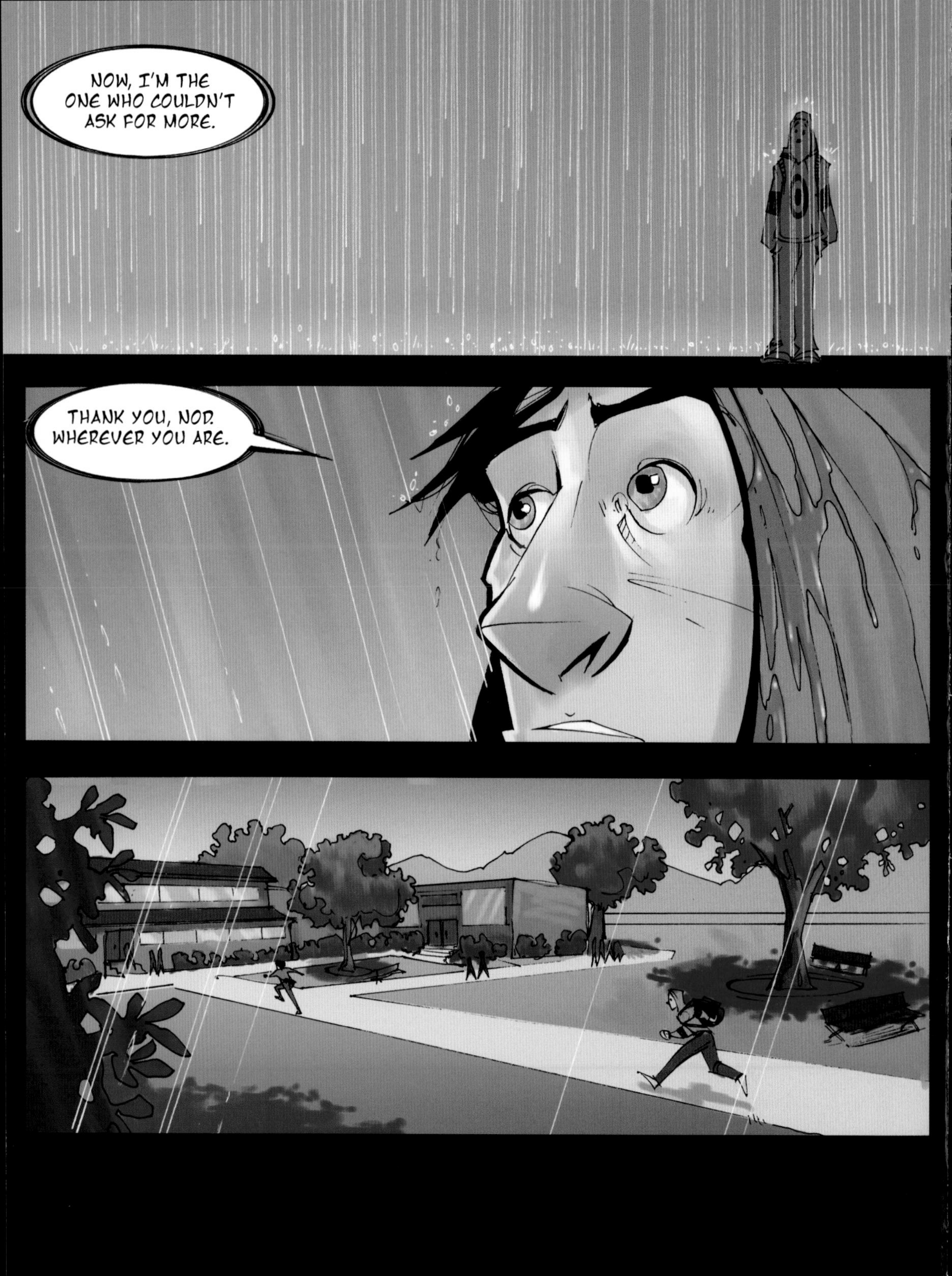
NOW, I'M THE ONE WHO COULDN'T ASK FOR MORE.
THANK YOU, NOD. WHEREVER YOU ARE.

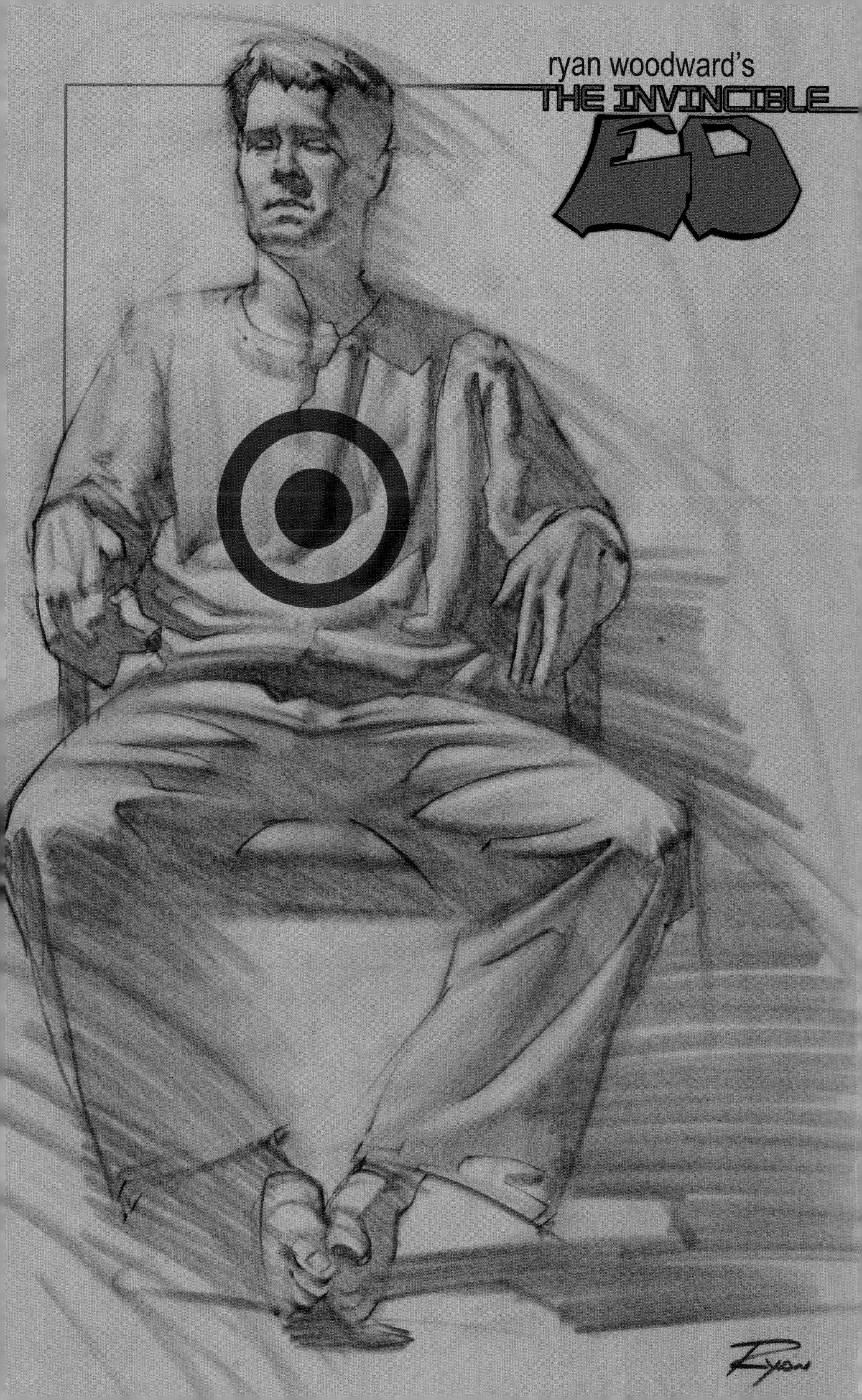
ryan woodward's
THE INVINCIBLE
ED
Ryan

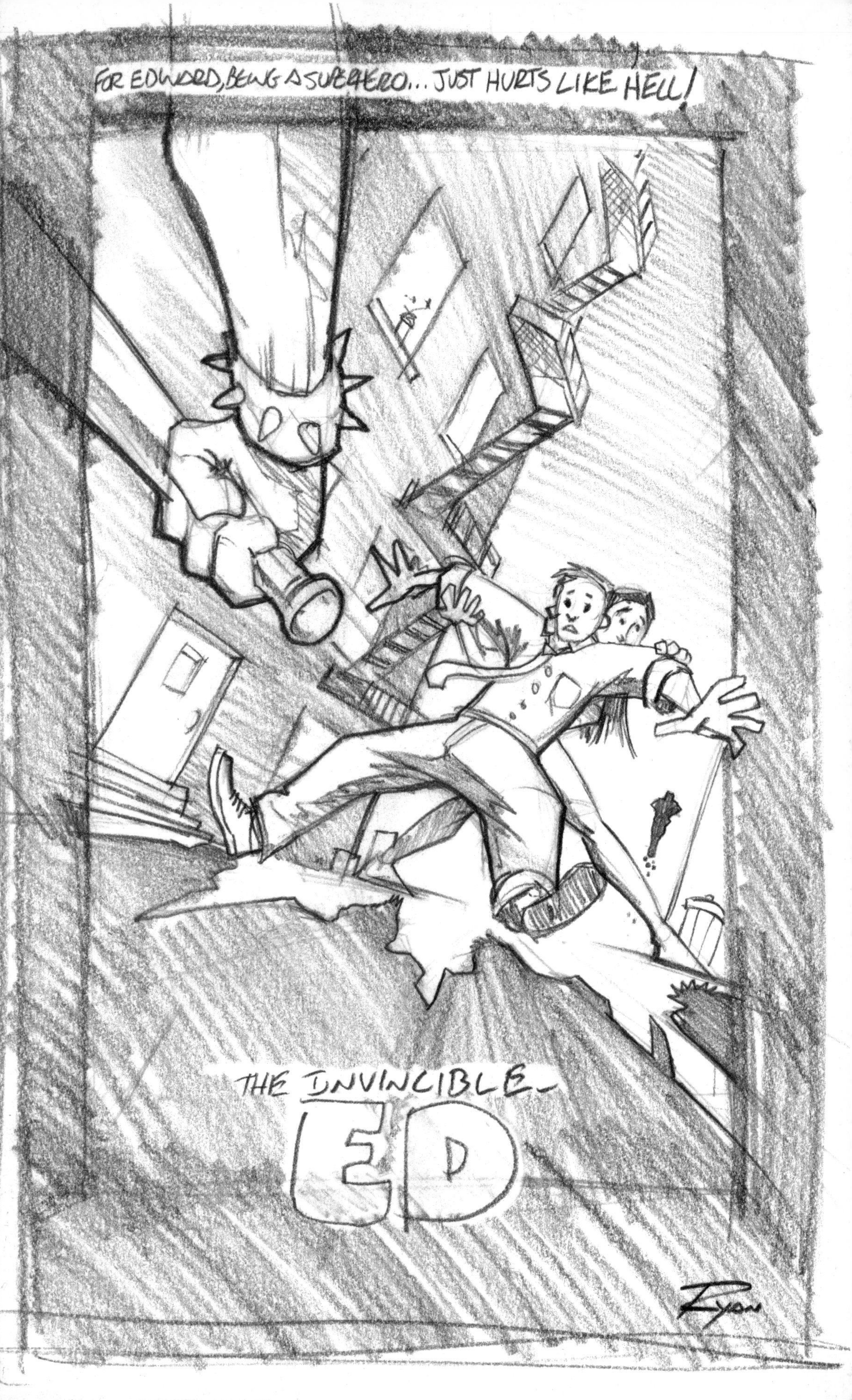
FOR EDWORD, BEING A SUPERHERO... JUST HURTS LIKE HELL!
THE INVINCIBLE
ED
Ryan

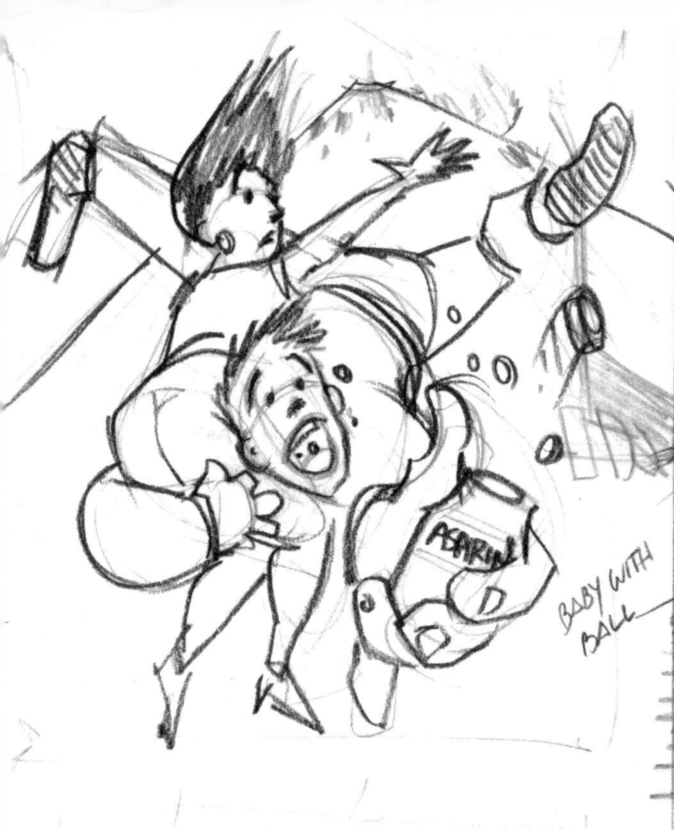
ASPIRIN
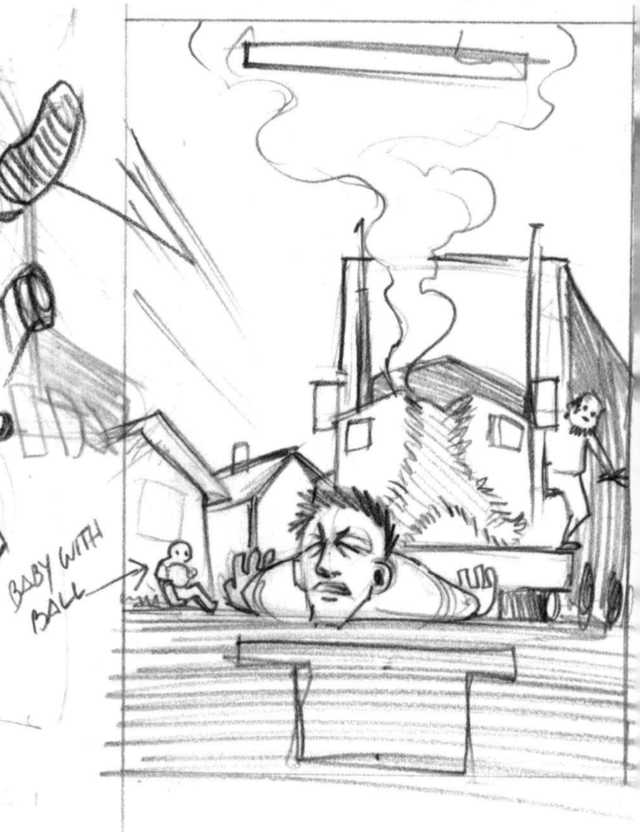
BABY WITH BALL
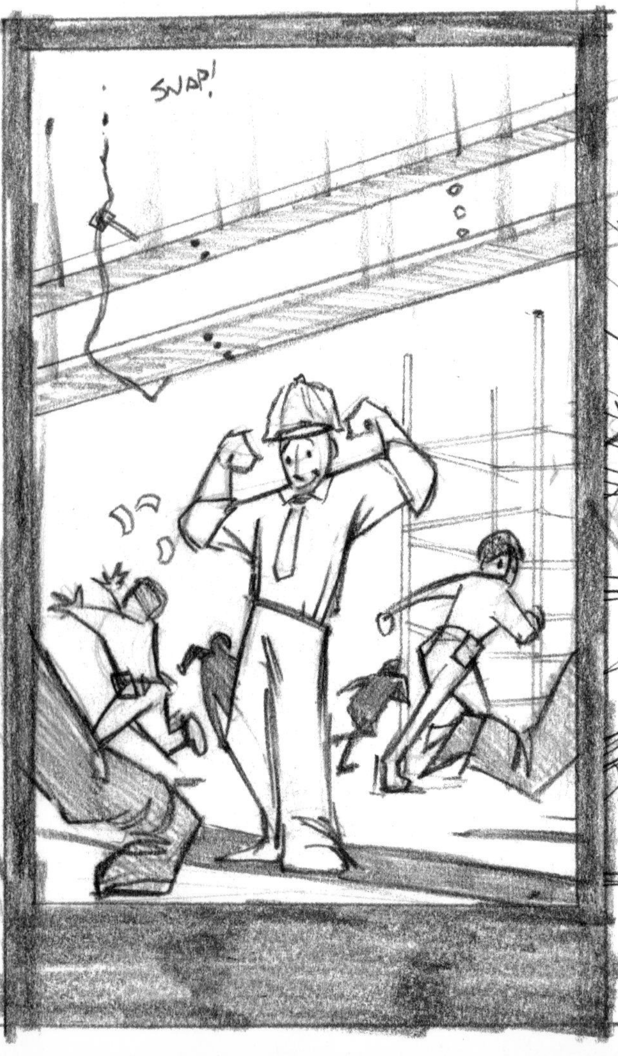
SNAP!
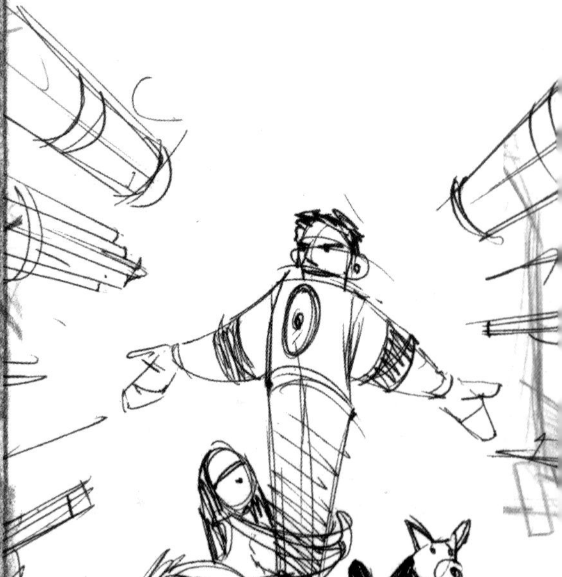